# More Resources from Nolo.com

### Legal Forms, Books, & Software
Hundreds of do-it-yourself products—all written in plain English, approved, and updated by our in-house legal editors.

### Legal Articles
Get informed with thousands of free articles on everyday legal topics. Our articles are accurate, up to date, and reader friendly.

### Find a Lawyer
Want to talk to a lawyer? Use Nolo to find a lawyer who can help you with your case.

NOLO
LAW for ALL

**19th Edition**

# Everybody's Guide to Small Claims Court

**Attorney Cara O'Neill**

| NINETEENTH EDITION | MARCH 2022 |
|---|---|
| Editor | CARA O'NEILL |
| Cover Design | SUSAN PUTNEY |
| Book Design | SUSAN PUTNEY |
| Proofreading | JOCELYN TRUITT |
| Index | ACCESS POINTS INDEXING |
| Printing | SHERIDAN |

ISSN: 2328-9848 (print)
ISSN: 2328-9856 (online)
ISBN: 978-1-4133-2953-7 (pbk)
ISBN: 978-1-4133-2954-4 (ebook)

This book covers only United States law, unless it specifically states otherwise.

**Please note**

This book's accurate, plain-English legal information can help you solve many of your own legal problems. But this text is not a substitute for personalized advice from a knowledgeable lawyer. If you want the help of a trained professional—and we'll always point out situations in which we think that's a good idea—consult an attorney licensed to practice in your state.

## Thank You

Thanks must go to Ralph Warner, the cofounder of Nolo and the original author of this book. While working as a Legal Aid lawyer in the late 1960s, it occurred to him that most Americans—not just the poor—were alienated from and oppressed by the legal system. Deciding to make a career out of working to provide better legal services, he cofounded Nolo in 1971. Ralph authored and coauthored many Nolo books, including *Leases & Rental Agreements*.

## About the Author

Cara O'Neill is a bankruptcy attorney in Northern California and a legal editor with Nolo. She has been practicing law in California for more than 20 years. Before joining Nolo, she served as an administrative law judge, litigated both criminal and civil cases, and taught law courses as an adjunct professor. She earned her law degree in 1994 from the University of the Pacific, McGeorge School of Law, where she served as a law review editor and graduated a member of the Order of the Barristers—an honor society recognizing excellence in courtroom advocacy. Cara has authored and coauthored several Nolo books, including *How to File for Chapter 7 Bankruptcy*, *The New Bankruptcy*, *Money Troubles*, and *Credit Repair*.

# Table of Contents

# Your Small Claims Court Companion

F iling a case in small claims court is a highly cost-effective strategy for resolving all kinds of disputes. In most states, the maximum amount you can sue for has increased substantially in recent years, and court judgments have become far easier to collect. Also, many states have implemented innovative mediation programs for small claims, which can spare you the time and tension of presenting your case to a judge. Although more can and should be done to make small claims court a true people's court, it is an efficient forum that allows participants to resolve many personal consumer and small business disputes.

This book aims to give people bringing a case and those defending one all the information they need to make the best possible use of small claims court. From deciding whether you have a case through gathering evidence, arranging for witnesses, planning your courtroom presentation, and collecting your money, you will find everything here.

*Everybody's Guide to Small Claims Court* has now been in print for more than 30 years. The goal is to make it the best possible tool to help you answer such questions as:

- How does small claims court work?
- Do I have a case worth pursuing or defending?
- How do I prepare my case to maximum advantage?
- What witnesses and other evidence should I present?
- What do I say in court?
- Can I appeal if I lose?
- How do I collect my judgment?

Proper presentation of your small claims action can often mean the difference between receiving a check and writing one. This isn't to say that we can tell you how to take a hopeless case and turn it into a winner. It does mean that with the information contained here, and with your own creativity and common sense, you will be able to develop and present your case as effectively as possible.

Just as important as knowing how to bring your small claims court action is knowing when not to. You won't want to waste time and energy dragging a hopeless case to court. And even if your case is legally sound, why pursue it if your chances of collecting from the defendant are poor.

In addition to studying the information you'll find here, review the materials made available by your state's small claims court. Crucial procedural details such as the types of evidence allowed and the cost of collecting a judgment are covered in more detail in those materials than here. Fortunately, accessing this material is easy—it's usually available online as well as in free pamphlets available at your small claims court clerk's office. You'll find information about your state's small claims court and website in the appendix.

Finally, keep in mind that Nolo is by far the most comprehensive publisher of self-help law materials in the United States. Because many legal issues can be litigated in small claims court, information in other Nolo books and on Nolo's website might be helpful. Nolo's books are available at most libraries, so it shouldn't be hard to look up any needed information at no cost.

# Basics of Small Claims Court

## Why Use Small Claims Court?

The purpose of small claims court is to hear lawsuits involving modest amounts of money without long delays and formal rules of evidence. Lawyers are prohibited in some states, including Michigan and California, but are allowed in most. However, the limited dollar amounts involved usually make it economically unwise to hire a lawyer, and disputes are typically presented directly by the people involved.

> **CAUTION**
> **Check your state's jurisdictional amount before you file.** We provide the most up-to-date information available at the time this book was published. But these amounts change, so be sure to check the rules for your state before filing. Freeadvice.com provides resources for people needing 50-state small claims court information (www.freeadvice.com/resources/smallclaimscourts.htm).

There are three significant advantages of small claims court:

- You get to prepare and present your case without having to pay a lawyer more than your claim is worth.
- Filing, preparing, and presenting a small claims case is relatively easy. The complicated legal forms and language found in other courts are kept to a minimum. To start your lawsuit, you need only fill out a few lines on a simple form (for example, "Defendant owes me the sum of $4,000 because the 2014 Neon he sold me on January 1, 2022, in supposedly 'excellent condition,' died less than a mile from the car lot").
- You can talk to the judge in plain English without any legal jargon when you get to court.
- Small claims court doesn't take long. Most disputes are heard in court within two or three months from the complaint filing. The hearing itself seldom takes more than 15 minutes. The judge announces a decision either right there in the courtroom or mails it within a few days.

## Will Small Claims Work for You?

Before you decide that small claims court sounds like the right place to bring your case, you will want to answer a fundamental question: Will it be worth the effort? Even in small claims court, a case will take at least 20 hours to prepare and, depending on your personality, could cause a few sleepless nights.

When assessing whether your dispute is worth bringing, you'll want to understand the details of how small claims court works, starting with who can sue, where, and for how much. You will also want to do the following:

- Learn enough law to answer critical questions such as whether you are likely to win and, if so, how much; what types of papers you must file; and who can sue. Part of this involves knowing the legal rules for different case types—for example, what you must prove in a personal injury claim will be different in a security deposit dispute.
- If you decide you have a winning case, understand how best to prepare and present it.
- Finally, and most importantly, a judgment won't be worth much if you can't get paid, so determine whether you'll be able to collect the money if you win. Unfortunately, some plaintiffs win but can't collect a dime because they sued someone judgment proof—that is, someone without collectible money or assets.

This book covers all of these issues. The first several chapters will help you decide whether you have a case worth pursuing. These chapters cover the basics, not the grand strategies that will baffle and confound the opposition—that comes later (well, sort of—keep in mind that a legal strategy is only as good as the facts of the case). The initial chapters deal with mundane tasks like locating the person you want to sue, suing in the right court, filling out the necessary forms, and delivering the documents to the person you're suing.

Below are checklists of issues plaintiffs and defendants should consider at this initial stage. The chapters that follow address each area in more detail and include targeted advice for both sides.

### Initial Stage Questions for a Plaintiff

☐ 1. Do you have a good case? That is, can you establish or prove everything required by the law (elements) to win your claim? (See Chapters 2 and 14–22.)

☐ 2. How much is your claim worth? If the value is more than the small claims maximum, do you wish to waive the excess and still use small claims court? (See Chapter 4.)

☐ 3. Have you made a reasonable effort to contact the other party and settle the case? (See Chapter 6.)

☐ 4. Are you within the deadline (statute of limitations) by which you must file your suit? (See Chapter 5.)

☐ 5. Who will you sue and how do you identify this person or business on your court papers? In some cases, especially those involving companies and automobiles, this can be a little trickier than you might have guessed. (See Chapter 8.)

☐ 6. Which small claims court should you bring your suit in? (See Chapter 9.)

☐ 7. If your small claims court offers or encourages mediation, do you understand how it works and how best to use it? (See Chapter 6.)

☐ 8. Can you make a convincing courtroom presentation? (See Chapter 15.)

☐ 9. And, assuming you can win, is there a reasonable chance you can collect? (See Chapters 3 and 24.)

## Initial Stage Questions for a Defendant

☐ 1. Do you have legal grounds for a countersuit against the plaintiff? Or put another way, does the plaintiff really owe you money instead of the other way around? (See Chapters 10 and 12.)

☐ 2. Do you have a partial or complete defense against the plaintiff's claim? In other words, has the plaintiff filed a bogus lawsuit? (See Chapters 2 and 12.)

☐ 3. Is the plaintiff's money demand reasonable or excessive? (See Chapter 4.)

☐ 4. Has the plaintiff brought the suit within the proper time limit? (See Chapter 5.)

☐ 5. Has the plaintiff followed the correct procedures in bringing suit and delivering the court papers to you? (See Chapters 11 and 12.)

☐ 6. If your small claims court offers or encourages mediation, do you understand how it works and how to use it? (See Chapter 6.)

☐ 7. Have you made a reasonable effort to contact the plaintiff to arrive at a settlement? (See Chapters 6 and 12.)

☐ 8. Assuming you'll fight the case in court, you'll typically need proof that your version of events is correct. Do you have the evidence and witnesses to accomplish this? (See Chapters 13–15.)

☐ 9. Are you prepared to present your side of the case convincingly in court? (See Chapter 15.)

TIP
**Defendants may want to file their own lawsuit.** In addition to their right to defend themselves, defendants also have the opportunity to file a case against the plaintiff. (See Chapters 10 and 12.) If you're sued, you'll want to do this if you lost money due to the same events the plaintiff complained about, and the plaintiff is legally responsible for your loss. Defendants' claims commonly develop out of a situation in which both parties are negligent, such as a car accident. The question becomes each driver's percentage of fault. If your claim is for less than the small claims court maximum, you can file there. If it's for more, check your state's rules. You'll probably have to file your case in a different court (and have your opponent's case transferred there). (See Chapter 10.)

## How to Use This Book

This guide covers the procedures that both plaintiffs and defendants should use to successfully bring or defend a small claims case. Unlike other guides, it also contains step-by-step instructions for preparing common small claims cases.

Chapters 2 and 3 help you answer the fundamental question of whether you should even file suit by asking two crucial questions: Do you have a good case? Can you collect any money from the defendant if you win? If your answer to either of these questions is "no," then you should read Chapter 6 to see whether you might be able to settle your dispute without going to court or should consider dropping the idea of a lawsuit.

Chapters 4–9 walk you through the procedural details. Small claims court is meant to be easy, but it still has rules about how much money you can sue for, who you can sue, what court you should bring your lawsuit in, and so forth.

Chapters 10 and 11 are about the actual paperwork: How do you fill out your papers and deliver them to the defendant? Chapter 12 explains what a defendant should do after being sued. Chapters 13-15 get you ready for your day in court, and Chapters 23 and 24 address how the judge issues a ruling, how to appeal, and how to collect your money if you're successful.

In Chapters 16–22, we discuss strategies you can use to handle common cases. Even if your situation doesn't fit neatly into one of the categories, read this material. By picking up a few hints here and a little information there, you should be able to piece together a good plan of action. For example, many of the suggestions on how to handle motor vehicle repair disputes can also be applied to cases involving major appliances such as a television, dishwasher, or dryer. However, these days, it would probably be cheaper to buy new.

Appendix A contains a summary of small claims court information and rules for every state. You'll find the name of the small claims court and a website link, relevant state statutes, lawsuit dollar limits, service of process rules, time limits for responding to claims, how to appeal a decision, and more. You will want to check your state's small claims court website early in the process, whether you're a plaintiff or a defendant, for valuable information about how your state handles small claims cases. Be sure to also check the local small claims court clerk's office for local rules.

Appendix B is a glossary of legal jargon you might come across in small claims cases and courts. Fortunately, there is not a lot of it, but a few terms might be new to you. If you can't find what you need, check Nolo's Free Dictionary of Law Terms and Legal Definitions at www.nolo.com/dictionary.

Because state law establishes small claims procedures, the operating rules differ from state to state, including the maximum amount you can sue for, who can sue, and the what, where, and when of filing papers. States even call small claims court (or its equivalent) different things, like "justice," "district," "municipal," "city," "county," and "magistrates" court.

Even so, the primary approach necessary to prepare and present a case is remarkably similar everywhere. But details are important, and you should do three things to make sure you understand how small claims court works in your state:

- Look up the summary of your state's rules in Appendix A of this book.
- Obtain your local small claims rules from your small claims court clerk's office.
- Check out your state's small claims rules online. See Appendix A for information on how to find your state's small claims court.

# Do You Have a Good Case?

## Stating Your Claim

One of the advantages of small claims court is that when you file, you aren't required to present theories of law—instead, you simply state the facts of the dispute, that you have suffered monetary loss, and that the person or business you are suing caused your loss.

In your complaint or claim, you will give a simple description of the dispute. (We'll go over the forms you must file to start your lawsuit in Chapter 10.) Depending, of course, on the facts of your case, you will state your claim more or less like this:

- "John's Dry Cleaners ruined my jacket on December 13, 20xx."
- "His dog bit me on the corner of Rose and Peach Streets in West Covina, California, on April 27, 20xx."
- "The car repairs that Joe's Garage did on my car on July 11, 20xx, were done wrong, resulting in an engine fire."
- "Landlord refused to return the cleaning deposit when I moved out of my apartment on August 11, 20xx, even though I left it clean."
- "The used car I purchased from her on January 26, 20xx, in 'tiptop condition,' blew a gasket the next day."
- "The $5,000 I lent defendant has not been repaid by November 12, 20xx, as promised."

### Time to Get Organized

Before filing your case, you should set up a system to safeguard key papers and evidence. It's no secret that more than one case has been won (or lost) because of good (or bad) record keeping. One excellent approach is to get a couple of manila envelopes or file folders and label them with the name of your dispute (*Lincoln v. Williams*). Use one folder to store all documentary evidence, such as receipts, letters, names and addresses of potential witnesses, and photographs. The other is for your court papers. Once organized, make sure you conscientiously store your folders in a safe place.

TIP
**Don't argue your case until you get to court.** When you state your case on the court papers, your goal is to notify the other party and the court of the issue in dispute. You don't need to list your evidence or try to convince anyone that you are right or that the law is on your side. Your chance to do this will come later in court.

## But Is My Case Any Good?

There's no denying that, as stated above, you can rely on the judge to do the heavy legal lifting. For instance, it's okay to:

- briefly state the nature of your dispute
- organize any evidence and witnesses you think will help back up your version of events
- come to court on time
- be polite, and
- let the judge decide if your case is any good.

However, the problem with this approach is that the judge will not decide your case based on what seems morally "right" (although it never hurts to seize the high moral ground) or on whose presentation and witnesses are more convincing. Instead, the judge must apply the same legal rules to your case as would be followed if your dispute was heard in a formal court. The judge must follow the law.

JUDGE'S TIP
**"Unfair" doesn't automatically mean "illegal."** Unfortunately, the mere fact that you have suffered a trauma at the hands of another person does not automatically entitle you to a legal judgment. The law must support your position that you were harmed by the *illegal* actions of another.

Obviously, this means there are problems with this "stay ignorant and trust the judge" approach. Here are the biggies:

- If you don't understand the legal rules the judge will apply to decide your matter, you might waste time and energy pursuing a loser case.
- If you don't understand the legal realities of your case, you might not present the evidence you need to win.
- If you win—and especially if you lose—you won't know why.

If none of this sounds good to you, perhaps you are open to considering a more informed approach. Take the time to understand the legal—as well as the moral—issues involved in your case. Or, put another way, evaluate your case the way a judge will ultimately view it. Doing so will increase your chances of winning exponentially—and it isn't as hard as you might think. Knowing that you're well prepared has another benefit, too—it will boost your confidence tremendously.

**TIP**

**Defendants need the same legal knowledge as plaintiffs.** Every law has several parts, called "elements," that a plaintiff must prove to win a case. A plaintiff who fails to prove an element must lose. To defend a case well, a defendant needs to understand the essential legal elements of the case the plaintiff is attempting to prove. Once armed with this information, the defendant will be in good shape to try to convince the judge that at least one legal requirement is missing.

The rest of this chapter reviews the legal theories most commonly used to establish legal liability in small claims court. In many instances, this information will be all you need to prepare your case. But occasionally, you will want to do additional legal research, especially if the exact wording of a statute or key court decision has a direct bearing on your case. (See Chapter 25 for more on how to do legal research.)

**CAUTION**

**Check your state's small claims court rules.** Many small claims courts limit the types of cases they will decide in addition to restricting the dollar amount of damages you can claim. For example, your small claims court might only allow breach of contract claims and claims by consumers for damages connected with retail products or services. Ask your small claims court clerk or review your small claims court's rules to make sure your case can be heard. (See Appendix A for your state court's website for contact and other information.)

Below is a list of common legal theories and what you need to prove to establish each one. The rest of this chapter reviews each key legal theory in more detail, so you can determine whether the facts of your case fit the requirements of at least one of them.

**Bad Debt.** A type of contract case. To prevail, you need to prove the debt exists, its amount, when payment was due, and that the person you are suing hasn't paid it or has only partially paid it.

**Breach of Contract.** One or more terms of a valid contract (written, oral, or implied) has been broken by the person you are suing. As a result, you have suffered a monetary loss.

**Breach of Warranty.** A written or implied warranty (assurance) extended to you by a merchant has been breached and, as a result, you have suffered a monetary loss—for example, a new or used car suffers mechanical problems while still covered by warranty.

**Failure to Return a Security Deposit.** Another variety of contract case that commonly arises between tenants and landlords. As discussed in more detail in Chapter 20, the tenant needs to prove that a deposit was made, that it was not returned (or only partially returned), and that the premises were sufficiently clean and undamaged when the tenant left so the landlord owes the tenant some or all of the amount withheld.

**Libel or Slander (Defamation).** To prove a libel or slander case, you must show that the other party said or wrote something untrue about you or your business, that others heard or read it and understood it was about you, and that it really did damage your reputation. (Public figures must also show that the person defaming them knew the offending statement or writing was false or was made in "reckless disregard of the truth.")

**Nuisance.** Someone's conduct creates a health or safety hazard to you or interferes with your ability to use and enjoy your property—for example, a factory makes so much noise that it keeps you and other nearby residents awake all night.

**Personal Injury.** The negligent (careless) or intentional behavior of the person you are suing has caused you to suffer personal injury.

**Product Liability.** You or your property were injured by a defective product. If so, you qualify for recovery under the legal doctrine of strict liability, which holds the manufacturer and seller responsible for the damages you suffered, without your having to prove negligence.

**Professional Malpractice.** A lawyer, a doctor, or another professional's failure to use the ordinary skills of members of that profession results in you, as a client or patient, being harmed (in the case of a lawyer or an accountant, you must suffer a monetary loss).

**Property Damage.** The negligent (careless) or intentional behavior of the person you are suing has damaged your personal property.

CAUTION

**Other legal theories exist.** The legal theories listed above are involved in more than 99% of small claims cases. There are dozens of more obscure types of lawsuits, each with specific legal requirements. If your case isn't covered here, you will want to do some research to determine whether your case meets the qualifications of another legal theory.

TIP

**How to find other legal theories.** One way to review common causes of action is to thumb through your state's set of civil jury instructions. Many of the legal theories will apply in small claims court. The beauty of using jury instructions is that the elements you'll need to prove will be listed in plain language, and you'll find citations to the law as well. You can find most state jury instructions online or at your local law library. If you're not sure where they are, ask the librarian for help.

Before considering each legal theory individually, this illustration will help you understand why you must establish that you have suffered a loss and that the defendant is legally required to compensate you.

**EXAMPLE:** One night, someone entered the garage in Sarah's apartment complex, smashed her car window, and stole the purse she left in it accidentally. The purse and its contents were worth $600. After discovering and reporting the theft, Sarah filed suit against the landlord in small claims court. Sarah prepared for her court trial by finding several witnesses willing to testify that her car had been vandalized. She also obtained a copy of the police report she made, several repair estimates for the car window, and proof of the value of her stolen purse.

However, Sarah overlooked one crucial thing—the building owner wasn't liable for her damages. The contract didn't require him to keep the garage locked, and he hadn't orally promised to do so. Also, he had never locked the garage or otherwise led Sarah to believe that he would keep her property secure.

At the trial, the judge determined two important facts: The tenants knew or should have known that anyone could gain access to the garage from inside or outside the building, and there were no previous instances of vehicle vandalism. The judge concluded that failing to lock the garage wasn't a contract violation, and that because the landlord had no reason to expect criminal activity, leaving the garage unlocked wasn't negligent. As the judge explained when ruling for the landlord, Sarah remained responsible, just as she would have if someone had damaged her car on the street.

The outcome might have been different if the facts were changed. Assume Sarah's lease entitled Sarah to an assigned parking place in a "secure garage" and that the landlord always locked the garage door. But, under the new scenario, the lock broke. Even though Sarah and other tenants asked the owner to fix the lock the next day, the landlord hadn't "gotten around to it" when the theft occurred a week later. In this situation, Sarah should win. The landlord failed to keep the contractual promise to lock the garage even though he'd had plenty of time to fulfill his obligation. A judge could reasonably conclude that the landlord's breach of contract allowed the thief access to the car.

## Breach of Contract Cases

A contract is an agreement between individuals or businesses in which one side agrees to do something for the other in exchange for something in return. For example, A asks B to paint his kitchen for $3,000 and B agrees. Agreements can be written or oral or implied from the circumstances. Contracts made by minors might be invalid if made before the minor turns 18. However, in most states, if a minor makes a contract and then honors it after turning 18, the contract is valid and can no longer be annulled.

All contracts come with an obligation that each party carry out its terms in "good faith," and that each contracting individual or business will deal with the other fairly and honestly under the circumstances. On the other side of the coin, courts have found "bad faith" when one party does something that isn't in the spirit of the agreement or violates community standards of fairness and reasonableness. Practically, all contracts contain an unwritten good faith requirement. A small claims judge often won't find in favor of a party who sues based on a highly technical—but obviously unfair or unreasonable—interpretation of contract language. For example, if X agrees to landscape Y's yard in two weeks, but on the last afternoon doesn't quite finish because she is called to the bedside of a sick child, a court will not agree with Y's contention that he doesn't have to pay for any of the work because X technically missed the 14-day deadline. Instead, a judge will almost surely rule that Y's duty to carry out the agreement in good faith requires him to allow X to finish the job a few days late.

## Common Contract Rules

Before someone can collect on a contract, that person must show that a contract actually exists. You'll need to prove three elements: One person must offer to sell goods or services; the other person must agree to accept the goods or services; and finally, something of value—such as money or something else—must be exchanged. The exchange is known as "consideration." If the offer, acceptance, or consideration is missing, a contract can't be formed.

> **TIP**
>
> **Quid pro quo isn't just for employers and politicians—it will help you spot consideration.** Quid pro quo occurs when one party agrees to give something in exchange for something else. Some quid pro quo transactions are forbidden. For instance, a politician can't agree to give a country foreign aid in exchange for dirt on a political rival. And an employer shouldn't promise a special employee a raise or promotion in exchange for a back rub behind closed doors. But quid pro quo doesn't always indicate illegality. Just that both parties are getting something out of the deal. You can use the quid pro quo concept to help you remember to look for value being exchanged between the parties.

This short summary of familiar situations should help you understand whether you've got a valid contract:

- **A gift is not a contract.** A promise to make a gift is not a contract. The reason is simple: The person receiving the gift hasn't promised to do anything in return. The problem would be the lack of consideration. An enforceable contract must include an exchange or a promise to exchange something of value, such as money for services.

  > **EXAMPLE 1:** Elizabeth tells Steven she is in a bad way financially, so Steven promises to give Elizabeth $750 on January 1. Later, Steven changes his mind after deciding he doesn't like Elizabeth after all. Can Elizabeth sue Steven for the $750? No. This is not a contract. Elizabeth didn't promise to do anything for Steven in return for his promise. Steven had only indicated that he would give Elizabeth a gift in the future.

- **A loan is a contract.** By contrast, a loan is usually a valid contract. Each party provides the other something of value: The lender advances the borrower the money, and the borrower agrees to pay it back with interest. The borrower gets the use of the funds, and the lender receives the interest.
- **An agreement to exchange goods, services, or money is a contract.** The most common type of contract occurs when A agrees to pay money to B in exchange for B agreeing to work for A or provide A with valuable goods.

EXAMPLE 2: Steven promises to pay Elizabeth $750 on January 31 in exchange for Elizabeth's promise to tutor Steven's oldest son. This is a valid contract because each person has promised to do something for the other (remember quid pro quo?). If Steven fails to pay Elizabeth on January 31 and Elizabeth has kept her part of the bargain, Elizabeth can go to court, claiming breach of contract.

- **Most oral contracts are valid but can be hard to prove.** If a spoken agreement contains all three elements, then it will be valid and enforceable. The problem? Oral contracts can be hard to prove. Even if you can prove it—and you might, so don't give up—you'll have to get over a few more hurdles. Generally speaking, oral contracts are not valid if they: (1) can't be accomplished within a year, (2) are for the sale of real estate, or (3) involve the sale of goods or property worth more than $500. (But this third type of transaction needs very little written proof—a faxed order or a letter confirming a deal will be enough.) Because the great majority of oral consumer contracts—whether to fix a kitchen, repair a car, or deliver a bed—can easily be carried out in less than a year (even if it actually takes longer), if you can prove its existence to the satisfaction of a judge, it can be enforced in small claims court.

- **Proving a contract by showing someone received a benefit.** A contract can be implied where one party has benefited from the other (known as "unjust enrichment"), and the other expects to be paid for goods or services. This is a tricky area of contract law that occasionally surfaces in small claims cases. The judge will be particularly interested in evidence that the party who received the benefit knew that the service provider expected to be paid.

EXAMPLE 3: Paul asks Gianna if she wants her house painted. Gianna says "Yes," and Paul paints her house. However, Giana refuses to pay, claiming that they never agreed on a price so there was no contract. Gianna is wrong. A contract exists when one person does work for another in circumstances where payment is usually expected and the second person accepts it. Consent can be stated, as in this example, or even implied, as would be the case if Gianna simply watches Paul paint her house. In other words, even though one or more technical parts of a contract are missing, when work is involved, the law will require that a person who knowingly benefits from another person's work pay for it unless it is absolutely clear the work was donated.

## Unpaid Debts

Often, a contract that has not been honored involves a failure to pay money. Hardly a day goes by in any small claims court when someone isn't sued for failing to pay a phone bill, an overdue credit card balance, or even a friend (former, probably) or relative. (See Chapter 18 for more on small claims suits where money is owed.) In many situations, getting a money judgment for an unpaid debt involves no more than stating that the defendant made a commitment to buy certain goods or services, that they were, in fact, provided, and that a legitimate bill for X dollars has not been paid.

A plaintiff should be ready to prove:
- the identity of the debtor
- the existence of a contract with the debtor
- that you kept your promises under the deal by providing the goods or services, and
- that the debt hasn't been paid.

If you are a defendant and believe you have a good defense, you'll typically need to prove:
- the goods or services you were supposed to receive were delivered late or not at all or were seriously defective
- the plaintiff never lent you the money in the first place
- you already paid back some or all the money the plaintiff lent you, or
- the plaintiff agreed to a subsequent contract to forgive the debt or give you more time to pay.

If you are sued because you owe money for consumer goods or consumer services (as opposed to a business purpose), research your state's consumer protection laws. (See Chapter 25 on painless methods of legal research.) Also, if a seller of consumer goods or services violates a consumer protection law, then you might be able to get your money back or cancel your deal with no obligation to pay.

## The Cooling-Off Rule

If you buy a product or service from a seller at a location that's not the seller's permanent place of business, you have three business days to change your mind and cancel the sale, as long as the purchase exceeded $25 and occurred at your residence. If it didn't take place at your home, it must exceed $130. (16 CFR Part 429.)

The Cooling-Off Rule applies if you buy something from a door-to-door salesperson (even if you invited the salesperson to make the presentation), at work, and at temporary sales locations like convention centers, fairgrounds, and restaurants.

The Cooling-Off Rule does not apply to sales of real estate, insurance, securities, motor vehicles sold at temporary locations as long as the seller has at least one permanent place of business, or arts or crafts sold at fairs, shopping malls, civic centers, and schools. The Cooling-Off Rule also doesn't apply to goods or services that:

- cost less than $130 (or $25 if purchased at your residence)
- are not primarily intended for personal, family, or household use
- are sold entirely by mail or telephone
- are sold after prior negotiations at the seller's permanent business location
- are needed to meet an emergency, or
- are made as part of your request for the seller to do repairs or maintenance on your personal property.

The Cooling-Off Rule requires the salesperson to tell you about your cancellation rights at the time of sale and give you two copies of a cancellation form and a copy of your contract or receipt. The contract or receipt must be in the same language used in the sales presentation, be dated, show the name and address of the seller, and explain your right to cancel. If you'd like to learn more, go to the Federal Trade Commission website at www.consumer.ftc.gov/articles/0176-buyers-remorse-when-ftcs-cooling-rule-may-help.

If fraud is present as part of a transaction, the deal can be canceled and your money refunded. Fraud can be:

- intentional misrepresentation (a deliberate, false statement about a product or service)
- negligent misrepresentation (a statement about a product or service made without investigating its truth)
- fraudulent concealment (suppression of the truth) or,
- a false promise (a promise with no intention to perform), or any other act designed to deceive.

If you make certain purchases, you have a "cooling-off" period under federal law during which you can cancel the contract or sale. (See "The Cooling-Off Rule," above.)

## Failure to Perform

Sometimes, a breach of contract suit results not from a refusal to pay a bill, but because one party claims that the other failed to carry out one or more of the terms of a contract. Such would be the case if:

- A tenant sued an apartment owner who agreed to rent an apartment but instead rented it to someone else. (Leases and rental agreements are discussed in more detail in Chapter 20.)
- A small business sued a caterer who showed up four hours late with the food and drink for an important party.
- A customer sued a tattoo artist who began an elaborate skull pattern on his back but couldn't find the time or inspiration to finish it— leaving the customer with what looked like a lumpy potato tattoo and the prospect of paying someone else to finish or remove it.

TIP
**In court, you'll need to convince the judge that the contract existed.** If the contract is in writing, bring it to court. If it's oral, be prepared to prove its existence through witnesses and circumstantial evidence. Be creative—if you lent money to a debtor using a check, bring a copy. Along with your testimony that the borrower promised to repay you, this should work, but bring everything you have that might help you establish the existence of a contract.

You'll also have to prove "damages," or how much money you've lost. Damages resulting from a breach of contract aren't usually difficult to prove, but they're easily forgotten. If you forget to put on evidence proving your damages, the judge won't issue a money judgment. All your effort will be for nothing. So, after you show that the contract existed and that the other party failed to meet its terms, you should testify as to the dollar amount of damages you have suffered as a result. Plan to introduce evidence to convince the judge that you really did lose this amount.

> **EXAMPLE 4:** Luca and Juliette, millennials with substantial student loan debt and skepticism for traditional marriage, planned a June commitment ceremony. Because both of their families were spread across the country, they thought it would be a great idea to turn the event into a family reunion catered by their favorite gastropub, Bittersweet Pubhouse. The pub prepared a written list of their food and drink orders, and Juliette signed it. When the big day arrived, everything went well until the 200 guests arrived at the local park only to find that the Bittersweet Pubhouse hadn't shown up with the food. The best man improvised by buying ten cases of champagne at the local liquor store and the maid of honor ordered 30 pizzas. Two hours later, Bittersweet Pubhouse showed up full of apologies. Juliette and Luca accepted the cake. But because everyone had already eaten and had plenty to drink, they turned down everything else. When Bittersweet Pubhouse sued the couple for $10,000 for breach of contract, Luca and Juliette countersued for $11,000 for emotional distress. The judge agreed with the couple that by being two hours late to a time-sensitive event, Bittersweet Pubhouse had breached its contract, and Juliette and Luca owed them nothing. But the judge also dismissed the couple's emotional distress claim, stating that the reception went well and the couple didn't prove they suffered emotional damage.

The fact that many contract cases are easy to win doesn't mean that all result in victory. A good number of plaintiffs lose cases that they assumed were open and shut. Why? Usually, it's because they:
- failed to show that a contract existed (see Examples 1 and 5)
- failed to show that a contract was broken (see Example 6)
- failed to sue the right defendant (again, see Example 5), or
- failed to establish that they really suffered a monetary loss (see Example 4).

**EXAMPLE 5:** Ben, a landlord, sued John, the parent of one of his tenants, for damage John's daughter and her roommates did to their rental unit. John was sued because he had cosigned his daughter's lease. Ben quickly convinced the judge that the damage had occurred, and the judge seemed disposed toward giving him a judgment for the $980 requested until John presented his defense. John showed that the lease between his daughter and the landlord had been rewritten three times after he originally cosigned it and that he had not added his signature to any of the revised versions, one of which involved replacing several of his daughter's original roommates with others. The judge agreed that because John had not cosigned any of the subsequent leases, he wasn't liable. The reason was simple: There was no longer a contract between Ben and John. (Leases and rental agreements, including a detailed discussion of the rights and responsibilities of cosigners, are discussed in more detail in *Every Landlord's Legal Guide*, by Janet Portman and Marcia Stewart (Nolo).)

**EXAMPLE 6:** Stephano sued Casual Cleaners for $650, the cost of replacing a suede jacket that Casual shrank. Stephano established that he had taken the jacket to Casual for cleaning and had agreed to pay Casual $80. Casual, by accepting the jacket, clearly implied it would properly clean it, so there was no question that a contract existed. Stephano showed the judge that the sleeves barely came to his elbows.

Unfortunately, Stephano made critical errors. His first mistake was asking for the jacket's $650 replacement value, not the jacket's fair market value based on the age and condition when the damage occurred. Because the jacket was eight months old and well worn by the time Casual received it, the fair market value was likely $400 or less.

Stephano's second mistake was failing to anticipate Casual's defense. Charlotte, Casual Cleaners' owner, testified that she was amazed when she saw the jacket after cleaning. Her cleaning shop specialized in leather goods, and the cleaning process should not have resulted in such shrinkage. She also testified that she had examined several other items in the same cleaning batch and found no similar problem. She then sent the jacket to an "independent testing laboratory." The report, which she presented to the court, stated that it was the jacket itself, not the cleaning, that was the problem. According to the report, shrinkage occurred because the leather had been severely overstretched before assembly.

The judge was convinced by the testing lab report and felt that Casual had breached no contract as far as the cleaning was concerned. However, the judge also felt that Casual, as a leather cleaning specialist, had some responsibility to notify Stephano that the jacket should not have been cleaned in the first place. Therefore, the judge mainly held for Casual but did award Stephano $100. He also suggested that Stephano might want to consider suing the store that sold the jacket. The judge explained that Stephano could claim the store breached an implied warranty by selling clothing made from seriously defective material. He could use as evidence the very lab report that lost him his original case.

**RELATED TOPIC**
**More material concerning contracts:**

- How much you should sue for in a breach of contract case (how to value your damages) is discussed in Chapter 4.
- Breach of warranty (based on a written or oral contract) is covered below.
- Leases and rental agreements (a specialized type of contract) are covered in Chapter 20.
- How to collect on contracts involving unpaid bills is covered in Chapter 18.
- If your contract involves fraud, undue influence, or a simple mistake—for instance, if $2,000 was mistakenly written as $20,000—you might have a right to have the contract ended or rewritten or to get your goods back under the legal doctrine of equitable relief. (See Chapter 4.)

# Personal Injury and Property Damage Cases

Most personal injury cases are based on a claim that someone has been negligent (careless). A few are based on allegations of intentional injury. Another category of small claims disputes occurs when a defendant negligently (carelessly) or intentionally damages the plaintiff's property.

Many plaintiffs will claim both personal injury and property damage in the same case. For instance, a bicyclist struck by a neighbor would likely seek compensation for physical injuries and repairs to the bicycle. To prevail, you must show that someone's negligent or intentional behavior caused your personal injury or property damage (or both). The same legal standard will apply to both the personal injury and property damage aspects of your case. (If your injury was caused by a defective product, a different legal doctrine applies—see "Defective Product Cases," below.)

## Negligence

A technical definition of negligence could—and does—fill entire law texts. Here's the short version: If someone injures you or damages your property as a result of failing to act reasonably under the circumstances, you'll have a valid negligence claim.

> **EXAMPLE:** Jake knows the brakes on his old Saab are in serious need of repair but does nothing about it. One night, he parks his car on a hill, and the brakes fail. The car rolls across the street and destroys Keija's persimmon tree. Keija sues Jake for $225, the reasonable value of the tree. Jake will lose because he did not act with reasonable care under the circumstances.

Negligence can also occur when a person with a duty or responsibility to act fails to do so. For example, an electrician who promises and then fails to check the wiring in a room where you tell him you saw some frightening sparks would be negligent.

Another obvious situation involving negligence would be one where a car or bus swerves into your traffic lane and sideswipes your fender. The driver of the offending vehicle has a duty to operate it in such a way as not to damage other vehicles. By swerving into your lane, it is extremely likely that he has failed to do so.

On the other hand, a situation in which negligence could be difficult to show would involve your neighbor's tree that falls on your car while it is properly parked in your driveway. Here you have to be ready to prove that the tree was in a weakened condition for some reason (such as age, disease, or a bad root system), and the neighbor knew about it but was negligent in failing to do something about it. If the tree looked to be in good health, your neighbor probably wasn't negligent and had no reason to remove it or prop it up.

Here are some additional examples in which a person or business failed to act with reasonable care and, as a result, was negligent:

- While playing with his kids in his small backyard, Kevin hits a ball over the fence, smashing a neighbor's window.
- While upgrading Mia's computer, Rhonda carelessly installs the wrong chip, which crashes Mia's hard drive and ruins the computer.
- RapidMail, Inc., a local courier service, loses several time-sensitive deliveries and fails to notify the sender of the problem.

Negligence also exists where more than one person is responsible for the damages you suffer—for example, if two coworkers break your vase while playing keep-away. When dealing with a situation in which more than one person might have contributed to your loss, sue them all.

EXAMPLE 1: Linda, a human resource consultant, comes home to find her new fence knocked over and Fred's Chevy Blazer in the middle of her herb garden. Fred admits he hit the fence when his brakes failed. To Linda, this might seem like a simple case against Fred. But what if Fred had just picked up his car from Great Escape Auto Repair, where he had his brakes worked on? Fred's liability could be minimal if Great Escape is only 50 feet away, and Fred just left the shop with the assurance that the brakes were fixed. Or, it might be extensive if Great Escape is located across town, and, at the last two stop signs Fred's brakes acted "funny" but he continued to drive anyway. Although Linda might not know all these details, if she learns that Fred recently had his brakes worked on, she would be well advised to sue both Fred and Great Escape and let the judge sort out who is more at fault.

EXAMPLE 2: Suppose Fred's brakes are fine, but he claims he was rear-ended at the stop sign by Dana, whose pickup truck pushed his vehicle through Linda's fence. Again, Fred's liability could be minimal if Dana was drunk and speeding. Or it could be extensive if Fred ran a stop sign while turning and was rear-ended by Dana, who had the right of way. Again, Linda would be wise to sue both parties and let the judge sort out who was more at fault.

To help you determine whether you have a good case based on someone else's negligence, answer the following questions:

- Did the person whose act (or failure to act) damaged your property behave in a reasonable way? Or to put it another way, would you have behaved differently if you were in that person's shoes?
- Was your conduct a significant cause of the injury?

If the person who damaged your property behaved in an unreasonable way (ran a red light when drunk) and you were acting sensibly (driving at 30 mph in the proper lane), you probably have a good case. If you were a little at fault (slightly negligent) but the other person was much more at fault (very negligent), you can probably still recover most of your losses, because most states follow a legal doctrine called "comparative negligence" (but not all do, so check your state's laws). The judge will subtract the percentage of your negligence from 100% to find out how legally responsible you and the other party are for the damage. For instance, if a judge finds that one person (drunk and speeding) was 80% at fault, and the other (slightly inattentive) was 20% at fault, the slightly inattentive party can recover 80% of the loss.

**RESOURCE**
**Where to get more information about negligence.** It's a good idea to get more details of negligence theory by researching online (see Chapter 25 for information on legal research). Or, you can go to your nearest law library and review legal text on torts (wrongful acts or injuries). Most law librarians will be happy to help you find a good resource.

## Intentional Acts

Not all harm is the result of an accident. You also have the right to recover money if someone intentionally injures you or damages your personal property (which includes all property other than real estate).

**EXAMPLE:** Neighbors Basil and Shirley are prize-winning rose growers who can't stand the sight of each other. When Basil took first place in the local exotic rose contest, Shirley became angry and jealous. To retaliate, she left her hose running and drowned Basil's award-winning roses. If Basil brings a small claims case against Shirley, he will likely recover the value of his rose bushes, and possibly even money for emotional distress, although it's unlikely (see below).

TIP

**Don't argue yourself out of insurance coverage.** It's easy to get mad when someone hurts you or damages your property, and in the heat of the moment, you might think that a wrongdoer did it on purpose. Or that claiming intentional harm will strengthen your case. Give it careful thought. Unless you're sure the defendant intended to hit you or key your car, you'll likely be better off arguing negligence—especially if insurance is available to cover your claim. Most insurance policies won't cover the intentional acts committed by the policyholder. You'd have to collect payment from the defendant, instead.

In theory, at least, it's possible to recover punitive damages—money given to you solely to punish the other person—if your property is damaged by the malicious conduct of someone else. However, punitive damages are seldom awarded in small claims court because the small claims process isn't set up to allow enough time to evaluate whether the defendant's conduct was so egregious that the defendant should be punished financially.

RELATED TOPIC

**More material concerning property damage.** To determine how much to sue for, see Chapter 4.

## Why Punitive Damages and Small Claims Court Don't Mix

Most plaintiffs are somewhat angry and would like nothing better than to ask the court to punish the defendant and get extra money in the process. Unfortunately, small claims usually isn't the right forum for punitive damages.

In most cases, the plaintiff would need to present evidence demonstrating that the defendant not only had a history of doing something wrong but was aware that the act was wrong and continued doing it anyway, harming many, many people in the process. A famous example involves the golden arches and scalding coffee.

In that case, what most people don't realize is that the coffee spilled was so hot that the plaintiff suffered third-degree burns and required skin grafts. Also, the plaintiff presented evidence showing that the company received hundreds of complaints concerning injuries resulting from hot coffee spills, many of which also involved third-degree burns. Yet, the company did nothing.

To punish the company, and to encourage change, the jury awarded almost three million dollars in punitive damages. That's the point of punitive damages—to punish the defendant for egregious acts. And, if it's a big company, it takes a lot of bucks to get a message across. But in small claims court, most defendants won't have the ability to gather the reams of evidence required or the time to present it in court. That type of case would be best tried in a traditional court by experienced attorneys.

Even so, your state might have a statute (written law or code) that allows for punitive damages in certain instances. For example, California Civil Code § 1950.5(g) says that if a landlord keeps a security deposit in bad faith, a renter can get twice the amount back in a punitive damage award. Often, the easiest way to find out what you can claim in damages is by contacting your local small claims self-help clinic.

## Assessing Your Personal Injury or Property Damage Case

Start by understanding that most personal injury cases—and some property damage cases—involve amounts of money that are clearly over the small claims maximum and should be pursued in formal court. However, occasionally a minor personal injury or property damage case will be appropriate for small claims.

> ! CAUTION
> **Check your state's rules.** Remember, in some states you cannot file a personal injury case in small claims court, even if the amount of damages is less than the maximum.

Next, before you sue someone for an injury or property damage, consider whether it was really caused by negligence. If so, the person is legally liable to make your loss good by paying for costs you've incurred. If not—for instance, suppose you trip and fall down a perfectly safe set of stairs—you have no right to recover, no matter how serious your injury. (Again, there's one major exception to the rule that you must demonstrate the other side's negligence—when you are injured by a defective product.) If in doubt, go ahead and sue, but be prepared to deal with the negligence question as well as prove the extent of your injury. (In Chapters 14 and 15, you'll find some practical advice on how to prove your case.)

> **EXAMPLE 1:** Jen and Karen are playing softball in a picnic area of a park while many families enjoy their lunches. Jen, never a star fielder, misses a batted ball that hits seven-year-old William and chips his tooth. With the help of his parents, William sues Jen and Karen for the $2,000 it will cost to repair his tooth. Jen and Karen claim they were just playing a game and shouldn't be held liable. How will a judge decide this case? Almost surely in favor of William, who was eating lunch in a picnic area where he had a right to be. By contrast, Jen and Karen will likely be found careless (negligent). Why? Because picnic areas are for picnickers—not ballplayers—and Jen and Karen should have known that the game was inappropriate and dangerous to others. They will have to pay for their negligence.

> **EXAMPLE 2:** Now, assume that Jen and Karen move to a nearby ball field. Their skills haven't improved and again, Jen misses the ball. Like before, it hits poor William in the mouth and chips his tooth, but this time he had escaped his parents and wandered onto the field unobserved. Are Jen and Karen still liable to pay to fix William's tooth? Probably not. Jen and Karen took reasonable precautions to avoid hitting picnickers by playing on the ball field. Although they might have a responsibility to get little William off the field if they spot him, they are probably not legally responsible—that is, negligent—if he wanders onto the field unnoticed.

The critical point is that not every act of another person that upsets you merits a lawsuit. You must prove fault on the part of the person you intend to sue.

If you want to recover additional money for emotional distress, the other person's behavior must:

- be negligent, violate a law, be outrageous, be intended to cause you harm, or be done in reckless disregard of whether it will cause you harm, and
- cause you emotional distress that is serious (for a negligence case) or severe (for a case where you claim the person's actions were intentional).

This second element is sometimes the hardest to prove in a mental distress case. Proving that you suffered emotional harm can be difficult and expensive—often more so than a small claims case would warrant. If you have seen a doctor or therapist, you could use a written statement outlining your emotional distress as evidence. However, bringing in the expert to testify would be the strongest approach. The problem is that most professionals charge a lot of money to appear in court. You could also try testifying about your issues yourself. However, because most judges put more stock in expert testimony, it might not be effective. Simply put, expect proving up a mental distress case to get expensive fast.

Also, as discussed in more detail in Chapter 4, you don't have to suffer a physical injury to recover in court based on someone else's negligent or intentionally harmful behavior. Intentional or negligent infliction of mental distress lawsuits are based solely on nonphysical injuries.

**EXAMPLE:** Suppose your landlord enters your apartment without notice, permission, or good legal reason. You make it clear that this behavior is highly upsetting and ask her to cease invading your privacy. She nevertheless persists in entering your apartment with no good reason, causing you to become genuinely upset and anxious. You file a small claims case based on the intentional infliction of mental distress. Assuming you can convince the judge that you were truly and seriously upset, your chances of winning are good.

 **RESOURCE**

**More information on personal injury.** Check out www.nolo.com/legal-encyclopedia/accident-law for free personal injury articles. You'll find information on everything from proving liability to hiring a personal injury lawyer. Nolo also publishes a book on the subject: *How to Win Your Personal Injury Claim*, by Joseph Matthews.

## Workplace Discrimination

Two areas in which the number of small claims cases is growing are sexual harassment and other workplace discrimination. Both are illegal under federal and state law. Small claims court is a particularly helpful option for people having trouble finding an attorney because the case will be hard to prove or not worth much money (damages). Before going to court, you must first "exhaust your administrative remedies" by following the procedure provided by the government agency responsible for addressing the wrongful conduct. In other words, you must file a claim with the agency first. If you don't take this step, the small claims court judge will dismiss your case.

**CAUTION**

**Allow enough time to correct mistakes.** Not everyone realizes that some cases require the plaintiff to pursue administrative remedies first—and that if you don't, claiming ignorance won't get you out of trouble. Fortunately, a fix exists as long as enough time remains to file the claim with the agency, get a right to sue letter (it's what the agency will give you after rejecting the claim), and refile the small claims complaint. Once the statute of limitations period expires—the time limit to file an action—your case will be barred and you'll lose the ability to recover your losses. So if it expires before you complete these steps, you'll be out of luck. You can avoid this and other filing pitfalls by doing your research and not waiting until the last minute to file your case.

You'll likely start the process by filing an administrative action or formal complaint with either the federal Equal Employment Opportunity Commission (EEOC) or your state's equivalent. Wherever you file, you'll need to get a "right to sue" letter before proceeding to small claims court. The right to sue letter tells the court that the agency will not pursue the matter on its own—a likely outcome, given that these agencies get numerous complaints. Once you've got that letter, you can file a lawsuit in court.

**RESOURCE**
**More information on sexual harassment.** See the website of the U.S. Equal Employment Opportunity Commission (www.eeoc.gov) for information on laws prohibiting sexual harassment and filing a claim. Nolo also has helpful articles on the subject (www.nolo.com/legal-encyclopedia/hr-employment-law).

## Defective Product Cases

If you're injured by a malfunctioning vacuum cleaner, hairdryer, steam iron, lawnmower, or another product, you are entitled to recover from the manufacturer or the seller without proving that the defendant was negligent.

When an injury is serious, you'll want to file a product liability case in traditional court. However, if a defective product causes a minor injury, a small claims court lawsuit might be appropriate. Keep in mind that it's best to sue both the manufacturer and product seller, and be prepared to prove:
- the product malfunctioned
- you were using the product as intended or in a way they should have foreseen, and
- you suffered an injury as a result.

# Breach of Warranty Cases

 **RELATED TOPIC**
**Car warranties.** Chapter 17 discusses warranties as they apply to problems with new and used cars.

In simplest terms, a warranty is a promise by the manufacturer or seller of a product that the product is of a certain quality or that they will repair the product for a stated period. The manufacturer or seller is legally obligated to live up to its promise if the product turns out to have a defect that's covered by the warranty. Warranty law is extremely confusing, even to lawyers. A principal reason for this is that three separate warranty laws can apply to the retail sale of consumer goods. The unhappy result is that, short of presenting you with a major legal treatise, it's impossible to thoroughly explain warranty law. Here are the basic rules.

## Types of Warranties

A number of different types of warranties could apply to your defective product.

### Express Written Warranty

If a new or used consumer product comes with an express written warranty, you have the right to rely on what it says. The express warranty might be the seller's written description of the product that you relied on when deciding to purchase it (for example, a promise that a car is free of defects). Or, the express warranty could be the manufacturer's or retailer's written promise to maintain the performance of the product (for example, a promise to repair or replace defective parts for a stated period).

### Express Oral Warranty

If a seller makes an oral statement describing a product's features (for example, "these tires will last at least 25,000 miles" or "this car is in running condition") or what it will do ("it will work for two years"), and you rely on the statement when deciding to purchase the product, the oral statement is a warranty that you have the right to rely on. It is important to understand that this is true even though a more limited written warranty printed on the package states there are no other warranties. You must be able to prove that the seller made the oral statement; if you can't, the written warranty and its limitations will apply.

## Warranty Law: Where Does It Come From?

The Magnuson-Moss Warranty Federal Trade Commission Improvement Act (15 U.S.C. § 2302) is a federal law that applies in every state. Also, every state has a commercial code, which includes similar laws regulating retail sales and warranty protections for consumers. Some states have enacted separate consumer protection and warranty laws that go beyond the Magnuson-Moss Act and these commercial codes. For example, in California, a warranty or guarantee is still good even if the buyer doesn't fill out and return the manufacturer's form (Cal. Com. Code § 2801), and in Kansas an implied warranty exists even for goods sold "as is," unless the consumer has knowledge of the exact defects in the merchandise (Kan. Stat. Ann. § 50-639). To find out about your state's warranty laws, search your state statutes for "commercial code," "consumer protection," or "warranty" (see Chapter 25 for more on how to do this), or get in touch with your state consumer protection agency.

## Implied Warranty

In most retail sales of consumer products, a product must be fit for the ordinary purposes for which it is used. The item must do what it's supposed to do. For example, a lawnmower must cut grass, a tire must hold air, and a calculator must add and subtract. This warranty is called the "implied warranty of merchantability." It's implied because it isn't written down anywhere. It doesn't need to be. It's understood that the product must meet this basic standard. This warranty exists in addition to any express written and oral warranties regarding the product's performance.

Also, the implied warranty covers the product even if there is a statement (often called a "warranty disclaimer") printed on the product or packaging saying no warranties exist beyond the express written warranty, or that no warranty exists at all, or that all implied warranties are specifically disclaimed.

## When a Breach of Warranty Occurs

If you believe someone has breached a warranty—for example, your computer with a one-year warranty on parts and labor breaks the month after the purchase—you should notify the seller and manufacturer in writing, keeping copies of both letters. Give them a reasonable chance to make necessary repairs or replace the defective product. Thirty days to accomplish this is usually considered reasonable. If they fail to do so, it's time to think about filing in small claims court.

Keep in mind that small claims court judges tend to evaluate warranty disputes based on their own broad view of fair circumstances. In other words, if you purchase goods that are clearly defective or do not accomplish the task the seller claimed they would perform, and you have documented a good-faith effort to give the seller or manufacturer a chance to fix the problem by either providing you with a working product or refunding your money, your chances of winning are excellent—as long as you can prove:

- the warranty existed in the first place
- the defect is "substantial" (for example, a computer screen that won't light up would be substantial, but a loose letter on the keyboard would not be), and
- you did not cause the defect by misusing the product.

However, proving the existence of a warranty can be difficult when the promises were made orally and the other party will likely deny they were ever made.

**EXAMPLE:** Michael purchases a computer and an accounting software program from TechLand after explaining his needs to the salesperson and being assured that the computer and software setup will do the job. The computer comes with a 90-day written warranty against defects in parts and labor. All implied warranties are disclaimed. However, the software doesn't have a written warranty. After a couple of days' work, Michael realizes that the software isn't sophisticated enough to meet the needs he outlined for the salesperson, and he suspects that the salesperson said it was "perfect for the job" to close the deal.

Two days later, the computer crashes. Michael calls TechLand and asks for the computer to be fixed or replaced and a refund on the software. TechLand ignores the request, and Michael sues in small claims court.

Michael should have no problem recovering the price of the computer because it failed within the written warranty period. But the software raises a more complex problem. Michael is claiming a breach of an express oral warranty based on the salesperson's statement that the software would meet his needs, and a breach of the implied warranty of general fitness or merchantability. To succeed on the first claim, Michael must prove that the salesperson assured him that the software was right for his needs, which might be difficult. However, proving the second claim will be even harder. Michael must prove that the software falls below the reasonable standard for small business accounting packages. TechLand will likely counter Michael's claim with evidence that the software is widely used and can accomplish most accounting tasks. In short, Michael should focus on proving that he relied on the salesperson's oral statements that the software would meet his needs.

How should he do this? If Michael gave the salesperson a written specification detailing his accounting needs, he should show it to the judge. Even better, if he has a witness who heard the salesperson's overly optimistic promises, he could ask this person to testify in court or write a letter stating what happened. Unfortunately, if Michael has no convincing evidence supporting the salesman's statements, the small claims hearing will likely come down to his word against the salesperson's, with the judge left to decide who is telling the truth.

# Professional Malpractice Cases

An increasing number of people are filing small claims cases against doctors, lawyers, accountants, and other professionals because it can be difficult to get legal representation in a formal court action. As a result, the injured person must decide to either file without a lawyer in traditional court or scale down the claim's dollar amount to fit into small claims court.

To succeed with a malpractice claim, you must establish all of the following facts:

- **Duty.** The lawyer, doctor, dentist, or other professional owed you a duty of care. This is automatic if you were a patient or a client.
- **Carelessness.** The professional failed to use at least ordinary professional skills in carrying out the task (unless the person claimed to be a specialist, in which case the standard is higher). This one can be tougher to prove because unless the mistake is breathtakingly apparent, you'll typically need to get the opinion of one or more other professionals (experts) that your professional screwed up. In theory, you can do this by letter. Still, since the professional you are suing will almost surely be in court denying all wrongdoing, it is far better to have your expert witness testify in person.
- **Causation.** The professional's carelessness directly caused the harm or injury you suffered. For most types of malpractice, showing that the professional caused your injury isn't a problem. For instance, if a dentist stuck a drill through your cheek, the cause will be obvious. But when suing a lawyer, proving causation can be tricky. That's because you typically will need to show not only that the professional's mistake caused you to lose your case, and that you would have won if no mistake had been made. In other words, you need to convince the judge your underlying lawsuit was a winner.
- **Damages.** The harm you suffered at the hands of the professional resulted in actual economic loss to you. You can demonstrate that you lost money.

**EXAMPLE:** You consult a lawyer about an injury you suffered when you tripped and fell at a store. The lawyer agrees to file a lawsuit on your behalf but forgets to do so before the two-year statute of limitations runs out. Several malpractice lawyers you consult won't represent you in suing the incompetent lawyer because your injuries were fairly minor and they aren't sure that even if malpractice is established, you will be able to prove that you would have won your case against the store. (In other words, they believe you might not have been harmed by your lawyer's mistake in failing to file your case on time because your case wasn't so great in the first place.) You sue your lawyer in small claims court. His failure to file your case on time is clearly an act of carelessness (a lawyer using ordinary legal skills would have filed on time), but to win you'll also have to show that your lawyer's careless act resulted in monetary harm to you. This means convincing the judge that, in fact, your case against the store was a winner and that your injuries were serious enough to qualify for at least the amount of money you are requesting.

**RESOURCE**

**Further reading on malpractice cases.** *Represent Yourself in Court: How to Prepare & Try a Winning Case,* by Paul Bergman and Sara Berman (Nolo), explains how to bring a malpractice case in formal court.

## Nuisance Cases

You might have a private nuisance claim if someone prevents or disturbs your use or enjoyment of your property. For example, if your neighbor lets his dog bark all night, preventing you from sleeping, that's a private nuisance. If the barking persists and causes you real discomfort after you ask the owner to keep the dog quiet, you can sue.

To successfully sue someone for causing a private nuisance, you must prove that:

- you own, rent, or lease property
- the defendant created or maintained a condition that was
  - harmful to your health
  - indecent or offensive, or
  - obstructed your free use of your property
- you did not consent to the person's conduct

- the person's conduct interfered with your use or enjoyment of your property
- the conduct would be reasonably annoying or disturbing to an ordinary person
- you were, in fact, harmed (for example, your sleep was disturbed) by the person's conduct, and
- the seriousness of the harm outweighs the public benefit of the conduct.

A public nuisance, by contrast, means that someone is acting in a way that causes a group of people to suffer a health or safety hazard or lose the peaceful enjoyment of their property. For example, lots of noisy airplanes suddenly begin flying low over a residential area, or a chemical plant lets toxic fumes drift over a neighboring property. Public nuisance suits are often initiated by groups of individuals who all file small claims suits at more or less the same time.

To successfully sue a person or group of people for creating a public nuisance, you must prove all the facts listed above relating to private nuisance and also that:

- the condition affected a substantial number of people at the same time
- any social usefulness of the offending conduct is outweighed by the seriousness of the harm, and
- the harm you suffered was different from the harm suffered by the general public (for example, if a chemical plant's fumes are noticeable from the nearby freeway but ashes from the plant's smokestack fall into your swimming pool).

One fairly common example of this phenomenon involves people filing multiple small claims lawsuits against drug-selling neighbors or the drug-seller's landlords. (See Chapter 20 for more about these types of cases.)

TIP

**Try mediation before filing a lawsuit against a neighbor.** It is very difficult to put a dollar value on lawsuits against neighbors for antisocial acts, no matter how annoying. Also, filing a lawsuit usually makes long-term relationships worse. For these reasons, disputing neighbors should consider trying mediation before turning to small claims court. Some local law enforcement agencies provide mediation services for neighborhood disputes. (See Chapter 6 for more on mediation.)

# Can You Collect Your Money If You Win?

This is the shortest chapter in the book but one of the most important because it helps you to focus on a very simple question: If I win my small claims case, can I collect the money I'm owed?

You might be surprised to learn that you won't automatically receive the money when you win a judgment. If the defendant doesn't voluntarily pay, you'll have to use additional legal procedures to collect. And although collecting from solvent individuals or businesses isn't usually a problem—most will pay any judgments entered against them—if they don't, there are ways you can force them to do so.

But unfortunately, some people and businesses sued in small claims court are either broke (lawyers say "judgment proof") or so good at hiding assets that collecting your winnings might prove impossible. In fact, a significant percentage of people who aren't even "poor" are nevertheless judgment proof. Here's why.

Debtor protection laws prevent creditors from seizing the wages and property someone will need to work and live, such as the clothing from the closet, the TV from the living room, and in many cases, even the car from the driveway. So even though you can sue and get a judgment, you won't be able to collect a dime unless someone has more money and property than they need to get by.

What should these facts mean to you? You'll want to save yourself time and money by figuring out whether you'll be able to collect before moving forward with a lawsuit. Bill collectors go through this analysis early on. For instance, a creditor might be willing to sue on a $3,000 credit card debt if the debtor has a job or money in the bank, but a lesser amount might not be worth the effort. Ultimately, whether you sue should be a business decision based on facts and figures. Of course, you might feel that being proven right would be its own reward, but it would be best to decide that before getting started rather than finding yourself forced to accept it afterward.

To determine whether you might have trouble collecting from the debtor, start by finding out whether the defendant has a job. If so, that's good news—when someone fails to pay a judgment voluntarily, the easiest way to collect is to garnish the person's wages. But you usually can't garnish welfare, Social Security, unemployment, pension, or disability checks because they're exempt from collection efforts. So if the person's income is from one of these sources, try to locate nonexempt assets that you're free to collect.

---

### Wage Garnishments in a Nutshell

Under federal law and in most states, a creditor with a judgment can't take more than 25% of a judgment debtor's net earnings or the amount by which the debtor's net earnings exceed 30 times the federal minimum wage, whichever is less. (Net earnings are total earnings minus all mandatory deductions for such items as withheld income taxes and unemployment tax.)

The sheriff or marshal's office in your area usually can supply you with your state's rules. If you're a defendant and there's a judgment against you, strategies to cope with wage garnishment are covered in *Solve Your Money Troubles: Strategies to Get Out of Debt and Stay That Way*, by Amy Loftsgordon and Cara O'Neill (Nolo).

---

What about other collection sources? Can't a judgment be collected from assets other than wages? Sure. Real estate, bank accounts, stocks and bonds, and motor vehicles are other common collection sources. And if you've sued a business, you can often collect by ordering the sheriff or marshal to take the amount of the judgment right out of the debtor's cash register.

But remember, as mentioned above, many types of personal property are legally exempt from attachment. Most states exempt household goods and appliances necessary for everyday living (such as a stove, refrigerator, dishes, or TV); sentimental items and family keepsakes (such as photos, jewelry, or works of art); and tools or machinery the debtor uses to make a living (such as a computer, professional library, or power saw). A debtor's retirement account, life insurance, pension, and certain savings accounts are also protected. Even more significant, most states exempt a portion or all of the equity in a debtor's home from collections. Also, there will always be a reasonably significant cost associated with liquidating real estate or other property to satisfy a judgment.

What does all this boil down to? Simply this. Before you file your small claims court case, make sure that at least one of the following is true:

- The person or business you wish to sue is solvent and likely to pay a court judgment voluntarily.
- The person might be struggling now but will likely be solvent in the future. Judgments in most states can be collected for five to 20 years and renewed at least once and will earn interest until paid. In short, if you are willing to take a chance that an impoverished college student will eventually get a job, win the lottery, inherit money, or otherwise become solvent sometime in the next few years, go ahead and sue. You'll have to sit on the judgment for a while, but eventually, it should be collectible.
- You can identify assets that aren't protected by debtor exemption laws, such as a bank account or rental property that isn't the person's residence.
- If the defendant is a business, you can identify a readily available cash source you can collect from—the best being a cash register. Another good source is a valuable piece of equipment or machinery the judgment debtor owns free and clear that a judge will order sold to pay off your judgment.
- If your lawsuit involves a motor vehicle accident, some states allow the suspension of a nonpaying defendant's license for a period. Just the threat of a license suspension will prompt some debtors to pay. (See Chapter 24.)

RELATED TOPIC

**More information on collecting a judgment.** In Chapter 24, we deal in detail with the mechanics of collecting after you get your judgment. If you still think that collection may pose a problem, skip ahead and read that chapter before deciding to sue.

CAUTION

**Beware of bankruptcy.** If a person or a business declares Chapter 7 bankruptcy and lists you as a creditor, your right to recover a small claims court judgment outside bankruptcy will be cut off. You won't get paid unless the debtor has assets remaining after paying more critical debts, like taxes and support obligations, or if your claim arose from fraudulent or malicious behavior that injured you or damaged your property. In the second scenario, your right to collect should survive bankruptcy if you intervene by filing an adversary proceeding (a bankruptcy lawsuit) and win. But, if you have a lien on the debtor's property securing the money judgment (much like the security interest involved with a car loan, mechanic's lien, or mortgage), you'll have a right to recover the property securing the debt. That is unless the debtor files a motion asking the bankruptcy court to remove the lien. For more information, see *How to File for Chapter 7 Bankruptcy*, by Cara O'Neill and Albin Renauer (Nolo).

Here are situations that could make it more challenging to collect a money judgment:

- The defendant has no job or prospect of getting one.
- You can't identify any property to use as a collection source (for example, your opponent doesn't have equity in real estate, a valuable car, or investments).
- The defendant is a fly-by-night business outfit with no permanent address or obvious collectible assets, such as money in a cash register or lien-free fixtures or equipment. (Remember, many businesses lease equipment or take out a secured loan to purchase it. The lender will have a claim to the property superior to your money judgment and you'll be out of luck.)
- A contractor you want to sue is unlicensed and hard to track down.

# How Much Can You Sue For?

The maximum amount you can sue for in small claims court—or be sued for—varies from state to state. For example, it's $15,000 in Minnesota's "Conciliation Court" (small claims courts sometimes use different names), $2,500 in Kentucky, and $8,000 in Florida. You'll find the limits for other states in Appendix A, but because these can change, you'll always want to check by calling your local small claims court clerk or reviewing your local court rules. With some exceptions, small claims courts do not hear cases unless they are for money damages. You can't use small claims court to get a divorce, stop the city from cutting down your favorite oak tree, change your name, or do many of the other things that require a solution other than one side paying money to the other.

One exception to the "money only" rule involves equitable relief. Equitable relief is a court's power to order a person or business to do something specific, such as return a uniquely valuable piece of property or change a contract that contains an obvious mistake. These remedies are discussed in "Equitable Relief (or, Money Can't Always Solve the Problem)," below.

Another exception to the money-only rule involves evictions. In some states, a landlord can use small claims court to evict tenants in certain situations. (See Chapter 20 and Appendix A for more information.)

## Cutting Your Claim to Fit the Limit

Sometimes a claim might be worth more than the small claims dollar limit, but the plaintiff would like the convenience of litigating in an informal court setting. The plaintiff can reduce the claim amount to fit within the limits. For instance, if you wanted to recover a $5,300 debt in a North Carolina county that limits small claims awards to $5,000 (some counties allow awards as high as $10,000), you could ask for $5,000 rather than the entire amount. But if you do this, you forever "waive the excess," or the $300 difference between $5,000 and $5,300. You might want to do this if you don't like the alternative of filing your suit in a higher court where you'll have to follow complicated rules and will probably need to hire a lawyer who will charge considerably more than $300.

It is possible to represent yourself in formal court, of course, but doing so will require a good bit of homework. If you plan to go it alone, check out *Represent Yourself in Court: How to Prepare & Try a Winning Case,* by Paul Bergman and Sara Berman (Nolo).

TIP
**Check out the court just above small claims.** In most states, there are several levels of courts with different monetary limits. A case that doesn't fit into small claims court might be appropriately filed in a higher court (possibly called "circuit," "district," or "county court," depending on the state). These courts typically hear cases worth between $10,000 and $25,000.

## Calculating the Amount of Your Claim

Usually, determining how much you should sue for is relatively easy. But for some types of cases, it can be a little tricky. Before getting to the hard part, let's start with a basic rule: Always estimate your damages on the high side when in doubt. Why? Because even though many judges will have no problem awarding you less than you request, a judge is unlikely to order more, even if your state allows the judge to do so. But don't go overboard—if you sue for $2,500 on a $1,000 claim, you are likely to spur your opponent to furious opposition, ruin any chance for an out-of-court compromise, and possibly even lose the respect of the judge.

TIP
**Ask to amend your claim if you belatedly discover you should have requested more.** If you find yourself in court and realize you have asked for too little, ask the judge to allow you to amend your claim on the spot. Some judges will do this and, at the same time, offer the defendant extra time to prepare to defend against the higher claim. Other judges will allow you to dismiss your original case and start over, which is fine if your time to file (statute of limitations) hasn't run out. (See Chapter 5.)

## Contract Cases

To arrive at the exact figure to sue for in contract cases, compute the difference between the amount you were supposed to receive under the contract and what you received. For example, if Amanda agrees to pay Gary $4,200 to paint her house but pays him only $3,000, Gary has a claim for $1,200, plus the cost of filing suit and serving Amanda with the papers. (Court costs are discussed in Chapter 15.) The fact that Amanda and Gary made their agreement orally does not bar Gary from suing. As discussed in Chapter 2, oral contracts are generally legal as long as they can be carried out in a year and don't involve the sale of real estate or goods (personal property) worth more than the current legal cap. (Chapter 22 discusses written contract requirements for the sale of goods.)

> **TIP**
>
> **Write it down.** Because people embroiled in a dispute almost always remember an oral contract differently, oral contracts can be hard to prove in court. It's always wise to reduce agreements to writing, even if only in an informal note or letter that's dated and signed by both parties.

Unfortunately, some claims based on a breach of contract are harder to reduce to a dollar amount because of a legal doctrine known as "mitigation of damages." Don't let the fancy term throw you. Mitigation of damages means that the person bringing suit for breach of contract must take all reasonable steps to limit the amount of damages they suffer.

> **EXAMPLE:** Tiffany Tenant moves out three months before the end of her lease (remember, a lease is a contract). Her monthly rent is $950. Can Larry Landlord recover the full $2,850 ($950 x 3 months) from Tiffany in small claims court? Maybe not. Larry must try to limit (or mitigate) his damages by taking reasonable steps to find a new tenant in many states. If Larry can immediately rerent the apartment to someone else for $950 or more per month, he has suffered little or no damage and has fulfilled his responsibility to "mitigate damages." More typically, it might take Larry several weeks or months to

find a suitable new tenant unless he had plenty of advance notice, or Tiffany herself found a new tenant. For example, if it took Larry one month and $75 in advertising costs, he could recover approximately $1,025 (one month's rent + $75) from Tiffany, assuming the judge found that Larry had taken reasonable steps to find the new tenant.

The mitigation of damages concept applies to most contracts when the opportunity to limit losses exists. In the earlier house painting example, if Amanda had agreed to pay Gary $300 per day for seven days to paint her house and then had canceled after the first day, Gary could sue her for the remaining $1,800, the amount agreed to in the contract. However, in court, Amanda could ask Gary whether he had found a replacement job that earned him money during the six days. If he had, it would be subtracted from the $1,800. But what if Gary refused other work and slept in his hammock instead? If Amanda could show that he had turned down other jobs or had refused to make reasonable efforts to seek available work, the judge would likely consider this a failure to mitigate damages and reduce Gary's recovery accordingly.

## Loan Contracts

How much should you sue for if you lent money to a person who promised to repay it but failed to do so? In the complaint, you'd ask for the total you are currently owed, including unpaid interest (assuming it doesn't result in your claim exceeding the small claims maximum). People sometimes make the mistake of suing for the exact amount of the debt, thinking they could have the judge add the interest when they got to court. In most states, the judge doesn't have the power to make an award larger than the amount you request.

TIP
**Don't invent interest if none was provided as part of the loan.** As a general rule, you can only recover interest when it is called for in a written or oral contract. For example, if you loaned a friend $1,000 but never mentioned interest, you can sue only for the return of the $1,000.

CAUTION

**Understand special rules for installment loans.** If you are owed money under the terms of a promissory note (contract) that calls for repayment to be made in installments, you usually are only entitled to recover the amount of the payments that have already been missed (that is, what you are currently owed) and not those that aren't yet due. And this is true even if you are sure future installments will never be paid. But there is a notable exception to this rule: You can sue for the entire loan amount plus any interest your contract calls for if your installment contract contains what lawyers call an acceleration clause— language that states that the entire amount of the loan is immediately due if one payment is missed.

## Bad Checks

In some situations, a statute (law) establishes your right to receive extra compensation, over and above the amount of the financial loss. The most common of these involves a bad check or a check stopped in bad faith.

Most states have bad check laws allowing recovery of the check amount plus a penalty of two or three times more if it isn't made good within the time permitted by the statute—usually within 30 days after the written demand to do so. In some states, this law is mandatory—the judge must award the penalty.

Also, minimum and maximum penalties often exist:

- You can generally sue for some minimum amount in damages, no matter how small the bad check. For instance, if the state's minimum penalty is $100, you could sue for $125 for a $25 bad check.
- There is usually a top damage limit, too. For instance, if the maximum penalty is $1,500, the most you could sue for on a $600 check would be $2,100 (the amount of the check plus the $1,500 maximum).

TIP
**Don't forget to demand payment before you sue.** If someone gives you a bad check or stops payment on a check and you want to try to collect the maximum your state allows, start by sending a letter by certified mail demanding payment of the amount of the bad check, plus any applicable service charge and your mailing costs. Wait at least 30 days before filing suit to give the check writer time to pay.

TIP
**Cover yourself by documenting why you stopped payment on a check.** If you write a check and then stop payment because you believe the service or goods you purchased were substandard (or never provided), write a letter to the other party stating in detail why you were dissatisfied. If sued in small claims court, you could show a copy of the letter to the judge as part of your defense.

## Property Damage Cases

When someone negligently or intentionally damages your property, you have a right to recover the amount needed to fix the damaged item.

> **EXAMPLE:** John plows into Melissa's new BMW, smashing the left rear fender. How much can Melissa recover? Melissa is entitled to recover the amount it would cost to fix, or if necessary, replace the damaged part of her car. Melissa should get several estimates from reputable body shops and sue for an amount equal to the lowest one. (For more on proving car accident cases, see Chapter 19.)

However, a significant exception to this rule exists. Specifically, a plaintiff isn't entitled to a new or better object than the damaged property, so the cost of fixing the item cannot exceed its total value. For instance, suppose Melissa's car was ten years old, and the cost to fix the fender exceeded the car's value. In that case, Melissa would be entitled to the car's value, not what it would cost to repair it. In short, the most you can recover is the fair market value of a damaged item (the amount you could have sold it for) at the time the damage occurred. Also, you'll subtract the item's scrap value, if any, from the fair market value.

TIP

**Give yourself the benefit of the doubt when putting a value on property.** No one knows exactly how much any piece of used property is worth. Recognizing that reasonable minds can differ, it makes sense to place a fairly aggressive value on the destroyed property. But don't demand a ridiculous amount. Be sure to base it on reasonable comparables, or you'll likely offend the judge and weaken your case.

> **EXAMPLE:** In this example, Melissa's ten-year-old BMW is worth $12,000 after subtracting its $800 scrap value, and repairs would cost $13,000. Because the law limits her recovery to the cost of repairs minus the car's value in its damaged state, Melissa would be entitled to $12,000. But if Melissa had installed an expensive rebuilt engine a few weeks before the accident, she might legitimately argue that the car was worth $18,800. Assuming the judge agreed, Melissa could recover the entire $13,000 needed to replace the fender.

Unfortunately, knowing what something is worth and proving it are quite different. A car you believe is worth $4,000 might appear worth $3,000 to someone else. In court, be prepared to prove the property is worth every bit of the $4,000. You can do this by getting estimates from experts in the field. The expert can come to court and testify, or you can present a written estimate to the judge. Depending on the type of property involved, consider checking online marketplaces for the prices asked for comparable goods. For tips on proving the dollar amount of damage in specific cases, see Chapters 16–21.

CAUTION

**Replacement costs aren't relevant when figuring how much you are owed when property is destroyed.** Many people insist on believing they can recover the cost of getting a replacement object when theirs has been totaled. As you should now understand, this isn't necessarily true. If Melissa's $12,000 car was totaled and she claimed she couldn't get another decent car for less than $20,000, she would still be limited to a $12,000 recovery.

## Damage to Clothing Cases

Even though clothing is property, we discuss it separately because the logic judges apply in clothing cases can be different from that used in other property damage cases. It could be because clothing is personal and often has little or no value to anyone else, even in good condition. Plaintiffs would get little or no compensation if a judge strictly applied the rule limiting recovery to the damaged item's current market value. Recognizing this, some judges might bend the rules a bit and assess value based on the clothing item's original cost and current condition.

So when suing for damage to new or almost-new clothing, it follows that you should sue for the amount you paid. If you've already worn the item, determine the percentage of useful life remaining when damaged and sue for that percentage. For example, if you paid $900 for a suit two years ago and it would have lasted another two years, sue for $450.

To summarize, in clothing cases, most judges want answers to these questions:

- How much did the clothing initially cost?
- How much of its useful life had already passed when the damage occurred?
- Does the damaged item still have value to the owner, or was it ruined entirely?

EXAMPLE 1: Wendy took her new $250 coat to Rudolph for alterations. Rudolph cut the back of the coat incorrectly and ruined it. Wendy should sue for $250 because the coat was new.

EXAMPLE 2: The same facts as in Example 1, but the coat was two years old but in good condition. Here, Wendy should consider suing for $175 and be satisfied receiving a money judgment between $100 and $150.

EXAMPLE 3: Here, let's assume Rudolph slightly damaged Wendy's coat. Wendy should sue for $250, recognizing that the amount she'll recover will depend on the judge. Most would probably award a little less on the theory that the coat retained some value.

## Personal Injury Cases

Because a significant amount of money is usually at stake, most injured plaintiffs can find legal representation. Even so, some small personal injury cases end up in small claims court. Dog bite cases are a good example.

CAUTION
**Some small claims courts don't allow personal injury lawsuits.** Many states require that personal injury cases be filed in formal court. In other states, a small claims judge can award money for out-of-pocket losses, such as doctors' bills and lost time from work, but nothing for pain and suffering, no matter how legitimate. So check local and state rules before filing a personal injury case in small claims court.

TIP
**Try to settle or mediate your personal injury claims.** If you are seriously injured, you'll almost always want to sue for more than the small claims maximum. But to gain a fair recovery, you might not need to sue at all. Many people successfully negotiate or mediate a satisfactory settlement with an insurance company. For information on how to do this, see *How to Win Your Personal Injury Claim*, by Joseph Matthews (Nolo).

To determine how much to sue for, add up the dollar amount of the following losses:

| | |
|---|---|
| Out-of-pocket medical costs, including medical care providers | $_____ |
| Loss of pay, or paid time off, for missing work | $_____ |
| Pain and suffering | $_____ |
| Damage to property | $_____ |
| Total | $_____ |

Let's look at each of these categories in a little more detail.

**Medical/hospital bills.** Medical and hospital bills, including transportation to and from the doctor, can be recovered as long as you have established that the person you are suing is at fault. However, if you have health insurance, your policy will require you to turn over any money recovered for these costs. Knowing this, many judges are reluctant to grant judgments for medical bills unless the individual personally paid out of pocket for the treatment. But if you had uninsured expenses or deductible payments, by all means, include them.

**Loss of pay.** Lost income and paid time off due to injury works similarly. Assume that during your morning walk, the cocker spaniel down the block grabs a piece of your derriere for breakfast, and you miss a day of work getting yourself patched up. You are entitled to recover any lost pay, commissions, or vacation time.

**Pain and suffering.** When you read about big-dollar settlements, a good chunk of the recovery almost always falls into the "pain and suffering" category. No question, recovering from some injuries is a painful, miserable ordeal for which compensation is reasonable.

## Don't Count on Recovering Punitive Damages in Small Claims Court

Formal trial courts have the power to award extra damages (over and above out-of-pocket losses and pain and suffering) if an injury is caused by the malicious or willful misconduct (often a fraudulent or criminal act) of the defendant. When the defendant is wealthy, these damages—which are intended to punish the defendant—can run into the millions. About half the states do not allow punitive damage awards (sometimes called "exemplary damages") in small claims court. Even when it's possible to receive punitive damages, the small claims court's low dollar limit largely rules them out, except in a few instances where specific dollar amounts are established for bad checks or failure to return a tenant's security deposit on time (see Chapter 20). See a lawyer if you've been injured by conduct that would support a claim for hefty punitive damages.

But suppose you've suffered a minor but painful injury, and you want compensation for your discomfort. How much should you ask for? When valuing a client's pain and suffering, a lawyer will typically sue for three to five times the out-of-pocket damages (medical bills and loss of work). Using that measure, if you were out of pocket $500, you might ask for $1,500, the overage being for "pain and suffering." You'd have to convince the judge that you suffered real pain and inconvenience—often by presenting bills for medical treatment and testifying about your experience. A judge who concludes you suffered an injury will likely add an amount for pain and suffering.

> EXAMPLE 1: Melissa is drinking a soda when what appears to be a mouse part floats to the surface. She is immediately nauseated and, worried about infectious disease, goes to the doctor for an antibiotic. Melissa incurs a medical bill of $450 and loses an afternoon's pay of an additional $450. She sues the soda company for $3,000, claiming the extra money will compensate her for pain and suffering. Depending on the judge, she will probably recover most of this amount.

> EXAMPLE 2: The same thing happens to Ryan, but instead of getting sick, he throws the soda away and returns to work. He decides to sue a few weeks later after hearing about Melissa's case. How much is Ryan likely to recover? Because he didn't see a doctor and wasn't too upset by the incident, the judge might conclude he suffered little or no injury and award Ryan the price of the soda. On the other hand, seeing a mouse part is objectively disgusting enough that if Ryan can prove his case, a squeamish judge might toss in a bit more for good measure.

**Property damage.** Often a personal injury is accompanied by property damage. For instance, a dog bite might also ruin your pants. If so, include the value of your trousers when determining your losses.

## Emotional or Mental Distress Cases

There are all sorts of ways we can cause one another real pain without even making physical contact, especially in increasingly crowded urban environments. For example, if Tim lives in the apartment above you and pounds on his floor (your ceiling) for an hour at 6:00 a.m. every day, he will probably quickly reduce you to a raving maniac. What can you do about it without getting yourself in trouble?

One remedy is to sue in small claims court based on the fact that Tim's actions constitute the intentional infliction of emotional distress. (You could also sue for causing a nuisance; see Chapter 2.) But how much should you sue for? Unfortunately, it's impossible to provide a formula. It depends on how obnoxious his behavior is, how long it has gone on, and how clearly you have asked him to cease it (this should be done several times in writing). And if this isn't vague enough, it will also depend greatly on the judge's personality. For instance, the judge might be skeptical of neighbor disputes and believe they don't belong in court. At the very least, you'll need to convince the judge you are an extremely reasonable person and your neighbor is highly obnoxious before you will be eligible for any compensation.

One way to convince the judge you aren't a hypersensitive complainer is to sue for a reasonable amount. You'd probably do well to sue for far less than your state's small claims maximum except in the most extreme cases.

> **TIP**
>
> **Choose mediation when neighbors are involved.** As discussed in Chapter 6, the process of filing, preparing, and arguing a lawsuit tends to make both sides even angrier than they were initially. And, of course, the losing side is likely to stay mad for a long time. This might be fine if you are suing a large company or someone you don't intend to interact with again. Still, given the high value most people place on good relations with neighbors, it's usually best to at least try to settle your case through mediation before going to court. Even so, this tactic doesn't always work. As sad as it might be, it isn't unusual for such cases to escalate to the point of requesting restraining orders and never really end until one neighbor moves away. So before you bring a suit against a neighbor, consider whether it's worth it. It might make more sense to plant a fast-growing shrub, construct a decorative yet strong fence, or install a few well-placed yet noticeable cameras around the perimeter of your home.

## Malpractice Cases

In theory, most malpractice cases are worth far more than can be sued for in small claims court. But because legal rules (what it takes to prove liability, for example) are usually tilted to favor professionals and these cases are expensive to bring, it's often hard to find a lawyer to represent you on a contingency-fee basis (the lawyer doesn't charge you upfront but instead takes a percentage of the settlement). That means that malpractice cases can end up being scaled down to fit into small claims court.

You need to prove that the doctor's malpractice harmed you financially and physically for most types of malpractice. If a doctor negligently misdiagnosed an illness and as a result, you experienced serious medical problems, you would present the court with:

- all medical, hospital, and drug bills paid after the misdiagnosis that could have been avoided
- a second doctor's opinion that the original care didn't measure up to accepted medical standards (or, in plain language, that the first doctor screwed up)
- an estimate for your pain and suffering, and
- proof of any pay or vacation time lost.

> CAUTION
> **Special rules for legal malpractice.** As discussed in Chapter 2, if your suit is based on a lawyer's having failed to handle your case properly, you have to be able to prove not only that the lawyer was a bungler but that you would likely have won your original case if the lawyer had done a reasonably competent job. And you must also show that you would have won at least as much money as you are suing for in small claims court.

# Equitable Relief (or, Money Can't Always Solve the Problem)

Many states allow judges to grant relief in ways that do not involve the payment of money, if equity (fairness) demands it. In small claims court, equitable relief is usually limited to one or more of four categories: rescission, restitution, reformation, and specific performance. Let's translate these legal terms into English.

> **CAUTION**
>
> **You might need to do more research.** If you think you may want to sue "in equity," you'll need to look up your state's small claims court law. (See Chapter 25 for tips on easy legal research.)

**Rescission.** This remedy can wipe out a grossly unfair or fraudulent contract under the following conditions:

- It was based on a mistake as to an important fact.
- It was induced by duress or undue influence.
- One party simply didn't receive what was promised, through the fault of the other.

> **EXAMPLE:** If a merchant sues you for failure to pay for aluminum siding, the quality of which you contend the merchant seriously misrepresented, you could ask that the court rescind the contract and order the merchant to return the money you paid. Don't hesitate to ask for this remedy whenever you've been unfairly treated in a contract dispute.

**Restitution.** This valuable remedy allows a judge to order the return of property to its original owner when fairness requires restoring the contracting parties to their original positions. The judge can use restitution when someone sells a piece of property (say a motor scooter), but the other fails to pay. Instead of simply giving the seller a money judgment that might be hard to collect, the judge can order the breaching buyer to return the scooter to the original owner. If someone paid money under a rescinded contract, the judge could order its return, plus damages. For instance, suppose the judge rescinded a used car purchase based on the seller's fraud. In that case, the buyer could get a judgment for the amount paid, plus any money spent repairing the car and alternate transportation costs.

**Reformation.** This remedy is somewhat unusual. It changes (reforms) a contract when the parties agree that a term or condition was left out or misstated. A judge might fix an oral agreement that the contracting parties later wrote down incorrectly using reformation.

> EXAMPLE: Arthur the Author and Peter the Publisher orally agree that Peter will publish Arthur's 200-page book. They then write a contract, inadvertently leaving out the number of pages. If Arthur shows up with a 3,000-page manuscript and demands that it be published in its entirety, a court would very likely "reform" the contract to include the 200-page provision, assuming the judge was convinced that it should have been included in the first place.

**Specific performance.** This remedy comes into play when a contract involves an unusual or one-of-a-kind object. For example, suppose you agree to buy a unique antique jade ring for your mother's birthday because it is exactly like the ring she lost years before. If the seller refuses to go through with the deal, a court could rely on the doctrine of specific performance to order the seller to turn over the ring. The court will order specific performance when money won't adequately compensate the person bringing suit.

TIP

**The small claims dollar maximum applies to cases involving equitable relief.** When you fill out your court papers and ask for equitable relief, you still must indicate that the item in question's value is under the small claims maximum. For instance, you might describe your claim as follows: "I want the defendant to deliver the ring described as a 'one-of-a-kind' antique jade ring, worth approximately $4,000, as required by the terms of our written contract."

**Conditional judgments and equitable relief.** In some states, judges can issue conditional judgments in cases involving equitable relief. That is, they can order a party to perform, or stop, a particular act or else pay a money judgment. For example, suppose you agree to sell your baby grand piano for $3,000, but the buyer fails to pay and you sue. The judge can order the buyer to either return the piano or fork over the $3,000. If the buyer doesn't return the piano within the time limit set by the judge, you can enforce the money judgment. (See Chapter 24.)

# When Should You Sue?

E ach state's legislature sets up time limits within which lawsuits must be filed. These are called "statutes of limitations." Time limits are different for different types of cases. If you wait too long, your right to sue will be barred by these statutes.

Why have a statute of limitations? Because unlike wine, lawsuits don't improve with age. Memories fade, witnesses die or move away, and once-clear details become blurred. In other words, it's best to settle disputes relatively soon after they develop.

Statutes of limitations are almost always at least one year, so you should have little to worry about if you file promptly.

> **CAUTION**
> **Act fast for claims against a government agency.** To sue a city, county, state, or governmental agency (for example, a school district), you must promptly file a claim with the people in charge (for example, the school board, county board of supervisors, city council). Once the agency rejects your claim—and it usually will be— you can file in small claims court. Often, you must file the administrative claim within three to six months after your loss occurred, or you'll be out of luck.

## Statute of Limitations

You can't recover if you make a statute of limitations mistake. So it is imperative that you read your state's statutes of limitations laws before deciding which limitation period applies in your case. If you rely on the wrong statutory period and file too late, you will lose the ability to pursue your case. If you're not comfortable with your research abilities, consult with an attorney.

You'll find a chart of statute of limitation periods for four of the most common types of lawsuits on Nolo's website (www.nolo.com/legal-encyclopedia/statute-of-limitations-state-laws-chart-29941.html). However, do not rely on the chart without doing additional research. You'll need to read the text of the actual statute to ensure that your case meets all requirements.

Also, these statutes apply in very particular cases, and other limitation periods exist. For example, your state likely has separate statute of limitations periods for claims involving medical malpractice, eviction, child or spousal support, fraud, product liability, consumer sales contracts, faulty work by builders, and more. Your state might also distinguish between different types of property, such as real estate and personal property. Finally, be aware that the time limits in all statutes can be affected by other variables—see "How the Discovery Rule Works," below.

Again, we can't stress this enough—do not rely solely on the chart. You must research and verify statutes of limitations independently.

## Calculating the Statute of Limitations

Okay, now let's assume you have found the limitations period that applies in your case. How do you know what date to start counting from? Start with the day the injury to your person or property occurred. If a contract is involved, start with the day of the contract breach (when it was broken). If a contract to pay in installments is involved, start with the day the particular payment was missed. (See "Tricky Rules for Installment Contracts," below.)

### How the Discovery Rule Works

With some types of cases, such as medical malpractice, the limitations period starts from the date the harm was discovered or reasonably should have been discovered. This rule protects people who don't know they have a problem until well after it has occurred.

EXAMPLE: During an operation, a doctor leaves a small clamp in your abdomen. It isn't until a year later that you experience extreme pain and see a different doctor, who orders an X-ray that shows the clamp. In most states, the statute of limitations for suits based on medical malpractice begins from the date you learn of the problem, not the date of the original operation. However, if you walked around in pain for several years before seeing a second doctor and getting an X-ray, a court might rule that the limitations period started before actual discovery, based on the theory that you could and should have discovered the problem sooner.

## Voluntary Payment After Limitations Periods

Sometimes you can revive an expired statute of limitations period, although in most cases, only the person owed the money would want it to happen. For instance, suppose that the statute of limitations on an oral contract to paint a fence is two years. After it expires, the debtor voluntarily starts making payments. Does the voluntary payment have the effect of creating a new two-year statute of limitations period, allowing the person owed the money to sue if the debtor stops paying again? In most states, the answer is no. Simply starting to pay an obligation after the time to sue has passed doesn't create a new period for a lawsuit. All the creditor can do is hope that the debtor continues to pay.

However, signing a written agreement promising to make the payments will likely create a new statute of limitations period. In legal slang, this is called "reaffirming the debt."

> **EXAMPLE:** Michael borrowed $1,000 from Alexis in 2017 under the terms of a written promissory note. But he lost his job the next month and didn't pay anything on the debt. Alexis didn't file a lawsuit within the applicable four-year statute of limitations. In 2022, Michael got a job and sent Alexis $50, but he soon quit his job and reverted to his old ways. Is the applicable statute of limitations allowing Alexis to sue reinstated by Michael's payment? No. As we learned above, once the applicable limitation period for written contracts runs out, Michael can't revive it by making a payment. However, if Michael sent Alexis a letter saying that he would pay the remainder of the debt along with the $50, Alexis would again be able to sue and get a judgment if Michael failed to pay. Why? Because a written promise to pay a debt that the statute of limitations would otherwise bar has the legal effect of reestablishing the debt.

CAUTION

**Debtors—beware of waiving statutes of limitations.** If a debtor asks a creditor for lower payments, more time to pay a bill, or some other accommodation, the creditor will almost always require that the debtor waive the statute of limitations in writing. If the debtor fails to pay, the creditor will have more time to sue.

## Suspending the Statute of Limitations

In a few situations, the statute of limitations will be suspended or "tolled" for a period. For instance, if you sue someone in prison or living out of the state, or you sue someone who is insane or a minor (and occasionally for other reasons), the statute won't run while that status remains in place. The counting starts or resumes when the event (prison term, absence from state, and so on) is no longer in effect.

### Tricky Rules for Installment Contracts

When an installment contract is involved, the statute of limitations typically applies separately to each installment. For example, assume you lend Jacob $5,000, and he agrees in writing to pay back the loan in five installments of $1,000 each beginning on January 1, 2022, and continuing on January 1 of each following year through 2026. Because the state in question applies a four-year statute of limitations to contracts, if Jacob doesn't make his first payment, you can sue him in small claims court until January 1, 2026. (Note that you can sue him for only the $1,000 payment he missed, not for the entire $5,000.)

From Jacob's point of view, if you don't sue by January 1, 2026, you cannot recover for the first missed $1,000 payment because the statute of limitations bars the lawsuit.

Because Jacob's second installment payment isn't due until January 1, 2023, you have until January 1, 2027, to sue him if he misses that payment, and so on.

There is, however, a critical exception to this rule: If the written contract contains an "acceleration clause" stating that if Jacob misses one installment payment, all immediately become due, the statute of limitations expires for a lawsuit to collect all installments on January 2, 2026.

EXAMPLE 1: Jack borrows money from Tim under a written contract in a state with a four-year statute of limitations for written contracts. Jack fails to pay the money back on the day required. Six months later, Jack is sentenced to a year in jail. The four-year statute of limitations would be suspended during this period, and Tim would still have three and a half years after Jack gets out of custody to file suit.

EXAMPLE 2: Tyler, age 12, stars in a series on an online streaming site. Just before he turns 18, an accountant for the show tells Tyler's family that Tyler wasn't paid all the money due under his contract. Tyler wonders if he can still sue for compensation. The answer is yes. Tyler's time to sue starts on his 18th birthday because the statute of limitations period would be suspended or tolled while he was a minor. So if he lives in a state with a four-year statute of limitation for disputes based on written contracts, Tyler could file suit until his 22nd birthday.

## What If the Statute of Limitations Has Run?

What should a defendant do if the statute of limitations period on the plaintiff's lawsuit has run out? Tell the judge. Do this in court when stating your defense. Or, if your state requires a defendant to make a written response to the plaintiff's claim before the hearing date (see Appendix A), then include a statement that the statute of limitations bars the plaintiff's claim in your response. You can't count on the judge to know that the statute of limitations expired. Also, don't assume that the plaintiff filed on time because the court clerk accepted the papers the plaintiff served on you. Clerks rarely get involved in a statute of limitations issue.

# Settling Your Dispute

L awsuits should be a last resort. In addition to being time-consuming and emotionally draining, lawsuits—even the small claims variety— tend to polarize disagreements into win-all or lose-all propositions where compromise is difficult. It's not hard to understand how this happens. When forced to defend our actions in a public forum, we tend to adopt a self-serving view of our own conduct and attribute the worst motives to our opponents. When possible, it's best to work out disputes amicably and use the court system only after exhausting other options.

CAUTION
**In most states, you are required to ask for the money owed you before filing a small claims lawsuit.** For example, in California, the form you fill out to start a small claims lawsuit states, "You must ask the Defendant (in person, in writing, or by phone) to pay you before you sue. If your claim is for possession of property, you must ask the defendant to give you the property. Have you done this? If no, explain why not."

As discussed earlier, it is almost always wise to first look for a noncourt solution when the other party is someone you'll have to deal with in the future. Typically, this would include a neighbor, a former friend, or a relative. Similarly, a business owner will almost always benefit by working out a compromise settlement with another established local business, a long-term customer, or a client. For example, an orthodontist who depends on referrals for most new customers should think twice before suing a patient who has refused to pay a bill in a situation where the patient is genuinely upset (whether rightly or wrongly) about the services received. Even if the orthodontist wins in court, the patient will likely disparage the orthodontist, possibly even online, and cause a loss of potential clients. When figuring in the costs associated with preparing and presenting the case, there's a good chance it won't be worth the headache.

# Negotiation

Trying to negotiate a compromise with the other party can be a win-win situation. And, since many states require you to request payment before filing anyway, there's no reason why you shouldn't try to resolve your case without litigation. (For tips on writing demand letters, see "Formal Demand Letters," below.)

But, first things first. Before you reach for pen and paper, try to talk with the other person involved in the dispute. If you're not sure how to go about it, you can build your confidence by learning a few negotiation skills ahead of time. You might find yourself pleasantly surprised that you're able to reach an agreement.

Keep in mind, however, that safety always comes first. If the tension is such that you're worried about verbal escalation, or even assault, it's best to communicate in writing.

# The Negotiation Process

If you're in sales or negotiate contracts for a living, you're likely already an expert negotiator. Many people, however, aren't comfortable with the process. If you fall into the former category, there's no cause for worry. Once you understand the steps, you'll be ready to go toe-to-toe with the best of them.

## How a Negotiation Works

Negotiation is a simple process: Participants exchange offers and counteroffers until one side agrees to the other's deal. Going back and forth allows each side to consider a proposal, reject it, and suggest a "more reasonable" settlement.

While the process takes time, it works because each negotiator must feel that they've gotten the best deal possible and that they haven't "left money on the table." Only then will they be ready to settle the case. This is why in almost every case, you won't start a negotiation with your best offer—the amount you're hoping to settle for. You'll leave room to negotiate the deal.

## Trusting the Process

Many new negotiators aren't comfortable with the strategy involved in negotiating. They'd prefer to tell the other side exactly how much they want and avoid the hassle. Here's why the "take it or leave it" approach won't work:

- An experienced negotiator will assume you've left room to negotiate and won't believe it's your best and final offer.
- An inexperienced negotiator could find a "drop dead" number (a colloquialism commonly used to mean a final offer) offputting and aggressive.

In either case, the other side won't feel good about a settlement. Remember, negotiation isn't about forcing your position or achieving dominance. It's about getting what you want while helping your opponent feel that they took everything you had to give and that you sweetened the pot because of their superior negotiation skills. In other words, you want them to feel good about agreement. Then you'll be more likely to strike a deal.

TIP

**The "great case" exception.** Sometimes you know with certainty that you're going to win your case. And the other side knows, too. When power shifts to that degree, it makes sense to stand on your number. Even so, because it's still a good idea to help the other side feel good about the outcome, consider giving up a small amount toward the end. It will likely help wrap things up more quickly.

## Preparing for the Negotiation

Either side can initiate negotiations by offering to settle the case for a particular amount. Before getting started, you'll want to decide your bottom-line settlement number—the minimum amount you must get, or else you'll take your chances with the judge at trial. It's your walkaway number. You won't open negotiations with that number, of course. You'll start lower (or higher, if you're the defendant), leaving yourself negotiating room.

TIP

**A settlement offer is not binding.** Don't worry that offering to settle for less than what you'd really like will limit the amount you can get at trial—it won't. You'll still be able to ask for the full amount if you don't come to an agreement. An offer to settle a case—whether made orally or in writing—doesn't legally bind the person to sue for that amount. For instance, you can make an oral or written demand for $2,000, then offer to settle for $1,500. If the opposing side turns down your offer, you can still sue for $2,000. It won't matter if your opponent tells the judge you offered to settle for less because the judge will consider it irrelevant.

When determining your bottom-line number, estimate how much eliminating the time and aggravation of going to court would be worth to you and factor in the likelihood of losing or getting less than you'd like.

TIP

**Negotiate early.** The amount that a plaintiff asks for in the small claims lawsuit can influence a settlement negotiation. Simply put, a defendant with a copy of the suit in hand will not agree to settle for more than the amount requested. You'd have to offer to settle for less. You can avoid this issue by initiating settlement negotiations before filing your case. If you aren't comfortable doing so in person or by phone, you can include an invitation to negotiate in your formal demand letter. You'll find more information about writing a demand letter below.

Once the first offer is made, you'll decide whether you want to accept it, or reject it (it will be off the table) and present a counteroffer. If it's a great offer, you might want to take it right away. However, in most cases, it's a good idea to feel out whether the other side has room to offer something better while not rejecting the offer outright (once you reject an offer, you lose your right to accept it). You can try something like, "I appreciate your offer. We might be able to settle this more quickly if you could move a little more, though—is that possible?"

If the offer isn't acceptable, you can calculate a counteroffer using a strategy lawyers use regularly. First, determine where you'd like to settle the case. Then, set the counteroffer so that if you split the difference between the offer and counteroffer, your target settlement number would be in the middle. For instance, suppose the defendant offers to settle for $2,000, but you're hoping to get $5,000, you'd counteroffer with $8,000. If you and your opponent match each other's movement dollar to dollar, you'd have a good chance of settling on your target amount. If you move less than your opponent, you might do even better. This strategy also opens the door for "splitting the difference" when it's time to wrap up the negotiation (see tip below).

> **TIP**
> **Splitting the difference.** Typically, negotiations start to slow or stall when one or both sides get close to their settlement tolerance. A common way to solve the problem is by offering to meet halfway by "splitting the difference." Often, your opponent will see the wisdom of relinquishing a bit more if you're giving up the same amount and it will settle the case.

## More Negotiation Tips

It doesn't matter whether you negotiate orally or in writing, the process is the same. Here are a few more suggestions you can use or modify to increase the likelihood of a successful negotiation:

- Let the other side put out the first number, if possible. Your opponent might offer to settle for a better amount than what you'd have started with.
- Sweeten the pot with something you don't care about and the other side wants.
- Don't "bid against yourself." If you made the last offer, and you're told, "That's not good enough, give me another offer," don't do it. Tell them you made the last offer and ask them to counter.
- Try to get opponents to bid against themselves.
- See if you can resolve the case without exchanging money. For example, a print shop owner who refuses to repay you $2,000 might agree to redo the job.
- Remember that a sincere apology might get you a significant discount. For instance, a case about damaged property might really be about a damaged ego.

- Take your time. If you make a low offer and the other person gets mad, you can always wait a few days and try again. Once they've had time to cool off, call back and ask for a counteroffer (remember, you don't want to bid against yourself).
- Always be cordial and convey that you're willing to settle, if possible. Being aggressive and unyielding might work in the movies, but in reality, it won't be as effective as you hope. Your opponent might believe that talking with you will be a waste of time.
- If the negotiation becomes heated, you can salvage it by reminding the other side that you'd like to resolve the case amicably, if possible. Then move the discussion to more neutral territory—settlement numbers—by making another offer or asking for a counteroffer.
- Know that if you settle for less than you'd hoped, you've likely done well. A good settlement hurts both sides equally, so almost every negotiation ends with everyone feeling somewhat bruised. And if you have settlement remorse later, let it go. It's normal, too.

Above all, remember to trust the process. There's no way around it—negotiation is a "give and take" dance you can't rush. For instance, think about the techniques used in a transaction that you're likely familiar with—the new car purchase. A dealer knows that the longer you sit in the showroom, the more invested you'll be in leaving with a new car key in your pocket. Allowing a negotiation to unfold naturally will help you reach a good outcome.

If you think you won't have the time to use all of these practices in the hallway of the small claims court, you're probably right. These techniques will work best if you start negotiating well before your court date. Otherwise, adjust them to suit the situation.

TIP

**If you settle, sign a written agreement right away.** If you talk things out with your opponent, write down your agreement as soon as possible. Oral settlement agreements, especially between people who have little confidence in one another, are often not worth the breath used to express them. And writing down an agreement gives each party a chance to see whether they have arrived at a complete understanding. Often some details must still be hashed out. (See "Get Your Settlement in Writing (a Release)," below, for more on how to reduce a compromise agreement to writing.)

RESOURCE

**Learn more about negotiating.** To brush up on your negotiating skills, try reading *Getting to Yes: Negotiating Agreement Without Giving In*, by Bruce Patton, Roger Fisher, and William Ury (Penguin), or *Getting Past No: Negotiating in Difficult Situations*, by William Ury (Bantam). *Neighbor Law: Fences, Trees, Boundaries & Noise*, by Emily Doskow and Lina Guillen (Nolo), has excellent advice on negotiating neighborhood quarrels.

# Mediation

If you and the opposing party can't seem to resolve matters, mediation is the next best process you can use to avoid litigation. The disputants voluntarily meet with a neutral third party who helps them discuss the issues and arrive at a solution. For small claims disputes, mediation is available in the courthouse in many counties. In others, you might find low-cost services provided by community-based mediation programs.

## Why Mediate?

Many people wonder why they should waste time mediating with an opponent who they believe is unreasonable. When the parties to a small claims court case voluntarily agree to mediate, most disputes settle. Settlement is especially likely when, deep down, one or both parties realize they have an interest in arriving at a solution that's at least minimally acceptable to the other party. This is particularly common in disputes between neighbors or businesspeople who live or work in the same geographical area and who really don't want the dispute to fester.

Also, people who agree to have their cases mediated tend to be more satisfied with the case's outcome than litigants who go to trial. People who arrive at a mediated settlement are more likely to pay up than are people who have a judgment imposed on them after losing a contested trial, too.

Is mediating your case always a good idea? Not if you're determined to get the total amount you are asking for, and if you won't have an ongoing relationship with the other party anyway (for example, your dispute is with a large corporation or government agency). Bypassing mediation and going directly to court would make more sense.

## How Does Mediation Work?

A small claims mediation session typically lasts between 30 minutes and three hours. Although many mediators are ex-attorneys or even ex-judges, they have no power to impose a decision on you. The result is that mediation sessions tend to be much more relaxed than court proceedings, and they often result in compromises that both parties are better able to live with.

You can't force the other party into mediating—both of you must agree to engage in the process. However, many states now "strongly encourage" small claims litigants to mediate before they head into the courtroom. Your small claims court trial might even include an extra block of time before the hearing so that you and the other party can meet with the mediator. Your discussions during the mediation session are confidential— if the mediation fails, the judge won't learn what happened.

---

### Arbitration

A few states also offer binding arbitration before a volunteer lawyer as an alternative to having a case heard in small claims court. Typically, the arbitrator and the parties sit down at a table and discuss the case. If the parties don't arrive at their own solution, the arbitrator renders a decision just as a judge would. One advantage of arbitration over going before a small claims judge or a commissioner is that, in some areas, it's faster to meet with the arbitrator.

However, a possible disadvantage of arbitration is that a volunteer lawyer might be less knowledgeable than a judge about the broad range of laws that can apply to consumers and small businesses.

**Nonbinding arbitration.** In some areas, a procedure called "nonbinding arbitration" is available. It's much like mediation, in the sense that both parties must agree to any settlement. The only difference is that, unlike a mediator, who doesn't make a formal recommendation, the arbitrator will recommend— but not compel—a solution. It's often a good idea to try nonbinding arbitration. The arbitrator's recommendation can be a pretty good indication of what will happen if the case ends up going to court, and you get to try your hand at presenting your case.

Although it makes sense to approach mediation with an open mind and be ready to agree to a reasonable compromise, nothing requires you to agree on anything. It's your right to have your case presented to a judge if you wish. You can even stop negotiating if the other party refuses to accept fault or will only settle for an unreasonable amount. Also, watch out for result-oriented mediators who make you feel like you have to give up a large chunk of your claim just to reach a settlement. Being reasonable doesn't mean giving away the farm.

Assuming you want to mediate, how can you get a reluctant opponent to the table? Often you can get help from your local court-sponsored or community mediation program. Typically, as soon as you notify a mediation program that you have a dispute and would like to try mediation, an employee or volunteer with the mediation program will contact the other party or parties and try to arrange a mediation session.

If you and the other party agree on a mediated settlement, the mediator will likely record it on a form called a "Mediated Agreement" or something similar. The agreement, signed by both parties, will spell out the settlement terms and the deadlines for payments or other actions. If the mediation occurs after the plaintiff has already filed a small claims case, some counties will add the agreement into the court record in a sealed envelope.

## Should Defendants Mediate?

Suppose that you are a defendant in a small claims case or have received a letter threatening a lawsuit. Should you ask for mediation? The answer is almost always a resounding yes, assuming you have a defense to all or part of the plaintiff's claim or believe the plaintiff is asking for too much money even though it's a decent case. Mediation will give you an excellent opportunity to present your side of the dispute and try to arrive at an acceptable compromise. It can also allow you to bring up other issues that could be poisoning your relationship with the plaintiff but would not be considered relevant in court. Finally, even if you don't settle, you'll likely learn more about the plaintiff's case, and you'll be in a better position to defend yourself at trial.

RESOURCE

**Preparing for mediation.** People ready to engage in mediation will likely achieve far better results than those who take a more casual approach. A good source of information on mediating is *Mediate, Don't Litigate: Strategies for Successful Mediation*, by Peter Lovenheim, available as a downloadable Nolo eBook (https://store.nolo.com/products/mediate-dont-litigate-medl1c.html). If you read it before you mediate, you will almost certainly achieve better results than would have been possible otherwise.

Assuming both parties honor the agreement you reached in mediation, that's the end of the case—no court judgment will be entered by the judge or reported to a credit agency. Some states will automatically set a second court date in case the agreement isn't honored. However, if your deal is completed as agreed, you can advise the court to cancel the second date.

If your opponent doesn't honor the obligations under the mediated agreement by the deadline, you must go back to court and obtain a judgment. That's easy in the states where a second court date was scheduled automatically. In other states, you will need to request a new court date or simply request a judgment.

TIP

**In case the mediated settlement agreement is broken, protect your right to ask for the full amount.** Most successfully mediated disputes result in a settlement for a lesser amount, such as when A sues B for $2,000 but agrees to accept $1,200. But if B fails to pay within the time allowed by the written mediation agreement, A might want a judgment for the full $2,000. After all, A no longer has an incentive to compromise if B isn't willing to end the dispute without a day in court. Add a sentence or two to your mediated agreement stating that if the other party doesn't meet the settlement obligations, you reserve the right to make your full, original claim in court.

## Formal Demand Letters

If you're not comfortable talking directly with your opponent, or if your efforts to talk out your problems fail and you decide not to propose or agree to mediation, your next step is to send your adversary a letter. Many courts require you to make a formal demand for payment. But even where writing a formal demand letter isn't legally required, there are two reasons why doing so makes great sense. First, your demand letter will serve as a catalyst to settlement in as many as one-third of all disputes. Second, even if no settlement results, setting out your case in a formal letter affords you an excellent opportunity to lay your case before the judge in a carefully organized way. Or, put another way, not only does it allow you to explain the facts in the way that best suits your position, but you might be able to use the letter in court if your case isn't settled.

> **EXAMPLE:** Sunita purchases a designer dress on eBay from Maya. When it arrives, she realizes that the dress was meant to come with a jacket and is too skimpy to be worn without it. Maya refuses to take the dress back. She hangs up the phone whenever she hears Sunita's voice on the line. Sunita writes a demand letter outlining all of this and sends it via certified mail. Maya doesn't respond. In court, Maya feigns complete surprise, claiming, "I had no idea you had a problem with the dress—why didn't you say something before?" Sunita's demand letter, with its complete account of events, can now be used as evidence to back up Sunita's account of the dispute—and it will make Maya look less believable on the whole.

## CAUTION

**You can be sued without first being sent a formal letter stating that a lawsuit is imminent.** Some people believe they can't be sued until they receive a formal letter asking for payment and saying that a lawsuit will be filed if it isn't forthcoming. This is not necessarily true. A simple past-due notice form from a creditor, stating that if the account isn't paid promptly, other action will be pursued, is usually sufficient. Also, a judge has the power to conclude that an oral demand for payment is adequate.

## Composing Your Demand Letter

Here are some pointers to keep in mind when writing your demand letter.

**Type your letter.** If you don't have a computer or typewriter, try to get access to one. Many public libraries have computers that you can use for free or for a minimal charge.

**Explain the main facts of the dispute.** Start with a short, concise statement that includes all of the important facts. It might seem a bit odd to outline these details; after all, your opponent knows the story. But remember—there are always two sides to every disagreement. If you end up in court, a judge will read the letter, and you want the judge to understand your version. Now is an excellent chance to make a record not only of the initial dispute, but of any subsequent phone conversations, unanswered calls, or inappropriate conduct by the defendant.

**Be polite.** Avoid personally attacking your adversary (even one who deserves it). The more you attack, the more you invite the other side to respond in a similarly angry vein. You also want to present yourself in a calm, rational manner at all times. It's more convincing.

**Write with your goal in mind.** The letter should encourage your opponent to make a businesslike analysis of the dispute and raise such questions as:

- What are my risks of losing?
- How much time will a defense take?
- Do I want the dispute to be decided in public?

**Ask for precisely what you want.** For example, if you want $2,000, don't beat around the bush—ask for it. Also, be sure to add a little more to allow some negotiating room if you'd like to open up negotiations (more below). Explain how you arrived at this figure. And be sure to set a deadline. One week (two weeks at the outside) is usually best; anything longer and your opponent has less motivation to deal with you right away. Supply the actual date, to remove any doubt.

**Consider inviting negotiation.** Although many courts require you to send a demand letter before filing your action, it isn't always effective. Unless your case is a clear winner, it's unlikely that the defendant will agree to pay your demand. You can use a demand letter as a way to open negotiations. But to do so, you'll need to signal that you're willing to settle for less. A sentence encouraging the other side to call and work out a mutually agreeable resolution will often do the trick.

**Conclude by stating you will promptly pursue your legal remedies if your demand is not met.** Remind the defendant that a court judgment could adversely affect their credit rating. Consider softening the wording if you're hoping to negotiate a settlement.

**Make and keep copies.** Make a copy of each letter before sending it, and keep a copy of the post office receipts (use certified mail, return receipt requested). Keep all correspondence from your adversary, also.

**Use certified mail.** Send the demand letter via certified mail with a return receipt requested. If you do end up in small claims court, you can use the return receipt to counter any claim that your opponent didn't receive the demand letter.

## After You Send Your Demand Letter

In legal practice, the purpose of the demand letter is to open the door for negotiation. Lawyers don't expect that it, in and of itself, will settle the case. Instead, it's usual for the opposing lawyer to submit a counteroffer, either in writing or by phone. Counteroffers get exchanged until a settlement is reached, or there's no choice but to proceed with litigation. There's no reason that you can't do the same. The negotiation techniques discussed earlier in the chapter apply at every stage of the process.

Sometimes the opposing side will let the demand letter date pass without contacting you. You can proceed to file your suit if you like—and in many cases, that will probably be the best bet. But there's also nothing wrong with making one last attempt to feel out a settlement possibility. Conveying interest in the other side's position, as well as suggesting the chance of avoiding litigation, is an excellent way to get the conversation started.

## A Real Small Claims Case

Now let's consider a real small claims case. The facts (with a bit of editorial license) are simple: Jennifer moved into Peter's house in August, agreeing to pay $550 per month in rent. The house had four bedrooms, each occupied by one person. The kitchen and other common areas were shared. Things went well enough until one chilly evening in October when Jennifer turned on the heat. Peter was right behind her to turn it off, explaining that heat inflamed his allergies.

As the days passed and fall deepened, the lack of heat became more and more of an issue, until one cold, late November night Jennifer returned home from her waitress job to find her room "about the same temperature as the inside of an icicle." She started packing and moved out the next morning. She refused to pay Peter any additional rent, claiming that she was within her rights to terminate her month-to-month tenancy without giving notice because the house was uninhabitable. It took Peter one month to find a suitable tenant and to have that person move in. Therefore, he lost rent in the amount of $550.

After calling Jennifer several times and asking her to pay the $550, only to have her slam down the phone in disgust, Peter wrote her the following letter:

---

61 Spring Street
Detroit, MI 12344

January 1, 20xx

Jennifer Tenant
111 Lake Street
Detroit, MI 12344

Dear Jennifer:

You are a real idiot. Actually, you're worse than that: You're malicious—walking out on me before Christmas and leaving me with no tenant when you know that I needed the money to pay my child support. You know that I promised to get you an electric room heater. Don't think I don't know that the real reason you moved out was to live with your boyfriend.

Please send me the $550 I lost because it took me a month to rerent the place. If you don't, I will sue you.

In aggravation,

*Peter Landperson*

Peter Landperson

---

To which Jennifer replied:

111 Lake Street
Detroit, MI 12344
January 4, 20xx

Peter Landperson
61 Spring Street
Detroit, MI 12344

Dear Mr. Landperson:

You nearly froze me to death, you cheap bastard. I am surprised it only took a month to rent that iceberg of a room—you must have found a rich polar bear (haha). People like you should be locked up.

I hope you choke on an ice cube.

*Jennifer Tenant*
Jennifer Tenant

Both Peter and Jennifer made the same mistake. Instead of being businesslike, each deliberately set out to annoy the other, reducing any chance of compromise. Also, they each assumed that they were writing only to the other, forgetting that the judge would be privy to their sentiments. As a result, they both lost a valuable chance to present the judge with a clear summary of their version of the facts. As evidence in a subsequent court proceeding, both letters were worthless.

Here are more sensible letters.

After having a friend review his draft letter in which he called former tenant Jennifer "an idiot" and "malicious," Peter wrote this more sensible letter:

61 Spring Street
Detroit, MI 12344
January 1, 20xx

Jennifer Tenant
111 Lake Street
Detroit, MI 12344

Dear Jennifer:

As you will recall, you moved into my house at 61 Spring Street on August 1, 20xx, agreeing to pay me $550 per month rent on the first of each month. On November 29, you suddenly moved out, having given me no advance notice whatsoever.

I realize you were unhappy that the house was on the cool side, but I don't believe this was a serious problem, as the temperature always exceeded 60 degrees, and I had agreed to get you an electric heater by December.

I could not get a tenant to replace you (although I tried every way I could and asked you for help) until January 1, 20xx. As a result, I am short $550 rent. If necessary, I will take this dispute to court. I hope that this isn't necessary and that we can arrive at a sensible compromise.

I am also willing to mediate this dispute, but you haven't answered my calls. Perhaps you could call next week to talk this over.

Sincerely,

*Peter Landperson*

Peter Landperson

To which our now enlightened Jennifer promptly replied:

> January 4, 20xx
> 111 Lake Street
> Detroit, MI 12344
>
> Peter Landperson
> 61 Spring Street
> Detroit, MI 12344
>
> Dear Peter:
>
> I just received your letter, and I am sorry, but I disagree with your version of the facts and your demand for back rent.
>
> When I moved in on August 1, 20xx, you never told me that you had an allergy and that there would be a problem keeping the house at a reasonable temperature. I would not have moved in had I known.
>
> From early October through November, I asked you to provide heat, but you didn't. Finally, returning from work to a cold house became unbearable. I indeed moved out suddenly, but I felt that I was within my rights under Michigan law, which allows tenants to sue landlords for constructive eviction when the landlord fails to provide a necessity such as heat. You are lucky that I am not suing you for damages for constructive eviction.
>
> Since you mentioned the nonexistent electric heater in your letter, let me respond to that. You first promised to get the heater over a month before I moved out and never did. Also, as I pointed out to you on several occasions, the heater was not a complete solution to the problem, as it would have heated only my room and not the kitchen, living room, or dining areas. You repeatedly told me that it would be impossible to heat these areas.
>
> Peter, I sincerely regret that you feel wronged, but I believe that I have been very fair with you. I am sure that you would have been able to rerent the room promptly if the house had been warm. I don't believe that any compromise is possible, so mediation does not make sense. If you wish to go to court, I'll be there with witnesses to support my position.
>
> Sincerely,
>
> *Jennifer Tenant*
> Jennifer Tenant

As you can see, while the second two letters are less fun to read, they are far more informative. In this instance, the goal of reaching a compromise or agreeing to mediation was not met. But both parties prepared a good outline of their positions for the judge. Of course, in court, both Peter and Jennifer will testify and present witnesses and possibly other evidence that will tell much the same story as is set out in the letters. However, court proceedings are often rushed and confused, and it's nice to have a written statement for the judge to fall back on. Be sure to give the judge a copy of your demand letter when presenting your case. The judge won't guess that you have it; you will have to state that you have it and hand it to the clerk. (For more about how to conduct yourself in court, see Chapters 13–15.)

## Sample Demand Letters

Below are letters a consumer might write to an auto repair shop after a shoddy repair job and a contractor who messed up a remodeling contract.

**Sample Demand Letter: Car Repair**

June 16, 20xx

Tucker's Fix-It-Quick Garage
9938 Main Street
Houston, TX 12333

Dear Mr. Tucker,

On May 21, 20xx, I took my car to your garage for servicing. Shortly after picking it up the next day, the engine caught fire because of your failure to properly connect the fuel line to the fuel injector. Fortunately, I was able to douse the fire without injury.

As a direct result of the engine fire, I paid the ABC garage $1,281 for necessary repair work. I enclose a copy of their invoice.

Also, I was without the use of my car for three days and had to rent a car to get to work. I enclose a copy of an invoice showing the rental cost of $145.

In a recent phone conversation, you claimed that the fire wasn't the result of your negligence and would have happened anyway. And you said that even if it was your fault, I should have brought my car back to your garage so you could have fixed it at a lower cost.

As to the first issue, Peter Klein of the ABC Garage is prepared to testify in court that the fire occurred because you didn't connect the fuel line you were working on to the fuel injector correctly.

Second, I had no obligation to return the car to you for further repair. I had the damage repaired at a reasonable price and will prove this by presenting several higher estimates.

Please send me a check or money order for $1,426 on or before July 15. If I don't receive payment by that date, I'll promptly file this case in small claims court and pursue all legal avenues to collect it. You can reach me during the day at 444-555-2857 or in the evenings until 10 p.m. at 444-555-8967.

Sincerely,

*Marsha Rizzoli*
Marsha Rizzoli

## Sample Demand Letter: Home Contractor

June 20, 20xx

Jane Brown
Beyond Repair Construction
10 Delaney Avenue
Seattle, WA 12355

Dear Ms. Brown:

Your firm recently did replacement tile work while remodeling my downstairs bathroom at 142 West Pine Street, here in Seattle. As per our written agreement, I paid you $4,175 upon completion of the job on May 17, 20xx.

On June 1, I noticed that the tile in the north portion of the shower had sunk almost half an inch. Now the shower floor is uneven, and the water pools in the downhill corner before draining.

In our telephone conversations, you claimed that the problem:

- was in my imagination
- was my fault, because the floor was always uneven, and
- was too minor to bother with.

I paid for a professional remodeling job, and I am entitled to receive it. Please contact me within ten days to arrange to pay me $1,200 (the cost of redoing the work per the enclosed estimate from ABC Tile) or redo the work. If I don't hear from you by July 1, 20xx, I will promptly file in small claims court.

Sincerely,

*Ben Price*

Ben Price

# Get Your Settlement in Writing (a Release)

If you and the other party agree to a settlement, either on your own or with the help of a mediator, it's important to write it down promptly. When a mediator is involved, preparing a written agreement is usually the last step in the mediation process. If you and your opponent negotiate your settlement, you'll need to cooperate to reduce it to writing. Lawyers call an agreement to settle a dispute a "release" because, in exchange for some act (often the payment of money), one person gives up or "releases" their claim against another. For instance, suppose Sandra, a neighboring property owner, damaged the paint on John's building while spray-painting her building on a windy day. In that case, John might agree to release Sandra from liability (not sue Sandra) if she agreed to pay $2,000 to repaint the damaged area of John's building.

A written release is valid if it is signed by both parties; is fair, in the sense that neither party was tricked into signing on the basis of misrepresentation; and provides each party with some benefit (if you pay me $500, I won't sue you and I'll keep my dog out of your yard). If either party later violates the settlement terms, the other can file a lawsuit and receive a court judgment for appropriate damages.

It's important to understand that settlement agreements are powerful legal documents. If you completely release someone who damaged your car for $500, only to later find out that the damage was more extensive, you'll be stuck with the $500 unless you can convincingly claim that the other party was guilty of misrepresentation or fraud in getting you to sign the settlement agreement. Of course, in most situations, where the details of a dispute are all well known, a settlement can be comfortably signed with the knowledge that the dispute will finally be laid to rest.

Below we provide a sample release ("Sample General Release") adopted from Nolo's book, *101 Law Forms for Personal Use*, by the Editors of Nolo. This general release is used to settle a dispute over a contract, debt, or minor personal injury when only one party is alleged to have suffered damages or been injured.

## Get the Court's Stamp of Approval

If a small claims case has been filed, you might have a choice as to whether your agreement is presented to a judge and made part of a court order or is simply written as a binding contract between you and the other party. Especially if it's less trouble (sometimes getting a court order involves an extra trip to court), you might be tempted to accept a contract and not bother with a court order. Keep in mind that a court order (judgment) is far easier to enforce than a contract, especially if you suspect that the other side might not do what they promise. Most people find that it's worth a little extra effort to have a settlement contract incorporated into a court judgment.

**RESOURCE**

**Where to get other types of release forms.** The Nolo book *101 Law Forms for Personal Use* contains specialized releases adapted to auto accidents, property damage, and personal injuries. It also has mutual release forms for use when both parties are giving up claims. In addition, release forms are often available from office supply stores that carry legal documents and lawyers' form books, available at law libraries.

No matter where you get your release, it should contain the following information:

- The names and addresses of the party being released (the potential defendant) and the party granting the release (the potential plaintiff).
- A brief description of the "what," "when," and "where" of the dispute or issue to which the release pertains. (The release below provides several blank lines for you to briefly describe the events giving rise to the need for the release.)
- A statement of what the person giving up a claim is getting in return. As mentioned, for a release to be a valid and enforceable contract, the person signing the release (releasor) must receive something of benefit (called "consideration" by lawyers) in exchange for agreeing to give up the right

to sue. The release below provides a space for this "consideration" to be described. Typically, it is money. If so, simply enter the amount. If it is an agreement by the releasee to perform or not perform some act (for example, stop his dog from barking at night), describe the act.

- A statement that the release applies to all claims arising from the dispute or issue, both those known at the time the release is signed and those that might come along later. This provision is standard in releases. It appears in essentially every release because without it, the release wouldn't be worth much.

- A statement that the release binds all persons who might otherwise have a legal right to file a claim on behalf of the releasor (for example, the releasor's spouse or heirs). Although we have included this provision in our releases for caution's sake, it is rare that it will ever prove relevant. Such persons are usually bound by the release anyway.

- The date the release is signed.

- The signatures of the parties. Legally, only the person granting a release needs to sign it, but we think it is a better practice for both parties to do so—after all, this critical document contains statements that affect both of their rights. In the case of mutual releases, which occur when both parties give up a claim against the other, both must sign.

TIP
**Use witnesses.** There is no legal requirement for a release to be witnessed, but the other person might later claim, "It's not my signature." A witness can help you avoid this situation. Also, if a release involves a lot of money or a potentially significant claim, signing in front of a witness or two— or even having it notarized—can increase the chances it will be upheld should it ever be challenged later. The witnesses can later testify that the other party was under no duress and appeared to know what they were doing.

## Last-Minute Agreements

Occasionally, disputes are settled while waiting for a case to be heard. Even on the day you go to court, it is proper to ask the other person to step into the hall for a moment to talk the matter over. If you reach a last-minute compromise, tell the judge about the agreement when the clerk calls your case. Typically, the judge will order that the case be dismissed if one person pays the other the agreed-upon amount on the spot. If payment will be made later, the judge will enter a judgment for the amount agreed on or set another date and enter judgment if the settlement isn't paid as promised.

Another possibility is that you and your opponent will agree to a last-minute attempt to mediate. If so, you will want to explain this to the judge, who in turn will typically delay ("continue," in legalese) your case until the mediation session takes place. If mediation works and your case settles, you and the other party should notify the court clerk jointly. Again, unless the agreed-upon amount is immediately paid, the debtor will typically want to return to court and have the settlement amount made part of an official court order (judgment).

## Sample General Release

1. [*person signing release and agreeing not to sue*], Releasor, voluntarily and knowingly executes this release with the express intention of eliminating and canceling Releasee's liabilities and obligations as described below.

2. Releasor hereby releases [*person being released*], Releasee, from all claims, known or unknown, that have arisen or may arise from the following occurrence: [*description of events giving rise to release, including location and date if appropriate—see box for sample language*].

**Sample Language:**
a. "Repair work incompletely done to Releasor's boat at the Fixmeup Shipyards on 5/6/20xx."
b. "Agreement by Releasee made during the week of June 6, 20xx, to deliver and install custom cabinets at Releasor's address no later than July 6, 20xx, which Releasee failed to keep."
c. "A tree growing on Releasee's property at 1011 Oak Street fell into Releasor's backyard at 1013 Oak Street on August 7, 20xx. It damaged Releasor's fence, which had to be replaced. The tree itself had to be removed."

3. Releasor understands that, as to claims that are known to the parties when the release is signed, any statutory provisions that would otherwise apply to limit this general release are hereby waived. Releasor also understands that this release extends to claims arising out of this incident that are not known by Releasor at the time this release is signed.

4. In exchange for granting this release Releasor has received the following payment or other consideration: [*amount of money, or description of something else of value that person signing release received from other party—see box for sample language*].

**Sample Language:**
a. "$150 cash."
b. "A used Samsung television set."
c. "An agreement by [*Releasee's name*] to desist from further activities as described in Clause 3 of this release."
d. "An agreement by [*Releasee's name*] to repair Releasor's iPad by January 1, 20xx."

## Sample General Release (continued)

5. By signing this release, Releasor additionally intends to bind his or her spouse, heirs, legal representatives, assigns, and anyone else claiming under him or her. Releasor has not assigned any claim covered by this release to any other party. Releasor also intends that this release apply to the heirs, personal representatives, assigns, insurers, and successors of Releasee as well as to the Releasee.

This release was executed on _____ , 20____ , at [*city and state*]

_____     _____
Releasor's signature                 Date

_____     _____
Releasor's name (print)              County of residence

_____
Releasor's address

_____     _____
Releasor's spouse's signature        Date

_____     _____
Releasor's spouse's name (print)     County of residence

_____     _____
Releasee's signature                 Date

_____     _____
Releasee's name (print)              County of residence

_____
Releasee's address

_____     _____
Releasee's spouse's signature        Date

_____     _____
Releasee's spouse's name (print)     County of residence

_____     _____
Witness's signature                  Date

_____     _____
Witness's name (print)               County of residence

_____
Witness's address

_____     _____
Witness's signature                  Date

_____     _____
Witness's name (print)               County of residence

_____
Witness's address

# Who Can Sue?

Who can sue in small claims court? The answer is easy. You can—as long as you:
- are 18 years of age or an emancipated minor
- have not been declared mentally incompetent in a judicial proceeding, and
- are suing on your own claim.

> **CAUTION**
>
> **Special requirements for some plaintiffs.** Some states do not let unlicensed contractors and other businesspeople who work without required licenses to bring suit on claims related to their business. Prisoners are allowed to sue in some states but not in others. In states where they can sue, their cases often must be presented in writing. (In a few states, prisoners can name an adult representative to appear on their behalf.) Check your state's small claims rules before bringing suit.

---

### What If You Want to Sue but Can't Appear in Court?

People who will find it difficult or impossible to show up in small claims court to present their case often ask whether there is another way to proceed. The answer might be yes for some people—prisoners, business owners, landlords, and certain military personnel stationed out of state—check your state's rules for details. Even if you don't fit into an approved category, a small claims judge has the discretion to hear your case through a nonlawyer representative if you convince the judge that for some good reason, such as bad health or advanced age, you need assistance and the person you send to court is familiar with what happened. Talk to your county's small claims court clerk to see whether this procedure will work in your case.

---

## Married Couples

What if you and your spouse co-own a car that your neighbor's teenager vandalizes? What if you and your spouse are both listed as payees on a bad check? These are called "joint claims," and you and your spouse can and should sue together. If you are a married couple with a joint claim, you should list both your names as plaintiffs. It is usually okay for one spouse to appear on behalf of both spouses if the following are true:

- the claim is joint
- the represented spouse has given written consent, which you should bring to court, and
- the court determines it would serve the interests of justice.

## Employees Can Appear on Behalf of a Business

States used to require the owner of a business to show up in small claims court personally. This discouraged the owners of many small unincorporated businesses from using small claims court. For example, a dentist who wished to sue on an overdue bill would have had to show up in court.

These days, many states are more understanding of business time pressures. If a business (incorporated or unincorporated) wishes to sue on an unpaid bill, it can often send an employee to court to testify about the debt as it is reflected in the written records of the business. For instance, in many states, a landlord suing for unpaid rent can send a property manager to court to establish that the rent was unpaid (but see cautions about bringing eviction cases in small claims court in Chapter 20). For a business owner to invoke this time-saving procedure, the employee must be familiar with the company's books and testify about how the debt was entered in them.

Also, ensure that anyone who goes to small claims court on behalf of your business has firsthand knowledge about the dispute. For example, suppose your rug store sues a customer who refuses to pay because a carpet was improperly installed. In that case, you will probably lose if you send to court only your bookkeeper, who knows nothing about what happened on the particular job. In this situation, some judges might postpone the case for a few days to allow the business owner to show up with the carpet installer and present testimony about the quality of the repair, but don't count on it—try to send the appropriate person the first time.

## Sole Proprietorships

If you own a small business and are the sole proprietor, you will list both your name and the name of your business on your court papers. Generally, a sole proprietor must appear personally at the court hearing.

> CAUTION
> **Does your business use a fictitious name?** Most states require companies that use a fictitious name (such as Tasty Donut Shop) to file a declaration stating that you have properly executed, filed, and published a fictitious business name statement as required by your state's law. Check with the small claims clerk.

## Business Partnerships

If you are filing a claim on behalf of a partnership, you should sue on behalf of the individual partners and the partnership itself. Most states allow either a partner or a regular employee to appear in court.

## Corporations

If you are filing a claim on behalf of a corporation, list the corporation itself as the plaintiff. In most states, the corporation can be represented at the hearing by either:

- an officer or director of the corporation, or
- an employee authorized to file claims on behalf of the corporation by the corporation's board of directors. If a nonofficer of a corporation signs the forms, the court clerk might want to see some documentation that the person suing is properly authorized.

Check your state laws for any special rules about corporations as plaintiffs.

## Limited Liability Companies

List the limited liability company (LLC) as the plaintiff. Most states allow any member to appear in court but check your local rules.

## Nonprofits and Unincorporated Associations

If you are suing on behalf of a nonprofit corporation or an unincorporated association, the plaintiff's claim should list the name of the corporation or association and the name of an officer or director who will appear in court (such as, "ABC Canine Happiness Society, by Philip Pup, Executive Director"). An officer can represent the nonprofit or unincorporated association at the hearing.

## Motor Vehicle Claims

When a claim arises out of damage to a motor vehicle, the vehicle's registered owner must file the small claims court case. So, if you are driving someone else's car and get hit by a third party, you can't sue for the cost to repair the vehicle damage. The registered owner must file the lawsuit. However, if you are injured in the accident, you can sue the other car's driver to recover money for your medical costs, lost wages, and pain and suffering.

## Government Agencies

Suppose you are suing on behalf of a government agency such as a public library, city tax assessor's office, or county hospital. In that case, you should list the organization's official name as the plaintiff. When you file the papers, you must show the court clerk proper authorization to sue.

## Special Rules for Prisoners and Military Personnel

In some states, prisoners are not allowed to bring small claims lawsuits. Other states have special procedures for prisoners who want to sue in small claims court. In California, for example, a prisoner who wants to sue in small claims court must file papers by mail and then either submit testimony in the form of written declarations or have another person appear on their behalf in court. (Cal. Civ. Proc. Code § 116.540(f).)

In some states, many military personnel who have been transferred out of state are also allowed to bring small claims court cases without appearing in court personally. Check your state rules for information on how to do this.

## Suits by Minors

If you are under 18 years old, your parent or legal guardian must sue for you. The exception is that, in some states, emancipated minors can sue on their own. When your parents or guardians sue on your behalf, they must fill out a form asking to have one of them appointed your guardian ad litem and have the form signed by the judge. "Guardian ad litem" means "guardian for the purposes of the lawsuit." Ask the court clerk for the rules in your state.

## Class Actions (Group Lawsuits)

In small claims court there is no such thing as an actual class action lawsuit, where several people in a similar situation ask a court's permission to join together in one lawsuit against the same defendant. However, as many communities and advocacy groups have discovered, if a large number of people with a particular grievance (pollution, noise, drug sales) sue the same defendant at the same time in small claims courts, something remarkably like a class action is created.

This technique was pioneered in the early 1980s by a group of determined homeowners who lived near the San Francisco airport. Several times, the group won more than 100 small claims court judgments against the City of San Francisco based on excessive noise. They hired expert witnesses, did research, ran training workshops, and paid for legal advice when needed as part of a coordinated effort to efficiently present their cases. The City of San Francisco tried to fend off these cases by arguing that the homeowners were, in effect, involved in a class-action lawsuit, and such suits are not permitted in small claims court. A California court of appeals disagreed, saying, "Numerous 'mass' actions against the City alleging that noise from the City airport constituted a continuing nuisance were neither too 'complex' nor had such 'broad social policy import' that they were outside the jurisdiction of Small Claims Court ...." *(City and County of San Francisco v. Small Claims Div., San Mateo Co.,* 190 Cal.Rptr. 340 (1983).)

A similar strategy has been widely used in many cities to shut down drug houses. Neighbors organize to sue landlords who rent to drug-selling tenants, claiming the legal theory of nuisance (use of property that unreasonably interferes with the rights of others—Chapter 2). In these cases, the neighbors claimed the nuisance was the emotional and mental distress that accompanied living near a drug house. Typically, each neighbor sues for the maximum amount. For instance, thirty neighbors who coordinate their small claims filings can, together, bring what amounts to a $225,000 case. Several drug house cases have resulted in large combined judgments, and problems that had dragged on for months or years were quickly cleaned up

Successful mass small claims lawsuits based on legal nuisance have also been brought against polluting refineries and factories.

**JUDGE'S TIP**
**Group lawsuits can lend credibility and weight to a "neighborhood quarrel."** One of the purposes of the small claims court is to provide a neighborhood forum to resolve group lawsuits that might otherwise clog up the higher courts. If neighbors can band together to address problems of barking dogs, rock bands, drug houses, and so on, each individual's case will be that much more credible to the judge.

**TIP**
**Select a small committee to coordinate your lawsuits.** When a good-sized group of plaintiffs all sue the same defendant based on the same grievance, it's wise to coordinate strategy. This typically involves creating an informal plaintiffs' organization to organize intergroup communications, find witnesses and, if needed, expert witnesses (see Chapter 14). It's also a good idea to conduct a training session for everyone who will testify in court, discuss settlement offers, and, if requested, meet with the judge to plan how to efficiently and effectively present your multiple cases in court.

CAUTION

**Losing defendants have the right to a new trial on appeal.** People who sue and beat corporations, governmental entities, and other defendants with deep pockets in small claims court are likely to be faced with a more arduous battle on appeal. That's because all losing small claims defendants have the right to appeal to superior court, where both sides have the right to be represented by a lawyer. (See Chapter 23.)

## Participation by Attorneys and Bill Collectors

In most states, you can be represented by an attorney in small claims court. In some states, attorneys are allowed only if the judge consents, and in other states, attorneys are required if the party is a corporation. Some states don't allow representation by attorneys at all. (See Appendix A for your state's rules.)

Even in states that don't allow lawyers in small claims court, it is still perfectly legal to get an attorney's advice about your small claims case.

Many states forbid the use of small claims court by "assignees" (a fancy term that usually refers to collection agencies). In other words, you cannot hire someone to sue for an unpaid debt in these states. But the majority of states still allow suits by collection agencies. Check with your small claims court clerk for information.

TIP

**Attorneys can always bring suits on their own behalf.** Even in states that don't allow attorneys to represent someone else in small claims court, attorneys can sue on or defend their own claims.

# Suing Different Kinds of Defendants

Y ou can sue just about any defendant in small claims court—a person, sole proprietorship, partnership, corporation, LLC, or government entity. Under certain circumstances, you can even sue out-of-staters. But figuring out where to sue (see Chapter 9) is often more difficult than figuring out whom to sue.

## One Person

If you are suing an individual, simply name the person on the form, using the most complete name that you know for that person. If the person calls himself J.R. Smith and you don't know what the J.R. stands for, sue him as J.R. Smith. However, if with a little effort you can find out that J stands for James, it's better to sue him as James R. Smith.

> **TIP**
> **What to do if a person uses several names.** Lots of people use two or more names. Jason Graboskawitz might also use J.T. Grab. When in doubt, list the name the person uses most often for business purposes first, followed by the words "also known as" (or "a.k.a.") and any other names. For instance, you might sue Jason Graboskawitz, a.k.a. J.T. Grab.

## Two or More People

When suing more than one person on a claim arising from the same incident or contract, list the complete names of all defendants. Then "serve" or deliver copies of court papers to each of them. It's the properly served paperwork that brings them before the court. (See Chapter 11.) Listing both names is also required when the defendants are married: List the defendants as John Randolph Smith and Jane Smith, husband and wife (or "spouses" if the partners are in a same-sex marriage). Or, if you don't know the name of one spouse: John Randolph Smith and Mrs. John Randolph Smith, husband and wife.

EXAMPLE: Jonathan and June Smith, a married couple, buy $1,200 worth of avocados from you on credit to start an avocado toast business. Unfortunately, shortly after receiving the fruit, the avocados begin to sprout. Believing the avocados aren't sufficiently fresh, Jonathan and June refuse to pay you what they owe. If you want to get a judgment against them, you should list them as Jonathan Smith and June Smith—not Mr. and Mrs. Smith. If, however, Jonathan bought $1,200 of avocados on credit in January, and June bought $1,000 of wedding flowers on credit a month later, and both bills went unpaid, you would sue each in separate small claims actions.

TIP
**Two defendants are better than one, and three are better than two.** If two or more people are responsible for your loss (for example, if three tenants damaged your apartment), sue them all. This will enable you to get judgments against several people. You'll be glad you did when you try to collect—if one defendant refuses to pay, you can go after the others. (For more information on collecting your judgment, see Chapter 24.)

## Individually Owned Businesses

List the owner's name and the name of the business (Ralph C. Jones, individually and doing business as [d.b.a.] Jones's Texaco). But never assume that the name of the business is the same as the name of the owner. For all you know, Jim's Garage might be owned by Pablo Garcia Motors, Inc. (more on suing a corporation below). If you get a judgment against Jim's Garage and there is no Jim, it will be worthless unless you take steps to have the judgment changed to reflect the correct name, which can take extra time and trouble. Suing the right person in the first place is a much better practice.

A few states have liberalized their rules and do not penalize plaintiffs who incorrectly state the business defendant's name. New York allows a plaintiff to sue a defendant under any name used in conducting business if it is impossible to find out the defendant's true name. California allows a plaintiff to correct a defendant's name at the time of the hearing and, in some cases, after judgment, if the defendant is a businessperson using a fictitious name.

---

### How to Find Out Who Owns a Business

Many states require that all people who do business using a name other than their own file a fictitious business name statement with the county clerk in the county or counties in which the business operates. This is public information that you can get from the county clerk. Another way to figure out who owns a business is to check with the business tax and license office in the city where the business is located. (If the business is not located in an incorporated city, try the county.) The tax and license office will have a list of the owners of all businesses paying taxes in the city. They should be able to tell you, for example, that Rufus Clod owns the Garden of Exotic Delights. Once you find this out, you sue Rufus Clod, individually and d.b.a. The Garden of Exotic Delights.

If the tax and license office or the county clerk can't help, many companies must register with the secretary of state or your state's department of corporations—a quick online check might tell you all you need to know. Otherwise, find a state agency that would seem to have jurisdiction over the type of business you wish to sue, call its public information number and explain your problem. It might take a little persistence, but eventually, you should get the help you need.

---

## Partnerships

All partners in a general partnership business are individually liable for all the acts of the business. You should list the names of all the business partners, even if your dispute is only with one (Patricia Sun and Farah Moon, d.b.a. Sacramento Gardens). Check with the local business tax and license office or recorder's office to find out who owns a particular partnership.

> EXAMPLE: You take your new blue suit to a local dry cleaner and, because they put too much cleaning fluid on it, it now has a small gray cloud on the right rear shoulder. After trying unsuccessfully to get the cleaners to take responsibility for the stain, you start thinking about a different kind of suit— a lawsuit. However, when you fill out the defendant's name in the court papers, you realize that all you know is that the store sign says "Perfection Cleaners" and that the unpleasant guy you were dealing with is named Bob. So you call the city business tax and license people and learn that Robert Johnson and Sal De Benno own Perfection Cleaners. You sue both owners and the business by listing them like this: Robert Johnson and Sal De Benno, d.b.a. Perfection Cleaners.

CAUTION
**Special procedures to sue limited partnerships.** Limited partnerships usually consist of one or more general partners who are subject to being sued, and a number of limited partners who, as investors, typically can't be sued. So if you sue a limited partnership, list the name of the partnership itself and the general partner or partners. Do not list the limited partners. Limited partnerships must register with the secretary of state. For information on who to sue and serve with papers, contact the secretary of state.

## Corporations and Limited Liability Companies (LLCs)

Corporations and limited liability companies (LLCs) are legal entities (like people). You can sue and enforce a judgment against the business entity itself. You should not sue the owners, officers, or managers of the corporation or LLC as individuals unless you have a personal claim against them that is separate from their role in the corporation or LLC. In most situations, the real people who own or operate the corporation or LLC aren't themselves legally liable to pay the corporation's or LLC's debts (unless there was fraud or a personal guaranty). This concept is called "limited personal liability" and is a big reason many people choose to incorporate or form an LLC in the first place.

Be sure to list the full name of the corporation or LLC when you file the lawsuit (John's Liquors, Inc., a Corporation, or John's Liquors, LLC). Here again, the name on the door or the stationery might not be the organization's real name, as corporations and LLCs sometimes use fictitious names. To be sure, check with the city or county business license office where the corporation or LLC is headquartered. Information is also usually available from either the secretary of state or your state's corporations commissioner's office.

You can sue a corporation or an LLC in your state if it does business there, even if its headquarters are in another state.

## Motor Vehicle Accident Cases

Special rules apply when it comes to motor vehicle accidents. In most states, if your claim arises from an accident with an automobile, motorcycle, truck, or RV, you should name both the driver of the vehicle and the registered owner as defendants because the vehicle's owner might be liable even if that person wasn't driving. Most of the time, you will obtain this information at the time of the accident. If the police make an accident report, it will contain this information. You can get a copy of any police report from the police department for a modest fee. If there was no police report—and assuming you have the license number of the offending vehicle—contact the Department of Motor Vehicles. Tell them you want to find out the name and address of the vehicle's owner for purposes of filing and serving a lawsuit based on a motor vehicle accident. This is a legitimate reason in most states, and you will get the information you need. However, in some states, you might need to complete some forms or jump through other hoops to learn the owner's name, and the owner of the car can be notified of your request.

When a business owns a vehicle, sue both the driver and the business owners. If a minor child is driving the car, find out the parents' names and, if possible, whether they gave their child permission to drive. (See "How to Sue Minors," below.) Remember, when you sue more than one person (in this case the driver and the owner, if they are different), serve papers on both.

EXAMPLE: You are involved in a car accident. The other driver first identifies herself as "Suzie Q" but then tells the police officer she is Suzanne Quigley. When you call Suzie about replacing your smashed headlight, she ignores your calls, so you request a copy of the accident report from the police. When reviewing it, you find out that Suzanne is 17 and was driving a car owned by her parents, George and Mary Quigley. You contact Suzanne's parents, but they also refuse to pay for the damage. However, during the conversation, you find out she was driving the car with their permission. When you sue, you'll list the defendants as follows: Suzanne Quigley, also known as Suzie Q, a minor; and George Quigley and Mary Quigley, husband and wife and parents of defendant Suzanne Quigley.

## How to Sue Minors

It is challenging to sue a minor for breach of contract because minors can disavow or back out of any contract they sign as long as they do it before they turn 18. The only exception is if the contract was for a necessity of life—for example, food—in which case the minor's parents are probably responsible. You can sue emancipated minors, that is, people under 18 who the law legally treats as adults. This includes minors who are on active duty in the armed services, married, or emancipated (freed from parental control) by court order.

What about damage caused by minors? Although it is legal to sue children for injuring you or damaging your property, it's rarely worthwhile, because most don't have money and can't pay the judgment. (There are exceptions, of course.) However, if you do sue someone under 18, do it like this: "John Jeffrey, a minor, and William Jeffrey, his father."

But what about suing the offending kid's parents? Typically, a parent is not legally responsible for damages negligently caused by children. However, exceptions to this rule exist. If the parent had a duty to watch the child and failed to do so, you might have a cause of action against the parents for negligent supervision. For instance, if you're injured after an unruly toddler knocks you down in the mall, the facts might show that the parents weren't correctly watching (and restraining) the child.

Also, in virtually all states, if a child is guilty of "malicious or willful misconduct," a parent could be liable up to a certain dollar amount per act for all property damage and sometimes for personal injuries. Parents can also be liable for damage done by their minor children in auto accidents if they authorize the child to drive—especially if they had reason to know they shouldn't do so.

Because this can be a complicated area of law, you'd likely want to consult with a lawyer before pursuing a small claims action. Otherwise, check the index to your state's laws under "Minors," "Children," or "Parent and Child" for the rules in your state.

> **EXAMPLE 1:** John Johnson, age 17, trips over his shoelace while delivering your newspaper and crashes through your glass door. Can you recover from John's parents? Probably not, as John is not guilty of "willful misconduct."

> **EXAMPLE 2:** John shoots out your glass door with a slingshot after you have repeatedly asked his parents to disarm him. Can you recover from the parents? Probably.

## How to Sue Government Agencies

Many states have special rules and procedures you must follow before bringing a lawsuit against a state or local government agency. Often, you have to act very quickly, or you'll lose your right to sue. Your local small claims court might have information on the procedures and time limits you must meet. Check your state's small claims court website (see Appendix A) or call your local small claims court. If you don't find the information you need, contact the government agency.

## Claims Against a City

Typically, before you can sue a city for an illegal tow or after a city employee injures you or damages your property, you must file a claim with the city and have it denied. To do this, get a claim form from the local city clerk. For cases involving personal injury or property damage, your claim usually must be filed within six months of the date of the incident—but be sure to check your city's deadlines. They are shorter than typical statutes of limitations because you must complete that step before filing a court action. It gives you time to complete the city's claim process and, if the city rejects the claim, file a court action against the city before the state statute of limitations expires.

Often, the city attorney will be in charge of reviewing your claim and making a recommendation to the city council. Sometimes the recommendation will be to pay you, but often it will be to deny the claim. After the city acts, you must file your small claims case before the statute of limitations expires— usually one to two years. Save a copy of your denial letter from the city; the small claims court will want to see it.

## Claims Against a County, District, or State

The rules for suits against all government entities, including counties and districts (for example, school districts) and the state are usually the same as the rules for claims against a city. You'll need to file a complaint against the government entity before you can go to small claims court. Get the complaint form and file it promptly. You'll usually have six months to file your complaint with the government entity but be sure to check the specific deadline. If the government entity denies your administrative claim, you must file your action in court before the statute of limitations period expires.

CAUTION

**No lawsuits against the U.S. government in small claims court.** You can't bring a small claims suit against the federal government, a federal agency, or even against a federal employee for actions relating to his or her employment. The federal government, like other governmental entities, cannot be sued in any state court without its consent. You'll file your administrative claim with the appropriate federal agency within six months or less—check the agency's deadlines for administrative actions. If the agency denies the administrative claim, you'll file your lawsuit in court—likely the federal district court. Be sure to file the lawsuit before the statute of limitations expires or you'll lose your right to sue.

## A Deceased Person's Estate

You can still file a lawsuit or collect a judgment even if the defendant has died. You will direct your efforts at the deceased person's estate—that is, the property the person left behind. Act promptly; if you don't, your claim could be barred by law.

Unless the defendant arranged for everything in the estate to pass outside of probate (by using a living trust or another probate avoidance device), there will probably be a probate court proceeding. It's conducted by the estate's "personal representative"—the executor named in the deceased person's will or, if there is no will, an administrator appointed by the court. Often, the surviving spouse or an adult child is the personal representative.

A personal representative who knows that you were owed money is required to send you a notification of the death. The notice will advise you to make a claim by a certain deadline, set by law. You will probably have at least two to four months in which to file your claim in the probate proceeding.

If you don't get a notice of the death, you can still submit a claim. Find out whether or not there's a probate proceeding (and if so, who the personal representative is) by checking probate records in the county where the defendant lived at the time of death. If you miss the deadline, a late claim might be allowed up to one year from the date of death.

You make an official claim by submitting a regular bill or using a court document called a "creditor's claim." Submit your claim directly to the probate court and serve a copy on the personal representative. If you file a formal claim and the personal representative rejects it, you can file suit against the estate.

What if there's no probate proceeding? In that case, your best bet is to present your claim to the deceased person's spouse, child, or close relative. If it is denied or ignored, you have the right to file suit against anyone who inherits from the deceased. Do it as soon as possible.

# Where Can You Sue?

S mall claims courts are local because the dollar amounts involved aren't large enough to justify people traveling great distances to go to court. Because your dispute will likely be with a person or business located nearby, the critical thing to remember is that you can sue in the county where the defendant lives or where a company's main place of business is located.

Occasionally, however, the person or business you want to sue resides at a considerable distance from your home. How you should proceed will depend on whether the defendant is in your state or another state.

## Out-of-State Defendants

Skip ahead to "Businesses," below, if you're planning to sue a business. Otherwise, read on.

### Individuals

The basic rule is that state courts—including small claims courts—only have the power or "jurisdiction" to hear cases involving individuals who live in or are present in the state. If you want to sue someone who lives in another state and doesn't travel to your state, you will have to sue in the state where the person lives, not in the state where you live. Often you can file papers by mail, but typically you'll need to show up in person on court day. (Some states allow people on active duty in the military and occasionally others to present their case entirely in writing.)

There are, however, circumstances under which you can use your state's small claims court to sue an out-of-state resident:

- Out-of-state residents can successfully be sued in state if you manage to serve them with court papers while they're physically within your state's borders *and* if the dispute arose in your state. For example, you live in Florida, and a nonresident injures you or damages your property while in Florida, or a contract with a nonresident was negotiated, performed, or violated in Florida. (For serving court papers, see Chapter 11.)

- A nonresident who has a vehicle accident in your state can be sued in your state's small claims court no matter where that person lives. Similarly, a nonresident owner of a vehicle can be sued no matter where the person lives if the car was being driven in your state by another person and was involved in an accident. Contact your small claims court clerk for details.
- The out-of-state owner of real property (including owners of apartments and other rental housing) located in your state can be sued locally on claims relating to the property.

## Businesses

When it comes to suing a business in small claims court, you can sue any business organized (incorporated or established as an LLC) in your state.

Also, you can bring suit against any business—whether incorporated or not—if one of the following conditions is true:

- the company was responsible for injuring you or damaging your property in your state *and* you can find a way to serve your court papers on the business in your state (see Chapter 11 for serving court papers)
- the business breaches a contract with you that was negotiated or was to be performed in your state *and* you can find a way to serve your court papers on the business in your state (see Chapter 11 for serving court papers)
- the business has an office, warehouse, retail establishment, restaurant, or another physical facility in the state, even if the business is headquartered or organized elsewhere, or
- the company does regular business in your state by selling products or services, employing a sales rep who calls on you personally or by phone to solicit business, sending you a catalog to solicit your business, or placing advertising in your state's media.

TIP

**The short story about suing out-of-state businesses.** What it comes down to is that most large national businesses can be sued in any state, but smaller businesses that are headquartered in another state, do no business in your state, and have no physical presence in your state can be sued only in the states where they operate.

EXAMPLE 1: While on vacation in Florida, you slip and fall in the ticket office of a small locally owned commuter airline operating only in Florida. When you return home to Maine, you file suit against the airline for your injuries in small claims court. The judge will toss out your case because Maine courts do not have jurisdiction (the power) to hear a case involving a defendant that doesn't operate, advertise, or solicit business in Maine. The only place you can sue the airline is in Florida.

EXAMPLE 2: You're at home in Maine planning your vacation to Florida when you slip and fall in the ticket office of a national airline headquartered in Florida. You can sue the airline for damages in a Maine small claims court because the airline does business in Maine. The fact that the airline is headquartered in another state is irrelevant.

EXAMPLE 3: You own a small graphic design company in Maine and negotiate a signage contract for a New York clothing store soon expanding into Maine. The negotiations take place by phone and email. After timely completing the work, the store refuses to pay. You can sue the store in Maine. Although the location of the contract negotiations is arguable, you performed the work in Maine. You can sue the store in a Maine small claims court if you can serve your court papers within Maine's borders.

## Defendants in Your State

If the person or business you want to sue resides or does business in your state, you must decide which small claims court should hear your suit.

Of all the aspects of small claims court that differ from state to state, the rules on where to sue seem to be the most variable. Some states let you sue only in the district or county where the defendant resides. Others also allow you to sue where an accident occurred, a contract was broken or originally signed, merchandise was purchased, a corporation does business, and so on.

You'll need to refer to the rules for your local small claims court (look at your state's listing in the appendix). The first thing to look at is the political subdivisions (judicial district, precinct, city, or county) your state uses to define the geographical boundaries of its small claims courts. Next, carefully study your local rules to understand the criteria used to define which district a particular lawsuit should be brought in (for example, suits can always be brought where a defendant lives). If this information isn't in the information sheet, call the clerk of the court and ask. You might be eligible to sue in more than one judicial district (for example, where a defendant lives or where a traffic accident occurred). If you have a choice, pick the court most convenient for you.

TIP
**In a few states you can sue for larger amounts in some areas.** In some states, such as New York, Pennsylvania, and Tennessee, you can sue for higher amounts in certain counties. If yours is a more significant claim, you'll want to see whether you can sue in one of these locations. (The rules for all states are set out in Appendix A.)

### General Rules on Where You Can Sue

Depending on the specific rules of your state, you can generally sue in any one of the following political subdivisions:
- the judicial district in which the defendant resides or has a place of business at the time you file your lawsuit
- the judicial district in which the contract underlying your lawsuit was supposed to be carried out
- the judicial district in which the injury underlying your lawsuit occurred, or
- the judicial district in which the rental property is located (for landlord-tenant security deposit disputes or evictions).

Now let's consider some typical rules about where you can sue within a state.

## Where the Defendant Lives or Does Business

Because most small claims disputes are local, most plaintiffs follow the most straightforward provisions of the rules. They sue individual defendants in the judicial district where they live and business defendants (corporations, LLCs, or unincorporated businesses) in the judicial district where they do business.

> **EXAMPLE:** Downhill Skier lives in City County, but also owns a mountain cabin in Snowy County, where he spends several months a year. Late one snowy afternoon, Downhill drives his new SUV from the ski slopes to his nearby cabin. Turning into his driveway, he executes a bad slalom skid right into Woodsey Carpenter's elderly but much-loved pickup. Where can Woodsey properly sue? Obviously, Woodsey can sue in City County where Downhill has his permanent address. He can probably also sue in Snowy County where Downhill's cabin is located, on the theory that Downhill also lives there. In many states, Woodsey is also eligible to sue Downhill in Snowy County because small claims cases can be filed where the damage occurred.

## Where the Contract Was Signed

Most states assume that the place where a written contract is signed is also where it will be carried out. Therefore, you can usually sue where the contract was signed, if a problem develops.

Arizona, California, Indiana, and a few other states are more thorough. (See Appendix A.) In these states, a suit can be brought either where the contract was signed or where the contract was to be performed. This is good common sense, as the law assumes that, if people enter into a contract to perform something at a certain location, it is probably reasonably convenient to both. If, for example, Downhill gets a telephone installed in his mountain cabin, or has the fender on his SUV fixed by a Snowy County mechanic, or has a cesspool put in at his cabin, or agrees to sit (and pay) for a portrait in

Snowy County, he can be sued in Snowy County if he fails to keep his part of the bargain. Of course, as we learned above, Downhill can also be sued in City County, where he resides permanently.

> **EXAMPLE:** John Gravenstein lives in Sonoma County, California, where he owns an apple orchard. He signs a contract to buy spare parts from Acme Mechanical Apple Picker Co., an international corporation with offices in San Francisco, New York, Paris, and Guatemala City. John signs the contract in Sonoma County. The parts are sent to John from San Francisco via UPS. They turn out to be defective. After trying and failing to reach a settlement with Acme, John wants to know if he can sue in Sonoma County. Yes. Even though Acme doesn't have a business office in Sonoma County, and didn't perform there in connection with their agreement to sell John the spare parts, that's where they signed the contract.

TIP

**If you have a choice of judicial districts, pick the most convenient one.** As you should now understand, there could be two, three, or more judicial districts where you could file your case. Choose the one that serves you best. As long as that district is proper, you have no obligation to pick one the defendant prefers.

Unfortunately, it isn't always easy to determine the location where a contract was entered into—particularly when the people who made the contract did so from different locations. If you enter a contract by phone or online, for example, there could be an argument that the contract was entered where you are or where the other party is. Rather than trying to learn and apply all the intricacies of contract law, your best bet is probably to sue in the place most convenient to you, claiming that the contract was made there. On the other hand, if someone sues you at the wrong end of the state and you believe there is a good argument that the contract was formed where you live (that is, where you accepted the other party's offer), write to the court as soon as you have been served and ask that the case be dismissed. (See "If You Are Sued in the Wrong Court," below.)

## Where the Injury or Event Occurred

Most states allow you to sue in the judicial district where the act or omission underlying the lawsuit occurred (see the appendix). "Act or omission" is a shorthand term that lumps together things that lead to lawsuits like automobile accidents, warranty disputes, and landlord-tenant disputes, for the purpose of deciding where you're allowed to sue. So if you are in a car accident, a dog bites you, a tree falls on your head, or a neighbor floods your cactus garden, you can sue in the judicial district where the event or injury occurred, even if it isn't where the defendant resides.

> **EXAMPLE:** Addison is returning to his home in Indianapolis from Bloomington, Indiana, following an Indiana University basketball game. At the same time, Lenore is rushing to Bloomington from her home in Brown County, Indiana, more than 40 miles west of Bloomington. Lenore runs a red light and demolishes Addison's Toyota near the Indiana University gym in downtown Bloomington, which is in Monroe County. After parking his car and taking a bus home, Addison tries to figure out where he can sue Lenore if they can't work out a fair settlement. Unfortunately, he can't sue in Indianapolis, as Lenore doesn't reside there, and the accident didn't happen there. Addison would have to sue either in Monroe County, where his property was damaged, or in Brown County, where Lenore lives. Luckily for Addison, Monroe County is just an hour from Indianapolis.

## If You Are Sued in the Wrong Court

Because the rules can be complicated, sometimes people and businesses are sued in the wrong court. If a plaintiff serves you with court papers and the case is located in the wrong judicial district, you have two choices:

- Show up and go ahead with the case. Although the court has independent authority to transfer the matter to the correct court, the judge will probably proceed with the trial if both parties are willing. Doing this might be a good choice if the location is reasonably convenient.

### Sample Letter by Defendant Challenging Venue

2100 Coast Drive
Beachtown, FL 12344
December 12, 20xx

Small Claims Court
600 Washington
Tallahassee, FL 12344

Re: *Upton v. Downey*
    # 987 321

Dear Judge:

I am the defendant in this case. Because I have been sued in the wrong court
and will be highly inconvenienced if I have to defend myself there, I request that
you please dismiss this court action.

My request is based on the fact I live in Beachtown, FL, and the car accident
that gave rise to this case occurred in Orange County. The fact that plaintiff
later moved to Tallahassee and chose to file suit in your court does not amount
to a valid legal reason to have it heard there.

Sincerely,

*Fred Downey*
Fred Downey

- Challenge the venue (location) of the case. You can challenge venue by:
  - promptly writing to the court explaining why the case is in the wrong place, and sending a copy to all other parties (while this would essentially be equivalent to a "motion to change venue," it's a good idea to contact the court to see if you're required to file a form or motion), or
  - showing up on the court date and challenging the location in person (some judges will consider your appearance a waiver of venue, meaning that by showing up, you consent to the judge hearing your case in that court, so be sure to check with your court before taking this approach).

A judge who determines the suit is in the wrong court will dismiss the case or transfer it to a proper court. A dismissal shouldn't be a problem if the plaintiff sued reasonably soon after the loss occurred, leaving the plaintiff enough time to refile before the statute of limitations—the time you have to sue—expires. If you find yourself in this situation, check the time limitations before agreeing to a transfer. (See Chapter 5 for information about statutes of limitations.) If the defendant challenges venue with a letter but the court rules that the matter is in the correct court, the judge will probably delay the hearing to give the defendant time to make arrangements to appear.

# Filing Fees, Court Papers, and Court Dates

## How Much Does It Cost?

Fees for filing a case in small claims court are very reasonable—usually not much more than $75. In some states, plaintiffs with very low incomes can ask to have court filing fees waived. Typically, a defendant doesn't have to pay anything unless the defendant files a claim or "counterclaim" against the plaintiff. There is usually an additional fee for serving papers on the opposing party unless you are in a state that allows personal service to be carried out by a nonprofessional process server and you have a friend who will do it for you without charge. (See Chapter 11.) Most states allow service by certified or registered mail, which doesn't cost much. In a few situations, you might have to hire a professional process server. How much this costs will depend partly on how hard it is to find the person you need to serve. You can get your filing fees and service costs added to the court judgment if you win. (See Chapter 15.)

## Filing Your Lawsuit

Now let's look at how you obtain and fill out the papers you need to file your lawsuit. You should be able to get the information and forms online (see Appendix A for your state's website). If you get the forms from your state's website, check whether the county or court where you plan to file has local forms or filing requirements (some do). If you're not sure you have everything you need, you can always visit or call the small claims court where you plan to file your lawsuit. If you do it this way, you will likely receive a package with the forms and instructions for completing and filing the papers.

You'll start the case by filing a complaint or claim which, in most cases, will include the following information:

- your full name, address, and telephone number
- the correct name and address of the person or persons you are suing (including whether this is an individual, partnership, sole proprietor, limited liability company, or corporation)
- the amount of your claim

- the reason the defendant owes you money, and
- whether you have any other claims against that person or other small claims cases.

Other information might be required as well. Follow the instructions on your forms and if you still have questions, ask your local small claims court clerk for help. In most states, small claims clerks will help people fill out these forms.

> ! **CAUTION**
> **Be sure you name everything properly.** Chapter 7 has details about the correct way to list yourself or your business as the plaintiff. In Chapter 8, we discuss how to name the defendant correctly.

When you're ready to file your papers and pay the filing fee, you'll follow the rules of the local court where you plan to file your case. In most jurisdictions, you can file papers in person or by mail by submitting the original signed document and required copies with the court. Some courts allow electronic filing (eFiling) for small claims cases, either by the plaintiff directly or through an approved online service provider (eFiling is becoming more widely used for small claims and is even required in some jurisdictions). If you can't afford the fee, you might be able to have it waived. Check with your local court for fee waiver instructions.

In most small claims courts, you don't need to provide written evidence until you get to court. Some small claims courts, however—such as those in Washington, D.C.—require that certain types of evidence (such as copies of unpaid bills, contracts, or other documents on which the claim is based) be provided at the time you file your first papers.

Whether or not your state's rules require written documentation of certain types of claims, it is wise to spend a little time thinking about how you will prove your case. Read ahead and figure out precisely what proof you will need to present before filing your first court papers. Being right is one thing—proving it is another.

## The Defendant's Forms

In most states, a defendant doesn't have to file any papers to defend a case in small claims court unless the defendant wants the case transferred to formal court. However, in a few states, a defendant must respond in writing. (See Appendix A for your state's rules.) In the majority of states, defendants simply show up for the hearing on the date and at the time indicated on the papers served on them, ready to tell their side of the story. (If you need to get the hearing delayed, see "Your Court Date," below.) It is proper, and advisable, for a defendant to call or write the plaintiff and see whether a fair settlement can be reached without going to court, or to propose mediation. (See Chapter 6.)

Sometimes a party you planned to sue sues you first (for example, over a traffic accident where you each believe the other is at fault). As long as your grievance stems from the same incident, you can file a defendant's claim for up to the small claims court maximum and have it heard by a judge at the same time that the plaintiff's claim against you is considered. However, if you believe that the plaintiff owes you money as the result of a different injury or breach of contract, you might have to file your own separate case.

In all states you must file any defendant's claim (counterclaim) in writing within a specific period after being served with the plaintiff's claim (usually ten to 30 days). When you file a defendant's claim, you become a plaintiff as far as this claim is concerned. In those states where only the defendant can appeal, this means that if you lose your defendant's claim, you can't appeal that part of the case. Of course, even in these states, if you lose on the original plaintiff's claim, you can typically appeal that portion of the judgment. Appeal rules vary from state to state and can be complicated. Research the amount of time you have to appeal carefully to ensure you don't lose your right to appeal. If you have any questions, consult with a local lawyer. (See Chapter 23 and Appendix A.)

In most states, if a defendant's claim is for more than the small claims maximum, the case will be transferred to a formal court. Some states allow transfers only at the discretion of a judge, who may inquire whether the defendant's claim is made in good faith. Check your court rules and your state's listing in Appendix A. A defendant who does not want to cope with the procedures of formal court might want to scale down the claim to fit under the small claims limit. (See Chapter 4.)

> **CAUTION**
> **A defendant might be required to file a defendant's claim or lose the right to do so.** A defendant who has a claim against a plaintiff arising out of the incident underlying the plaintiff's lawsuit will almost always want to promptly file it. Some states require defendants to file a counterclaim as part of the plaintiff's lawsuit; others allow defendants to file their own lawsuit later. If this is an issue for you, check your state's rules.

## Jury Trials

Jury trials are not available in small claims court in most states. Plaintiffs know this when they file and can usually opt for a different court if they want a trial by jury. Defendants, of course, aren't involved in this choice. To compensate, some states allow a defendant who wants a jury trial to transfer a case to a formal court no matter how small the claim. Others allow transfer when the defendant's claim exceeds the small claims court maximum. Usually, a defendant must request a jury trial or a transfer to a court where a jury is permitted promptly after being served with court papers. And jury fees (often ranging from $100 to $500) must typically be paid in advance, although fees are usually recoverable if you win. Asking for a jury trial also tends to delay proceedings, and some people make the request for this reason. Check your state's rules on jury trials in small claims court.

## Your Court Date

One of the great advantages of small claims court is that disputes are heard quickly. This is important. Many people avoid lawyers and the regular courts primarily because they can take what seems like forever. In small claims court, you should get a court date in a relatively short time frame.

It is sometimes impossible for a plaintiff or defendant to be present on the date the court sets for the hearing. If this happens, you should contact the court immediately and ask that the case be rescheduled. Ask the clerk of the court or check your local court rules for any specific requirements for rescheduling a case. Oftentimes, you'll be required to make your request in writing and explain why you need a delay. Here's a sample of a letter requesting a postponement. Be sure to also send a copy to the other party at the same time you give the letter to the court.

### Sample Letter Requesting Postponement

37 Birdwalk Boulevard
Trenton, NJ

January 15, 20xx

Clerk
Small Claims Court
Trenton, NJ

Re: Small Claims No. 374-628

Dear Clerk:

I have been served with a complaint (No. 374-628) by John's Laundry, Inc. The date set for a hearing, February 15, falls on the day of my son's graduation from Nursing School in Oscaloosa, Oklahoma, which my husband and I plan to attend.

I called John's Laundry and asked to have the case delayed one week. They did not return my call.

I feel that I have a good defense to this suit. Please delay this case until any date after February 22, except March 13, which is my day for a medical checkup.

Thank you,

*Sally Wren*

Sally Wren

cc: John's Laundry

Before making your request to the court, you can try to contact the other party to see if you can agree to a mutually acceptable time for a new court date. If you both agree to reschedule, you could give the court a joint request for postponement signed by both parties. Here's a sample (but check your local rules for any specific requirements in your jurisdiction).

### Sample Joint Request for Postponement

11 South Street
Denver, CO

January 10, 20xx

Clerk of the Small Claims Court
Denver, CO

Re: SC 4117 (*Rodriguez v. McNally*)

Mr. Rodriguez and I agree to request that you postpone this case to a date after March 1, 20xx. If possible, we would prefer that it not be scheduled on March 27 or 28.

*John McNally*
John McNally

*John Rodriguez*
John Rodriguez

What if an emergency occurs a few days before a scheduled hearing? The court has the power to reschedule your case if the judge is convinced that circumstances warrant it (for example, a key witness has left town to attend a funeral). Contact the court clerk immediately, explain the problem, and ask for guidance.

 RELATED TOPIC
**What if your opponent doesn't show up?** For detailed instructions on how to proceed if your opponent (whether you're the plaintiff or defendant) doesn't show up to the court hearing, see Chapter 15.

# Serving Your Papers

A fter filing a claim with the small claims clerk, the plaintiff must deliver a copy of the claim to each defendant. This is called "service of process," and no lawsuit is complete without it. The reason you must serve the other side is obvious: Defendants in a case need to know about any claims against them and must be notified of the day, time, and place that they can show up to defend themselves. Also, any defendant who files a defendant's claim against a plaintiff must serve copies of that claim on all plaintiffs in the case. Service of process rules also apply if you need to deliver a subpoena to a witness. (See Chapter 14.)

CAUTION

**Check to be sure your papers were served.** Never show up in court on the day of the court hearing on the assumption that your certified mail service has been accomplished. If the defendant didn't sign for the paper, you will be wasting your time. Call the court clerk a couple of days in advance and verify that the service of process has been completed. This means the certified letter has been signed for by the defendant, not by someone else at the address.

## Who Must Be Served

All defendants on the plaintiff's claim or all plaintiffs on the defendant's claim must be served. It is not enough to serve one defendant or plaintiff and assume that that person will tell the others. This is true even if the parties are married, live together, or do business together.

CAUTION

**If you don't serve a party, the judge will postpone the hearing or dismiss your case against that party.** If you sue only one person and don't serve that person according to the rules, the judge will probably postpone the hearing until after you can serve that person. If you sue more than one person but serve only one properly, the judge cannot enter a judgment against those you didn't serve and will dismiss your action against those parties. Some states will allow you to refile your claim against those parties if you wish.

## Where Can Papers Be Served?

Typically, you must serve papers in the state where you filed your lawsuit. For instance, you can't sue someone in a Massachusetts court and serve papers on them in Oklahoma. An exception involves suits involving motor vehicle accidents or lawsuits against out-of-state owners of real estate located in-state. Many states allow out-of-state service on this type of claim. Your small claims court clerk will show you how your state handles these situations.

If the person you want to sue resides or does business in your state, you can serve papers anyplace in the state. (See Chapter 9.)

## Serving an Individual

There are several ways to serve papers on individual defendants. (See "Serving a Business," below, for information on serving a business.) It all depends on knowing where the defendant is. If you can't find the defendant personally and do not know where the person lives or works, you won't be able to complete service, and it probably makes little sense to file a lawsuit.

---

### Serving Someone With a Post Office Box

If you know nothing more than the individual defendant's post office box, you'll need to get a street address to serve the person. To do this, you must give the post office a written statement saying that you need the address solely to serve legal papers in a pending lawsuit. (See "Sample Request to Post Office for Boxholder's Address," below.) This should work, but if it doesn't, refer the post office employee to the Post Office's Administrative Support Manual § 352.44e(2). There is no fee for the Post Office providing this information. (39 CFR § 265.6(d)(4)(ii).)

## Sample Request to Post Office for Boxholder's Address

June 1, 20xx

Postmaster
Minneapolis, MN 12333

REQUEST FOR BOXHOLDER INFORMATION NEEDED FOR SERVICE OF LEGAL PROCESS

Please furnish the name and street address of the following post office box holder:

> Don Defendant
> P.O. Box 0000
> Minneapolis, MN 12333

1. Capacity of requester (for example, process server, attorney, party representing self): Party representing self.

2. Statute or regulation that empowers me to serve process (not required when requester is an attorney or a party acting pro se—except a corporation acting pro se must cite statute): I am a party representing myself.

3. The names of all known parties to the litigation: Peggy Plaintiff and Don Defendant.

4. The court in which the case has been or will be heard: Hennepin County Small Claims Court, City Hall, Room 306, Minneapolis, MN 55415.

5. The docket or other identifying number if one has been issued: Case Number 000000.

6. The capacity in which this individual is to be served (for example, defendant or witness): Defendant.

WARNING: THE SUBMISSION OF FALSE INFORMATION TO OBTAIN AND USE BOXHOLDER INFORMATION FOR ANY PURPOSE OTHER THAN THE SERVICE OF LEGAL PROCESS IN CONNECTION WITH ACTUAL OR PROSPECTIVE LITIGATION COULD RESULT IN CRIMINAL PENALTIES INCLUDING A FINE OF UP TO $10,000 OR IMPRISONMENT OF NOT MORE THAN 5 YEARS, OR BOTH (18 U.S.C. § 1001).

**Sample Request to Post Office for Boxholder's Address (continued)**

I certify that the above information is true and that the address information is needed and will be used solely for service of legal process in conjunction with actual or prospective litigation.

*Peggy Plaintiff*

Peggy Plaintiff

123 Maiden Lane

Minneapolis, MN 12333

## Personal Service

Personal service means that someone hands the defendant the required papers. You have various options regarding who performs this task. Of course, if you use someone who doesn't personally know the defendant, the server will need to be particularly careful to serve the right person. These are your options for who can serve the defendant:

- **Sheriff, marshal, or constable.** All states allow personal service to be made by law officers, although not all officers will serve civil subpoenas. Using this method is often valuable for its sobering effect. The fee can be added to your judgment if you win.

- **Private process servers.** Many states also allow service by private process servers. Fees charged are usually based on how long the service takes. See your state's listing in Appendix A to find out whether your state allows service by private process servers.

- **Service by disinterested adult.** Some states (see Appendix A) allow service by any person who is at least 18 years old, except the person bringing the suit. Any person means just that—a relative or a friend is fine. However, states often require that this person be approved by the court.

### How to Find a Good Process Server

Unfortunately, sheriff's offices in some states are getting out of the process-serving business. So you might have to hire a private person or company. To make sure you're dealing with a business you can trust, do a little research first. One indicator of trustworthiness is how long the process server has been in business or ask the small claims court clerk for a list of registered process servers. If you know any lawyers, you can ask them for a recommendation.

CAUTION

**A mailbox isn't personal enough.** No matter who serves the papers, if personal service is used, the claim and a summons must be handed to the defendant. You can't simply leave the papers at the defendant's job or home or in the mailbox. The process server should never try to use force to get a defendant to take any papers. If the process server locates the right person, but the person refuses to accept the paperwork, acts hostile, or attempts to run away, the process server should put the papers down and leave. Valid service will have been accomplished.

---

### Serving Someone in the Military

It is proper to serve someone who is on active duty in the armed forces. If the person shows up, you'll be in good shape. If not, however, you'll have a problem. Although you can usually get a default judgment against a properly served defendant who fails to show up, this is not true if the person you are suing is in the military (other than the reserves).

Typically, the court won't issue a default judgment against someone on active duty in the armed forces because Congress has given our military personnel special protections. To get a default judgment, you will probably have to file a statement under penalty of perjury that the defendant is not in the military. This declaration is available from the clerk. Clerks almost always accept a Declaration of Nonmilitary Service signed by the plaintiff, as long as the plaintiff reasonably believes that the defendant is not on active duty.

---

## Certified Mail

In most states, you can serve papers by sending them to the defendant by certified mail with a return receipt requested. Service by certified (or registered) mail is one of several ways some states let you serve papers. Other states require you to try service by certified mail before any other method of service. (See Appendix A.) Typically, the court clerk does the mailing for you and charges a small fee that's recoverable if you win. (See Chapter 15.) The mail method is both cheap and easy, but the defendant will likely need to sign for the letter for this type of service to be effective. In a few states, service is accomplished even if the defendant rejects a certified letter. Most businesses and many individuals routinely sign to accept their mail. However, some people never do, knowing instinctively, or perhaps from past experience, that nothing good ever comes by certified mail. The consensus in an informal survey of court clerks is that about 50% of court papers served by certified mail are accepted. If you try using the mail to serve your papers and fail, and you have to pay a process server, tell the judge about it as part of your presentation. The chances are your costs will be added to the judgment.

## Regular First-Class Mail

A minority of states allow you to serve papers by first-class mail. The states differ, however, regarding what you must do if the defendant doesn't answer the complaint within the time limit. New York, for example, presumes that the defendant received the papers unless the envelope comes back as "undeliverable." Check with your court clerk to see if this method is available in your area.

## Substituted Service (or "Nail and Mail")

It can be difficult to serve some individuals. In some states, avoiding service no longer works, and a procedure exists allowing for "substituted service" if you make "reasonable efforts" to serve a defendant and fail. Often the slang for this type of service is "nail and mail," because in several states, if you can't serve the defendant personally, you don't have to leave the claim with a live person. Instead, you can tack one copy to the defendant's door and mail the second copy.

In a typical state, substituted service works like this:

1. Small claims papers can be served by an adult not named in the lawsuit by leaving a copy at the person's dwelling place in the presence of a competent member of the household who is at least age 18 (and who must be told what the papers are about) or at the person's workplace during normal business hours with the person in charge (who must be told what the papers are about).

2. On the same day, a copy of the papers must also be mailed to the defendant by first-class mail.

Service is complete ten days after mailing. Be sure that all steps, including mailing the extra copy, are carried out by an adult not named in the lawsuit.

## Serving a Business

When you sue a business, the same methods of service discussed above can be used. However, if you use the personal service or certified mail service methods, you'll need to know how the business is legally organized to determine whom you must serve. (See "Who Should Be Served," below.) And if you know only a business defendant's post office box, you'll want to get its street address. (See "Serving Someone With a Post Office Box," above.)

### Whom to Serve When Suing a Business

When suing a business, you need to serve your court papers on the owner, a partner, the president, vice-president, secretary, treasurer, or the business's agent for service of process. How do you find out who this person is?

A straightforward approach is to call the business and ask who and where to serve a lawsuit. If the company won't tell you, the city or county tax and license people where the business is located should be able to do so. (See Chapter 8.) For a corporation, limited partnership, or LLC organized in your state, you should be able to get this information from your secretary of state's office.

## Who Should Be Served?

No matter which method of service you choose, who you must serve depends on how the business is organized.

**Sole proprietorship.** Serve the owner.

**Partnership.** Serve at least one partner.

**Limited partnership.** Serve the partner who runs the business (the general partner) or the agent for service of process.

**Corporation (profit or nonprofit).** Serve an officer (president, vice president, secretary, or treasurer) or the agent for service of process.

**Limited liability company.** Serve an officer (president, vice president, secretary, or treasurer) or the agent for service of process.

## Substituted or Personal Service

If you need to serve papers on a business with a local office, store, or another physical location, personal service or substituted service is best if your state allows this type of service. (See Appendix A.) Have a process server or "disinterested adult" attempt to deliver the papers personally to the proper person at the business address. If the person is unavailable, the process server should leave the papers at the defendant's business during usual business hours with the person in charge (this is the first step in "substituted service"). Then, mail a copy of the summons and complaint, via certified mail, to the person to be served at the same address.

## Certified Mail Service

Service via certified mail is probably your best bet if the business doesn't have a local office, store, or other physical location and if your state allows this type of service. (See Appendix A.) To serve a business via certified mail, ask the court clerk to send the court papers to the proper person and address and pay the small fee. You can serve:

- the proper person as listed in "Who Should Be Served?" above, or
- the business's registered agent for service of process, if the business has its only address outside of your state.

## How to Serve a Government Agency

As discussed in Chapter 8, before you can sue a city, a county, or another government agency, you must first file an administrative (in-house) claim against that agency within a specified number of days after the incident that gave rise to your claim. (The fact that you have done this must be stated in your plaintiff's claim.) After your claim is denied—or if it is ignored—you can go ahead and sue in small claims court. To serve your papers, call the governmental body in question and ask who should be served. Then proceed, following the rules set out in "Serving an Individual," above.

## Time Limits for Serving a Claim

The plaintiff in a small claims case is responsible for making sure that the defendant receives copies of the lawsuit before the hearing date. Every state has its own rule about the deadline by which the defendant must be served; some states require as few as five days before the hearing, whereas others require as many as 30 days. Check with your small claims court clerk for the rules in your state.

If the defendant is served fewer than the required number of days before the trial date, they can either go ahead with the trial anyway or request a postponement. Call the court clerk if you're the defendant and it's impossible for you to show up in person to ask for a delay. Point out that the opposing party didn't serve you in the proper time and that you want the case postponed.

The clerk should see to it that a default judgment is not entered against you. (See Chapter 10.) But just to be sure, get the clerk's name and take thorough notes about your conversation. You'll need the information if the clerk fails to take action and you have to ask the court to set aside the default judgment.

To count the days to see whether service has been accomplished within the correct time, do not count the day the service is made, but do count the day of the court appearance. Also count weekends and holidays, unless the last day falls on a weekend or holiday. If so, the period extends to the next day that is not a holiday.

EXAMPLE: Jack serves Julie on July 12 in Los Angeles, California, with court papers listing a July 22 court date. California's rules require Jack to serve Julie with the court papers at least 15 days before the hearing. July 13 is a Sunday. To figure out the days, you do not count July 12, the day of service, but you do count July 13, 14, 15, 16, 17, 18, 19, 20, 21, and 22, for a total of ten days. Ten days is not enough time before the hearing date. Julie can either request a postponement because she wasn't served according to the rules, or she can choose to go ahead with the hearing.

If you are unable to serve the defendant within the proper time, simply ask the court clerk for a new court date and try again.

## Proof of Service—Letting the Court Know

If you have asked the court clerk to serve your papers by certified mail, you don't need to do anything further. The court clerk sends out the certified mail for you, and the signed post office receipt comes back directly to the clerk if service is accomplished. It's as simple as that.

However, a court has no way of knowing whether or not papers have been successfully filed by personal service, substituted service, or first-class mail unless you tell them. So, you are required to notify the court that you've accomplished service of process. Notification is accomplished by filing a form sometimes called a "Proof of Service" form with the court clerk after the service has been made. (See "Sample Proof of Service," below.)

The Proof of Service form must be signed by the person actually making the service. A Proof of Service is used both by the plaintiff and by the defendant if the defendant files a defendant's claim. It must be returned to the clerk's office.

## Serving a Defendant's Claim

A defendant's claim is the form filed by a defendant who wishes to sue the plaintiff for money damages. A defendant's claim should be filed with the clerk and served on the plaintiff within the correct number of days before the hearing. Days are counted in the same way as discussed above.

If you are a defendant who has filed a claim and you cannot serve the plaintiff, show up on the court hearing date with your papers and serve the plaintiff in the hallway (not in the courtroom). Then explain to the judge why it was impossible to locate the plaintiff earlier. The judge will typically delay the case for a few days unless both you and the plaintiff agree to proceed with your claim that day. Either way, the judge should accept your defendant's claim as having been validly served.

## Serving Subpoenas

In Chapter 14, we discuss subpoenaing witnesses and documents. The service rules are the same as those discussed in "Serving an Individual," above, with one crucial difference: Any person, including the person bringing the suit, can serve the subpoena. Also, in many states, the person making the service must be ready to pay the person subpoenaed a witness fee if it is requested. This is often a flat fee (normally $40–$100), plus a mileage fee based on the distance to the courthouse. If you hire a sheriff or marshal to do the service, expect to be asked to pay this fee, plus the service fee, in advance. In many states, if the witness doesn't ask for the fee, it will be returned to you. (See Chapter 14 for details.)

A witness must be served with a subpoena far enough in advance of the court hearing date to give the witness "reasonable time" to prepare for and travel to the hearing.

## Costs of Service

Professional process servers commonly charge from $30–$100 per service, depending on how far they must travel. You can usually get these costs of service added to your judgment if you win, but be sure to remind the judge to do this when you conclude your court presentation. However, a few courts will not give the successful party an award to cover a process server's costs unless the person first tried to have the papers served by the cheaper certified mail approach. Other courts prefer that you don't use the mail approach at all; they feel that it wastes time because too often the mail isn't accepted. Check the website of your small claims court for instructions. If you can't find the answer, contact the small claims clerk or small claims adviser in your district and ask how the court prefers that you accomplish service and how much the judge will allow as a service of process fee.

## Sample Proof of Service

---

### SC-104 | Proof of Service

Use this form to serve a **person**, a **business**, or a **public entity**. To learn more about proof of service, read *What Is "Proof of Service"?*, Form SC-104B. To learn more about how to serve a business or entity, read *How to Serve a Business or Public Entity*, Form SC-104C.

To serve a **business,** you must serve **one** of the following people:
- Owner (for a sole proprietorship)
- Partner (for a partnership) or general partner (for a limited partnership)
- Any officer or general manager (corporation or association)
- Any person authorized for service by the business (corporation, association, general partnership, limited partnership)
- Any person authorized for service with the Secretary of State (corporation, association, limited liability company [LLC], limited liability partnership [LLP], limited partnership)

To serve a **public entity,** you must first file a claim with that entity, then serve **one** of the following people:
- Clerk (of a city or county)
- Chief officer or director (of a public agency)
- Any person authorized for service by the entity

**(1)**    a. If you are serving a **person,** write the person's name below:

_____

     b. If you are serving a **business** or **entity,** write the name of the business or entity, the person authorized for service, and that person's job title:

**Acme Illusions, Inc.   Waldo Fergus, President**
Business or Agency Name

_____
Person Authorized for Service        Job Title

*Clerk stamps date here when form is filed.*

*Fill in court name and street address:*
**Superior Court of California, County of**
Alameda
600 Washington Street
3rd Floor
Oakland, CA 94607

*Fill in case number, case name, hearing date, day, time, and department below:*

**Case Number:**
002006

**Case Name:**
Printer v. Acme Illusions, Inc.

**Hearing Date:**
6/15/20xx

**Time:** 9:00 a.m.    **Dept.:** 304

**(2)**   **Instructions to Server:**
You must be at least 18 years old and **not be named in this case.** Follow these steps:
- Give a copy of all the documents checked in ③ to the person in ①, *or*
- Give a copy of all the documents checked in ③ to one of the following people:
  - a. A competent adult (at least 18) living with, and at the home of the person in ①, *or*
  - b. An adult (at least 18) who seems to be in charge at the usual workplace of the person in ①, *or*
  - c. An adult (at least 18) who seems to be in charge where the person in ① usually receives mail (but not a U.S. Post Office box), if there is no known physical address for the person in ①.
  - *and* mail a copy of the documents left with one of the adults in a, b, or c above to the person in ①.

THEN
- Complete and sign this form, and
- Give or mail your completed form to the person who asked you to serve these court papers, *in time for the form to be filed with the court at least 5 days before the hearing.*

**(3)**   **I served the person in ① a copy of the documents checked below:**

     a. ☒ SC-100, *Plaintiff's Claim and ORDER to Go to Small Claims Court*

     b. ☐ SC-120, *Defendant's Claim and ORDER to Go to Small Claims Court*

     c. ☐ Order for examination *(This form must be personally served. Check the form that was served):*

         **Note:** *The court can issue a civil arrest warrant if the served party does not come to court **only** if the order for examination was personally served by a registered process server, sheriff, marshal, or someone appointed by the court.*

         (1) ☐ SC-134, *Application and Order to Produce Statement of Assets and to Appear for Examination*

         (2) ☐ AT-138/EJ-125, *Application and Order for Appearance and Examination*

     d. ☐ Other *(specify):* _____

Judicial Council of California, *www.courtinfo.ca.gov*
Revised January 1, 2009, Optional Form
Code of Civil Procedure, §§ 116.340, 415.10, 415.20

**Proof of Service**
**(Small Claims)**

SC-104, Page 1 of 2 →

## Sample Proof of Service (page 2)

| | Case Number: |
|---|---|
| Case name: Printer v. Acme Illusions, Inc. | 002006 |

**(4) Fill out "a" or "b" below:**

a. ☐ **Personal Service:** I personally gave copies of the documents checked in ③ to the person in ①:

On *(date):* _____ At *(time):* _____ ☐ a.m. ☐ p.m.

At this address: _____

City: _____ State: _____ Zip: _____

b. ☒ **Substituted Service:** I personally gave copies of the documents checked in ③ *(a, b, or d)* to *(check one):*

☐ A competent adult (at least 18) at the **home** of, and living with the person in ① , or
☐ An adult who seems to be in charge where the person in ① usually **works**, or
☒ An adult who seems to be in charge where the person in ① usually **receives mail**, or has a private post office box (not a U.S. Post Office box), if there is no known physical address for the person in ①.

I told that adult, "Please give these court papers to (name of person in ①)."

I did this on *(date):* May 10, 20xx _____ At *(time):* 10:15 ☒ a.m. ☐ p.m.

At this address: 100 Primrose Path _____

City: Oakland _____ State: CA Zip: 94602 _____

Name or description of the person I gave the papers to: Donna Doolittle _____

After serving the court papers, I put copies of the documents listed in ③ in an envelope, sealed the envelope, and put first-class prepaid postage on it. I addressed the envelope to the person in ① at the address where I left the copies.

I mailed the envelope on *(date):* 5/11/20xx from *(city, state):* Fremont, CA

by leaving it *(check one):*

a. ☒ At a U.S. Postal Service mail drop, or
b. ☐ At an office or business mail drop where I know the mail is picked up every day and deposited with the U.S. Postal Service, or
c. ☐ With someone else I asked to mail the documents to the person in ①, and I have attached that person's completed Form SC-104A.

**(5) Server's Information**

Name: Margaret Middleman _____ Phone: 510-703-2220

Address: 23 Treelined Way

City: Fremont _____ State: CA Zip: 94536

Fee for service: $ -0-

*If you are a registered process server:*

County of registration: _____ Registration number: _____

**(6)** I declare under penalty of perjury under California state law that I am at least 18 years old and not named in this case and that the information above is true and correct.

Date: 5/11/20xx

Margaret Middleman ► *Margaret Middleman*
_____ _____
*Type or print server's name* *Server signs here after serving*

# The Defendant's Options

This chapter is devoted to the concerns of small claims defendants. A lot of this material has been discussed already from the plaintiff's perspective. This chapter gives an overview of a small claims case from the point of view of the defendant—the person being sued.

> !  CAUTION
>
> **A response may be required.** In some states, the defendant must make a written response to the plaintiff's claim to avoid having a default judgment entered. The deadline for submitting the response differs from state to state. Check Appendix A for your state's general approach and help finding resources. However, always read state and local small claims laws and rules personally.

## If You Aren't Properly Served

You might conclude that the plaintiff didn't serve you properly with the court papers. Perhaps the plaintiff's claim was left with your neighbors, or maybe you weren't given the correct number of days in which to respond. If you find one or more procedural defects in the plaintiff's case, you might be tempted to not show up in court. However, this would likely be a mistake and would undoubtedly cause you more work down the road. The judge won't be aware of the problem and will issue a default judgment against you—a decision in the plaintiff's favor. If this happens, your first step will be going to the trouble of requesting that the court vacate (set aside) the default judgment. Then, if you're successful, your next step will be addressing the defect, and, in many cases, the plaintiff will be able to fix it without much effort.

When the plaintiff fails to have court papers properly served on you or makes some other procedural error, your best course of action is to contact the court in writing, explain the problem, and ask the court to dismiss the case. If the court can't or won't help, you'll probably want to show up on the court date and make your request in person. However, you won't want the judge to believe that you've agreed to appear at trial, so the very first thing that you say should be about the problem you want to address. If the problem involves a failure to serve papers on you properly, chances are the plaintiff will re-serve you then and there. But the court will likely delay the trial to give you a chance to prepare your defense.

## If You're Sued in the Wrong Court

If you think the plaintiff has filed suit in the wrong small claims court or, in legal terms, "in the wrong venue," you can challenge the venue—the court's right to hear the case.

As discussed in Chapter 9, you can do this in two ways. First, you can go to court on the scheduled day and request a dismissal of the case. If the judge refuses, the judge will likely go forward and hear the case. However, a judge who agrees that the location is improper will dismiss the case or transfer it to the appropriate judicial district.

The easier option is to write to the court explaining why you think the claim was brought in the wrong place. If you choose this approach, consider finding out if you should file a form or follow some other procedure. Send a copy of your letter or form to each of the other parties. If the judge agrees the suit is in the wrong place, the judge will likely dismiss or transfer the case. You will likely receive notification of the court's decision by mail, but if your court date draws near and you haven't heard back, call the court to find out the status.

> **TIP**
> **Out-of-state defendants should ask for a dismissal.** As discussed in Chapter 9, if you don't live—or do business—in the state in which you are sued, the small claims court normally doesn't have power ("jurisdiction") to enter a valid judgment against you, unless court papers are served on you while you happen to be in the state. Exceptions to this rule exist for out-of-staters sued because of a dispute involving real property located in the state or because of a traffic accident occurring in the state. If you are an out-of-state resident and receive small claims papers by mail, promptly write a letter to the court explaining that you do not believe you are subject to the court's jurisdiction. Send a copy of your letter to each of the other parties. Stay in touch with the court until you are sure the court has dismissed your case.

## If the Statute of Limitations Has Expired

Plaintiffs don't have an indefinite period to sue someone for a perceived wrong. If the plaintiff is suing you about an event that happened long ago, check Chapter 5 to see whether the plaintiff has missed the deadline or "statute of limitations" for suing. Statutes of limitations are different for different types of lawsuits but are never less than one year from the date of the incident. The main exception to this rule is if the plaintiff is suing a government agency. In that case, the plaintiff must file an administrative claim form with the government within a shorter period—often six months, but it could be less, so be sure to find and read the statute.

## Try to Compromise

If you feel that the plaintiff is partly right but is suing you for too much, try to work out a compromise settlement. One good approach is to call or write the plaintiff and make a settlement offer. How much to offer depends on your case's relative merits compared to the plaintiff's, and whether the plaintiff is asking for a reasonable or inflated amount. Assuming the plaintiff has a pretty solid legal position (you probably are legally liable) and is asking the court for a fair amount, start by offering to pay about half of the request. Even with a strong case, the plaintiff might want to save the time and trouble it takes to prepare for and appear in court. More likely, your initial offer will start negotiations that end with the plaintiff accepting a compromise—between 65% and 80% of the original demand, if you're lucky. If you settle, be sure to memorialize your agreement in writing. (See Chapter 6 for more on how to negotiate.)

RELATED TOPIC

**More information on personal bankruptcy.** See *How to File for Chapter 7 Bankruptcy,* by Cara O'Neill and Albin Renauer (Nolo).

CAUTION

**Don't rely on being judgment proof.** Some defendants who have no money are tempted not to show up and defend a case in small claims court because they figure that, even if they lose, the plaintiff can't collect. If you have a decent defense, this is not a good idea. Judgments are good for anywhere from five to 20 years, depending on the state (see Chapter 24) and can be renewed, if necessary. Hopefully, you'll get a job or otherwise put a few dollars together sometime in the future and, if so, you probably won't want them immediately taken away to satisfy a small claims judgment that you believe shouldn't have been entered in the first place. So defend yourself while you can. One possible exception to this "always fight back if you have a decent case" advice is if you plan to declare Chapter 7 bankruptcy. Bankruptcy wipes out most debts, including small claims judgments. However, keep in mind that if possible, it's usually in your best interest to file for bankruptcy before the case goes to trial and a judgment is entered against you.

## Try to Mediate

Engaging in mediation is frequently beneficial to the defendant because mediation tends to encourage a settlement for a lower amount than the plaintiff has demanded. In addition, mediation gives the defendant a chance to raise issues that would not be considered relevant by a small claims court judge. For example, in a dispute between neighbors, local businesspeople, or relatives, mediation would allow the parties to raise and deal with both legal and emotional concerns. (See Chapter 6 for more on mediation.)

TIP

**Ask the small claims clerk for help setting up mediation.** Mediation of small claims cases works in various ways in different states. In many, it can take place in the courthouse itself and is encouraged by the small claims court. In others, it's available at a nearby community mediation project. Ask the small claims court clerk or check your small claims court website to find out where mediation is available in your area. Then, if necessary, contact the mediation project and enlist their help in bringing the plaintiff to the table.

## If You Have No Defense

Now let's assume that the plaintiff filed in the correct venue and served you properly. Also, you don't have a valid defense—for instance, you borrowed money under the terms of a written contract and haven't paid it back—and the plaintiff doesn't want to compromise. Because you know you'll lose, you might conclude that it makes little sense to defend yourself in court. Your decision not to show up will very likely result in a default judgment against you. This judgment will most likely be for the dollar amount demanded by the plaintiff, plus the amount of the filing fee and any reasonable costs to serve the papers on you. (In Chapter 15, you can read about default judgments and how you can probably get one vacated if you act immediately.)

> **TIP**
> **Even if you owe 100% of the plaintiff's demand, it never hurts to make an offer.** If you have the money, why not offer to pay 75%–90% of what the plaintiff requests? To save the trouble of going to court—or for some other reason you might never guess—the plaintiff might accept, even though it is almost certain that the plaintiff would win a judgment for the whole amount by going to court.

## Paying in Installments

If you don't dispute the plaintiff's claim amount but want to make installment payments rather than paying all at once, consider showing up on the court date. You'll want to tell the judge why it would be difficult or impossible to pay a judgment all at once. For example, you might explain that you're on a fixed income, are unemployed, or have a moderate income and a large family. After stating the facts, tell the judge how much you can afford to pay each month. The judge can order installment payments when appropriate. (See Chapter 23 for more on paying a judgment in installments.)

## If You, Not the Plaintiff, Were Wronged— File a Defendant's Claim

Finally, some defendants will want to dispute the plaintiff's claim and sue the plaintiff back. Perhaps you are outraged because you are the person wronged. To assert your claim against the plaintiff, promptly file a defendant's claim. (See Appendix A.) If you want to sue for more than the court's limit, ask the small claims clerk to transfer the case to a higher court.

## Transferring Your Case to a Higher Court

Depending on state law and the facts of your case, you might be able to have your case transferred out of small claims court to a higher court, such as a municipal, superior, district, county, justice, circuit, city, or civil court. Whatever the name used in your state, this court will allow lawyers and require far more paperwork than necessary in small claims court.

Transfer rules vary significantly from one state to the next. Some states allow any defendant to transfer any case, while others allow it only if the defendant files a claim for an amount greater than the small claims limit or makes a request for a jury trial. Still, other states allow a case to be transferred only with the discretionary approval of a judge. And some states don't allow transfers at all.

If you are interested in transferring your case, look at the brief summary for your state in Appendix A to see if it's possible. Then, you need to consult your state's rules. But first, it makes sense to ask yourself why you would want to transfer a case out of small claims court. Some attorneys believe it's rarely a good idea. Because small claims court is cheaper, more user-friendly, and far less time-consuming than formal court, you'll usually want to defend your case right there. The exception is when filing a defendant's claim (counterclaim) for an amount significantly over the small claims limit. Here are some other situations in which it might make sense to transfer your case:

- To get a jury trial in states that allow transfers for this reason. Nonlawyers are almost always better off trying a case before a judge under relaxed small claims rules than submitting to the extra level of formality a jury trial adds to the already complicated court rules. But some people disagree, believing that there is no justice without a jury.
- Because you know how to navigate formal court far better than the plaintiff—or are willing to hire a lawyer to represent you. Some people do quite well representing themselves. Others find the cost of attorneys' fees worthwhile if defending the case means enough to them.

## Fight Back

You believe you don't owe the plaintiff anything and want to fight the case. To do this, file a response to the plaintiff's claim if required (see Appendix A but check your court rules personally), then show up in court on the date stated in the papers served on you, ready to present your side of the story.

 **RELATED TOPIC**
**Defendant's claim.** For more on what to do if you wish to sue the plaintiff, see Chapters 10 and 11.

If your case stays in small claims court, the court will hear all claims together. You should prepare and present your case just as you would if you had filed first—that is, understand the legal basics that underlie your case, make a practical and convincing oral presentation, and back it up with as much hard evidence as you can find.

Before considering the merits of the plaintiff's case, your first job is to check that the plaintiff brought it within the time allowed by the statute of limitations. (See Chapter 5.) If not, request that the judge dismiss the plaintiff's case at the beginning of your presentation. It should be the first thing you say.

To successfully present your defense, you'll want to be prepared to make a well-organized, convincing oral statement backed up with as much evidence as possible. Good case presentation strategies, including how to present witnesses, estimates, diagrams, and other evidence are discussed in Chapters 13–22 and apply both to defendants and plaintiffs. If the plaintiff has asked for too much money, you'll also want to be sure you tell the judge exactly why it is too much. (See Chapter 4.)

**Take apart your opponent's case.** To do this, you will typically want to focus on any facts that show you are not legally liable. Reread Chapter 2 to see what the plaintiff must prove for all the common types of small claims cases and see whether you can disprove any key points. If, after doing this you conclude the plaintiff might have a winning case, consider whether the plaintiff has asked for the right dollar amount. If you can convince a judge that you only owe a couple of hundred dollars— not the several thousand requested by the plaintiff—you will have won a substantial victory. (On calculating damages, see Chapter 4.)

> EXAMPLE 1: The plaintiff sues you for a breach of contract. You reread Chapter 2 to understand what the plaintiff must prove to win the case. Then, assuming the facts support your position, you might present evidence that no contract existed in the first place or that, even if a contract did exist, the plaintiff violated its terms so thoroughly that you were justified in considering it void. And even if you have to admit that you broke a valid contract, you might claim the plaintiff is asking for far too much money.

> EXAMPLE 2: Someone sues you, claiming your negligent conduct resulted in his property being damaged (as would be the case in a fender bender). To successfully defend, you want to convince the court that you were not negligent (careless) or, if you were, that the plaintiff was more negligent. And even if the judge decides that the accident was your fault, you might want to claim that the plaintiff paid far more than was necessary to have the car fixed.

**Gather evidence.** As emphasized in Chapters 13 and 14, the key to winning (or not losing) in small claims court is very often to convince the judge that your version of the facts is correct. To do this, you'll typically need to back up your oral presentation with convincing evidence. One approach is to present the testimony of an eyewitness (if you are lucky enough to have one) or an expert witness who agrees with your position (for example, a mechanic who can explain how the plaintiff damaged your engine). Also, you will want to show the judge any available documentary evidence such as letters, photos, and opinions of experts—or sometimes even damaged property—that backs up your version of events. For example, suppose you are a computer repair person sued by someone who claims you ruined their computer. In that case, you might want to get a written opinion from another repair shop that the computer problem has nothing to do with the defect you fixed. In addition, it would make sense to present any advertisements or trade pricing data showing the plaintiff overvalued the ruined but old computer. And don't forget that you can also bring along physical evidence. For instance, if you're sued for nonpayment on a handmade ceramic tea service that you commissioned from the plaintiff, showing the judge that it doesn't pour properly would likely be a crucial part of your defense strategy.

**Be prepared to make a convincing courtroom presentation.** The plaintiff gets to talk first. Patiently wait until it's your turn. Then make a short and logical presentation explaining why the plaintiff should receive little or nothing. It's a good idea to practice what you plan to say with a friend or family member until it is perfect. One trick to keeping the judge's attention is not to repeat uncontested facts presented by the plaintiff. Instead, immediately focus on why the plaintiff's case is misguided.

> EXAMPLE: Tom, the landlord, listens patiently as Evie, the tenant, spends five minutes presenting a lengthy, sometimes incorrect history of their landlord-tenant relationship. When it's Tom's turn, he ignores Evie's irrelevant remarks and focuses on the exact point of the dispute by saying, "Your Honor, the key to my defense is that the plaintiff left the rental at 127 Spring Street in a dirty and damaged condition. I have pictures to demonstrate this and a reliable witness to back it up. But first, I would like to list the three worst problems."

# Getting Ready for Court

O nce you've filed papers with the small claims clerk and properly served the other party, you'll be ready to prepare for the main event—your day in court.

Chances are good that, like most of us, your idea of what a court proceeding is like comes mostly from television and movies. If so, put everything you think you know aside—especially the dramatics—and just be yourself.

To succeed in small claims court, you don't need to wear a suit, use legal jargon, or put on a particular attitude. Just use plain English and tell the judge what happened and why you are right. If you're like most people who present or defend small claims cases, you'll do pretty well. But it's also true that only a few make outstanding presentations. What sets this elite group apart from the others is no secret—practice and preparation—and with a bit of effort, you too can present a clear, well-organized case backed up by convincing evidence.

The rest of this chapter and Chapters 14 and 15 cover preparing for your small claims court date.

**JUDGE'S TIP**

**Watch small claims court in action before your own hearing.** If you're nervous about your court date or if you want to see how the court might approach your dispute, consider visiting the court while it is in session and observe how judges handle the cases presented to them. You might even see an example of your type of case.

**TIP**

**Need an interpreter?** If you do not speak English, you can bring a friend or relative to translate for you in small claims court. If you don't have a personal contact who can serve as interpreter, contact your small claims court to see if there are interpreters available to translate the court proceedings. If no court interpreter is available, there are nonprofit and other organizations that offer interpreter services to low-income persons free of charge. Be sure to contact the appropriate organization well in advance of your court date to ask for help.

## Using a Private Lawyer

In many states, lawyers can represent clients in small claims court. However, the amount at stake often doesn't justify paying a lawyer's legal fee. In such cases, people who need help sometimes find it cost-effective to hire a lawyer for advice only. If you are worried about some legal aspect of your case and can't get an answer from the court clerk or through research (see Chapter 25), it might make sense to discuss the problem with a lawyer. It should not cost more than $150–$250 for a short consultation.

> **TIP**
> **It's perfectly proper to get assistance from a lawyer.** A lawyer can be extremely helpful in preparing your case, especially if it's complicated. For help finding a lawyer, check Nolo's Lawyer Directory at www.nolo.com/lawyers. It offers comprehensive profiles of the lawyers who advertise there, including the area of expertise, such as personal injury or landlord-tenant law. For advice on hiring and working with a lawyer, including what to ask a prospective attorney, see the article "Tips on Hiring and Working with Lawyers" at www.nolo.com/legal-encyclopedia/lawyers-lawfirms/tips.html

## Consider Mediation—Again

As discussed in considerable detail in Chapter 6, free or low-cost mediation services are available in many communities. Usually, the choice of whether to mediate is yours. However, the courts in some judicial districts might require it or so strongly encourage mediation that it seems required. Ask any small claims clerk for information on how to contact local mediation programs.

Mediation programs help people settle their own disputes. A mediator won't impose a decision as the judge will in small claims court. Especially if you will inevitably have a continuing relationship with the person with whom you have a dispute—as is the case with a neighbor, family member, or many business relationships—trying to achieve a compromise settlement is almost always wiser than fighting it out in court.

Even if your opponent refused to engage in mediation previously, you could raise this possibility again by telling the judge you are still willing to mediate. The judge, who has the power to postpone the case to allow the parties to try to settle it, might attempt to talk the other party into giving mediation a try. As part of doing so, the judge might point out that settling the case will keep the judgment off of the loser's credit record.

## Be Prepared

Once you are pretty sure you can't settle your case and avoid trial, you'll want to start practicing presenting it. Line up an objective, tough-minded friend and run through your entire case just as you plan to on court day. Ask your friend for suggestions, not compliments, on ways to improve. For example, your friend might tell you that you need a witness or written documentation, a better grasp of the legal technicalities involved, or a better-organized presentation. Make all possible improvements and practice again.

The four key phrases to remember as you prepare and practice your courtroom presentation are:

- **Be polite** to the judge, your opponent, the clerk, and the bailiff.
- **Bring evidence** from witnesses or documents to supplement your verbal statement of the facts.
- **Organize your presentation** so you present the necessary facts logically.
- **Keep it short** because the person deciding your case has heard thousands of similar stories and will get bored or annoyed if you are needlessly repetitive.

Finally, don't let the robe and other trappings of judicial office cause you to forget that you are dealing with a human being. A judge is like anyone else and will be sympathetic to your point of view if you can show that you are calm, respectful, and well-intentioned.

## Getting to the Courthouse

Before you locate the right courtroom, you have to get to the right building. Don't assume that you know where your small claims court is unless you've been there before. Be sure to review the route on your GPS or ask the court clerk for specific directions. If you can, check it out in advance so you know where to park and how far you'll walk to the courthouse. Finding parking can be especially challenging early in the morning and after lunch when most cases begin, so give yourself extra time. And be sure to let your witnesses know where and when to show up. People who rush in flustered and late have a more difficult time presenting their case effectively.

Multiple cases will be set for the same time and heard in turn. So your case might be scheduled for 9 a.m. but not get started until about 10 a.m. Arrive early and use any wait time to watch other matters before yours begins. Courts in larger cities might also hold Saturday or evening sessions. If it is not convenient for you to go to court during business hours and night court is an option, ask the court clerk to schedule your case during one of these sessions.

## The Courtroom

Most small claims proceedings are conducted in standard courtrooms also used for regular trials.

> CAUTION
> **Leave sharp metal objects at home.** This may seem like common sense, but remember that all visitors to courthouses must pass through metal detectors. If you have scissors, metal knitting needles, a knife, or any other weaponlike object with you, it will be confiscated or held for you by security.

## Courtroom Etiquette 101

Most of us know that lawyers often dress in expensive, formidable-looking suits, but you won't be required to wear formal clothing to your small claims appearance. Although it's polite to dress neatly and professionally, it's not mandatory. For instance, if you're a house painter and come directly from work to court, the judge will probably understand and excuse your paint-splattered appearance.

It is also polite—but not required—for parties and witnesses to stand when they address the judge. The respectful and recommended way to address the judge directly is "Your Honor." If you refer to the judge in the third person, say "the judge."

Other suggestions for showing respect to the court and the other litigants come from Commissioner Douglas G. Carnahan:

- Don't walk in the "well" of the courtroom, which is the area between the lawyers' table and the judge's bench. This is a security zone, and the bailiff will prevent you from entering it, sometimes rather aggressively.
- Turn off your cell phones before entering the courtroom.
- Keep courtroom chitchat to a minimum. Many judges find it distracting.
- Even while waiting for your case to be called, an attentive, pleasant demeanor will make a good impression on the judge. So pay attention, don't check your phone, chew gum, or listen to music.

Most judges still sit on an elevated platform (called "the bench") and wear black robes. In addition to the judge, a clerk and a bailiff will usually be present. They usually sit at tables immediately in front of or next to the judge. The clerk's job is to keep the judge supplied with necessary files and papers and ensure that proceedings flow smoothly. The bailiff is there to keep order in the courtroom if tempers get out of hand.

Courtrooms are divided by a short fence lawyers call the "bar." The public must stay behind the bar on the opposite side from the judge, clerk, bailiff, and the presenting parties, unless asked to come forward. This invitation occurs when the clerk calls your case by name (for instance, *Smith v. Jones* or

*Abercrombie v. Lee*). That's when you will step to the front of the room and sit at a table known as the "counsel table." Your witnesses will stay in the audience until needed unless the court instructs you to bring them to the front with you.

You will then face the judge with your back to the spectator section of the courtroom. In a few courtrooms, judges try to hurry things along by asking everyone to stand while presenting their case. The idea seems to be that if people can't sit down, they will present their cases faster.

In small claims courts, you must affirm that you will tell the truth. Often this oath is administered before the first case is heard to everyone who will testify during the morning or afternoon session. However, occasionally the oath will be administered to participants separately.

In most small claims courts, you, your opponent, and your witnesses will present the entire case from the counsel table. No one will sit in the witness box next to the judge.

> **JUDGE'S TIP**
> **Be nice to the clerk and the bailiff.** The clerk organizes the paperwork, and the bailiff keeps order, although sometimes each person shares some of the other's work. Don't antagonize them; they will often report their positive or negative impressions to the judge. And they can be helpful, too, so be sure to be polite and respectful.

## The Judge or Commissioner

The person who hears your case might be a regular court judge who also presides over other types of cases. But, increasingly, full-time commissioners and referees are hired for small claims cases. Commissioners are attorneys trained to preside over small claims cases but who are paid lower salaries and benefits than judges (a bit like colleges hiring nontenured instructors instead of full professors). By and large, commissioners and referees—who usually hear small claims cases daily—do a competent job, sometimes better than judges who have other duties.

## Temporary Judges (Judges Pro Tem)

In addition to commissioners and regular judges, volunteer lawyers are also routinely appointed when a judge or commissioner is ill or on vacation. The legal term for a temporary judge is "judge pro tem." If your case comes up on a day when only a pro tem judge is present, you will be given a choice as to whether you want to go ahead or have your case rescheduled on a day when a regular judge or commissioner will be present.

If your case is contested and you feel it involves fairly complicated legal issues, you might not want to accept a pro tem judge. Pro tem judges are not paid, and often do not have as much practical experience in the legal areas commonly heard in small claims court. They receive some training, but usually don't have the experience or training that a regular judge or commissioner has. Although some are excellent, you might not want to risk accepting one. It is your choice, so make sure you think it through.

> CAUTION
>
> **Pay attention to any forms you are asked to sign about the judge for your case.** In some courtrooms, before court begins for the day, a clerk will ask you to sign a form accepting a particular judge, without clearly explaining that the judge is a local lawyer serving on a temporary (pro tem) basis and that you have the right to say no. Whenever you are asked to approve a judge, the person is a substitute for the real judge, and you have the right to say no.

> CAUTION
>
> **You can't appeal from an arbitrator's decision in New York.** To save time, residents of the Empire State are often encouraged to have their cases heard by a volunteer lawyer arbitrator instead of a small claims court judge. But beware of this alternative. In addition to getting a less experienced decision maker, there is no right to appeal from an arbitrator's decision, as there is from the decision of a regular small claims judge.

## Disqualifying a Prejudiced Judge

What if your case will be heard by a regular judge or commissioner whom you don't like, either because you know the person or because you don't like the way the person has handled other cases? For example, you might live in a small town or city and be convinced a particular judge, whose reputation you know, is likely to be hard on you (perhaps you are a landlord and the judge is known to be pro-tenant). Laws exist in nearly all states that allow you to "disqualify" a regular judge based on your honest belief that the judge is "prejudiced" against you. No one will ask you to prove it. To disqualify a judge, in some states when your case is called you can say something like this: "Your Honor, I believe you are prejudiced against my interest, and I request a trial before another judge." In other states, you need to put your disqualification request in writing and file it in advance. If you think you might want to take advantage of a disqualification procedure, check with the small claims clerk before your court date to be sure you understand the rules.

If you have a lot at stake—perhaps you're part of a group of people filing nuisance cases based on drug dealing or noise (see Chapter 20)—it often makes sense to do some research on the judge likely to be assigned your case well ahead of your court date. Start by asking the small claims court clerk for a list of the judges who might be assigned to your case. One good way to check them out is to do a bit of online research. You can also have someone in your group (or perhaps a friend or relative) who has the necessary contacts talk to several local lawyers who have practiced before the listed judges. Many lawyers will readily share their opinions, especially if they consider a particular judge to be unfair or incompetent. If you discover reliable information about a particular judge that makes you doubt that person's ability to be fair, be prepared to challenge the judge.

**JUDGE'S TIP**
**If you're going to reject a temporary or regular judge, you must do it before the judge does anything with your case.** You cannot "test" a judge's opinion about the case, decide you don't like it, then try to reject them. This is not only ineffective but also rude.

> **JUDGE'S TIP**
> **You don't have to say why you believe a judge is prejudiced.** After you state your challenge, the judge may have you take the oath again and ask you to repeat your challenge. You aren't expected to say why you challenged the judge, just that you believe the judge is prejudiced against you or your cause.
> —The late Judge Roderic Duncan

# Your Courtroom Strategy

The plaintiff will be asked to present first and introduce any witnesses, who will also get a chance to have their say. When the plaintiff finishes, it will be the defendant's turn to speak and present witnesses. Both sides should have any papers or other evidence that backs up their story carefully organized and ready to present to the judge. This can include bills, receipts, estimates, photographs, contracts, letters to or from your opponent, and other types of documentation or physical evidence. At the appropriate place in your presentation, tell the judge you have evidence you want to present, and then hand it to the clerk, who in turn will give it to the judge. Appropriate documentation is often the key to winning your case.

> **TIP**
> **Copies of documents.** You should bring at least three copies of each document you plan to show the judge: one for you, one for the judge, and one for your opponent. You can highlight or otherwise make notes on your copies to remind yourself why the particular document is important. Also, try organizing your documents in a binder in the order that you intend to present them. It will be easier for you to stay focused and on track.

As you plan your courtroom strategy, give thought to your opponent. What sort of presentation will the person make? And even more important, how can you best counter any arguments? Figuring out how to cope with your opponent's best points is an effective way to flesh out your case.

Also, always be polite when presenting or defending your case. If you are hostile or sarcastic, you run the risk of losing the respect of the judge. Never interrupt when your opponent is speaking—you will get your chance.

Instead, write down any inaccurate statements made. When it's your turn, lay out the key facts that support your position directly to the judge and correct any of your opponent's statements that you don't agree with. The last thing you want to do is get into an argument with the other side. It's the judge you need to convince, not your opponent.

## Organize Your Testimony and Evidence

It's essential that you organize what you have to say and the physical evidence you wish to show the judge. Do this by dividing your testimony into a list of the main points you want to make. Under each heading, note any items of physical or documentary evidence you plan to show the judge. List the evidence in the appropriate order so you can find each item quickly.

Let's assume you are the plaintiff in a case that is based on a hotel's failure to return your deposit when you canceled a wedding reception three months before the event date. Your list of key points—and the evidence to back them up—might look like this:

- Valley View Hotel refused to return my $500 deposit when I canceled my wedding reception.
- This was true even though I canceled 83 days before the event.
- The contract I signed with the hotel allowed a full refund if the cancellation occurred more than 60 days before the event. (Show contract to the judge.)
- When I canceled, Valley View claimed they sent me a letter the previous month stating they changed their cancellation policy and now required 90 days' notice for a refund.
- I never received a letter and had no idea of the policy change until I canceled and asked for my money back.
- Even if Valley View did send me a letter, the change should not affect my contract, which I signed before the policy change. Because I never signed a new contract, the existing contract is still valid.
- Also, the hotel has a duty to try and rerent the banquet room to mitigate any damages they suffered. And 83 days was plenty of time to do so.
- Ninety days is an unreasonably long cancellation policy.

- Here is a list of the cancellation policies of five other hotels in the area, demonstrating that the industry practice allows a full refund on much shorter notice. (Give the list to the judge.)

Because Valley View will present after your case, its representative won't know in advance what you will say or the evidence you will present. Valley View will need to be flexible. Still, because Valley View's reps will have talked to you and read your letters, they'll have an idea of what to expect. Accordingly, Valley View's list might look something like this:

- It's true that we didn't refund the $500, but it was because we turned down two other receptions for that same day before the plaintiff canceled. Even though it was a sought-after date, we ended up without a function and lost at least $500.
- Although the written contract stated that cancellation must occur 60 days before the event, we notified the plaintiff of the 90-day policy in the following two ways before the contract signing:
  - A sign on the reservations desk where the plaintiff sat when signing the contract. (Show sign to judge.)
  - Testimony of Angie Ells, who booked the reservation. Angie will testify that she included a written notice of the change with the contract package. (Show judge a copy of the notice.)

TIP

**How to cope with the big lie.** Although it doesn't occur everyday, big lies told in small claims court can influence the judge in your opponent's favor, so you'll want to be prepared to poke holes in them. If your adversary tells a whopper, wait calmly for your turn to speak and then say something like this: "Your Honor, almost everything the defendant (or plaintiff) has said about X is untrue. Here is what happened." Then present your testimony and evidence. If you've already shown the judge key evidence, explain why it proves that your opponent's story is false. For example, if your former landlord who failed to return your security deposit swears you left the apartment filthy, provide the judge with photos showing how clean it was when you left. Fortunately, if you demonstrate that your opponent has told one big lie, the judge will likely distrust the rest of what that person says. And it's perfectly appropriate to suggest that the judge do just that.

# Witnesses

t can be extremely helpful to have someone in court with you who knows the facts of your case firsthand and can support your point of view. In many cases, such as car accidents or disputes over whether a tenant left an apartment clean, witnesses are particularly valuable. However, in other situations, witnesses aren't as necessary. For example, if a friend borrowed $500 and didn't pay it back, you don't need a witness to prove that your now ex-friend's signature on the promissory note is genuine, unless you expect the person to claim that the signature was forged.

## What Makes a Good Witness

A good witness should have firsthand or personal knowledge of the facts in dispute. The person saw something that helps establish your case (for example, the car accident, dog bite, or dirty apartment) or is an expert you have consulted about an important aspect of your case (for example, a car mechanic who testifies that your engine wasn't fixed properly). The judge will not be interested in the testimony of a person repeating secondhand or generalized information such as "I know Joe is a good, safe driver and would never have done anything reckless," or "I didn't see Joe's apartment before he moved out, but both Joe and his mother, who couldn't be here today, told me that they worked for two days cleaning it up."

Above all, a good witness is believable, which isn't always an easy quality to define. For example, a police officer might be a symbol of integrity to some people, but others will automatically discount much of what a member of law enforcement says.

But remember, it's the judge you are trying to convince, and judges tend to be establishment folk. They make comfortable salaries, own their own homes, and generally like the existing order of things. Most judges would likely believe a police officer.

In many types of cases, such as a car accident, you won't have a lot of witnesses at your disposal. You will be lucky to have one person who saw what happened. Often this will be a close friend or family member. There is no rule that says you can't have these people testify for you. Indeed, a person's spouse, roommate, or close friend can often give very convincing testimony. But given a choice, it is usually better to have a witness who is neither buddy nor kin. That's because a judge might discount the testimony of people to whom you are close on the theory that they would naturally be biased in your favor.

> **TIP**
> **Try to dispel a judge's cynicism about friends or family who are witnesses.** Have a closely related witness bend over backward to treat the other side as fairly as possible. For instance, if your brother is your only witness to the fact that ABC Painting splashed paint on your boat, he might point out to the judge not only that he saw ABC employees screw up, but that it was a very windy day and so the painter understandably had a hard time keeping the paint on the dock where it belonged.

When you need an expert who can explain what went wrong, you can locate witnesses ahead of time. Keep in mind that a judge will only believe this type of witness if the person has good credentials and relevant knowledge. For instance, in a dispute over whether or not car repairs were properly done, it's preferable to bring a letter from a car mechanic with 20 years' experience who has completed a load of training courses rather than one from your neighbor "who knows a lot about cars."

You'll want to be sure that your expert is prepared to address all necessary points. As long as the expert's testimony is honest and accurate, it isn't a problem to practice before appearing in court. Doing so will go far to limit any surprises, such as your expert's not understanding your questions and providing irrelevant testimony at the small claims court trial (it can happen).

## Selecting and Preparing Witnesses

- Educate your witness thoroughly about your legal and factual position and what your opponent is likely to say. In court, witnesses will be on their own, and you want to be sure that the story comes out the right way. It is entirely legal to discuss the case with your witness beforehand, as long as you do not coach or encourage the witness to lie or exaggerate.
- Never ask a witness to testify in court unless you know exactly what the person will say. And don't assume that you know what that will be. People have lost cases because their witnesses got mixed up, or even supported the other side.
- It's not a good idea to use a subpoena to require a witness to be present unless you make sure that it is okay with the witness, as might be the case if the person needs a good reason to take off a few hours from his or her job. (For more about subpoenas, see "How to Subpoena Witnesses," below.) Otherwise, you could end up with a "hostile witness" who won't be eager to help you, and might even be mad enough to testify against you.
- Do not offer to pay an eyewitness to testify on your behalf except for the small witness fee allowed by law. If discovered, your payment will likely be seen as a bribe.
- On the other hand, it's proper and perfectly legal to pay an expert witness—say, a car mechanic who has examined your engine—a reasonable fee for the expert's time in court. However, if you can't afford to pay an expert to attend, you can ask an expert to write a letter to the judge explaining their findings and present it as part of your case. Be sure to have the expert include credential, schooling, and other pertinent information that will help establish the expert's credibility.

For tips on selecting and preparing witnesses for specific types of cases, see Chapters 16–22.

## How to Subpoena Witnesses

In small claims court, you should be wary of using a subpoena to compel a witness to come to court and testify unless the witness has already agreed to testify. The very act of dragging someone into court who doesn't want to come can set that person against you.

However, there are unusual circumstances when you might need to subpoena a witness. For example, your witness might need proof that they are testifying for you in court on a specific day to get approval to miss work. Or, in rare cases, you might need testimony from a reluctant witness, in which case you can compel the witness to show up by using a subpoena and informing the witness that the court can impose a fine for failure to appear.

In most states, you can require a witness with firsthand knowledge to be present if that person resides within a certain distance from the courthouse. The distance varies from state to state. It is often about 150 miles, but in some states subpoenas reach only within county boundaries.

Expert witnesses cannot be subpoenaed. For this reason, they often submit their opinions in writing, a practice that is allowed in most courts, but check your court rules to be sure the court will accept a letter as evidence before relying on this approach.

Below is the standard California subpoena form. The one in your state should look quite similar. You'll likely need to prepare an original and two copies. Once prepared, you'll take the subpoena form to the clerk, who will issue it. Service must be made personally, and you must return the proof of service, which is often on the back of the subpoena, to the clerk's office. (Rules for service are discussed in Chapter 11.)

A subpoenaed witness is usually entitled to a modest fee upon demand. You must pay your witness this fee ahead of time if the witness asks for it.

If you pay your witness transportation fees (as required by law), write a short receipt so that you can prove how much you paid when it comes time to ask the judge to reimburse you for the expense.

## Sample Small Claims Subpoena

Name and Address of Court: **Small Claims Court, County of Alameda
Berkeley-Albany Judicial District
2000 Center Street, Berkeley, CA 94704**

**SC-107**

SMALL CLAIMS CASE NO. **(123456)**

PLAINTIFF/DEMANDANTE *(Name, address, and telephone number of each):*

**Public Library
100 Allston Way
Berkeley, CA 94704**

Telephone No.:

DEFENDANT/DEMANDADO *(Name, address, and telephone number of each):*

**John O'Gara
100 Scenic Drive
Berkeley, CA 94702**

Telephone No.:

Telephone No.:

Telephone No.:

☐ See attached sheet for additional plaintiffs and defendants.

### SMALL CLAIMS SUBPOENA
#### FOR PERSONAL APPEARANCE AND PRODUCTION OF DOCUMENTS
#### AND THINGS AT TRIAL OR HEARING AND DECLARATION

THE PEOPLE OF THE STATE OF CALIFORNIA, TO *(name, address, and telephone number of witness, if known):*

**Jane Doe**

1. **YOU ARE ORDERED TO APPEAR AS A WITNESS** in this case at the date, time, and place shown in the box below UNLESS your appearance is excused as indicated in box 4b below or you make an agreement with the person named in item 2 below.

   a. Date:                Time:          ☐ Dept.:          ☐ Div.:          ☐ Room:

   b. Address:

2. **IF YOU HAVE ANY QUESTIONS ABOUT THE TIME OR DATE YOU ARE TO APPEAR, OR IF YOU WANT TO BE CERTAIN THAT YOUR PRESENCE IS REQUIRED, CONTACT THE FOLLOWING PERSON BEFORE THE DATE ON WHICH YOU ARE TO APPEAR:**

   a. Name of subpoenaing party: **John O'Gara**          b. Telephone number: **510-555-1212**

3. **Witness Fees:** You are entitled to witness fees and mileage actually traveled both ways, as provided by law, if you request them at the time of service. You may request them before your scheduled appearance from the person named in item 2.

#### PRODUCTION OF DOCUMENTS AND THINGS

*(Complete item 4 only if you want the witness to produce documents and things at the trial or hearing.)*

4. YOU ARE *(item a or b must be checked)*:

   a. ☒ Ordered to appear in person and to produce the records described in the declaration on page two. The personal attendance of the custodian or other qualified witness and the production of the original records are required by this subpoena. The procedure authorized by Evidence Code sections 1560(b), 1561, and 1562 will not be deemed sufficient compliance with this subpoena.

   b. ☐ Not required to appear in person if you produce (i) the records described in the declaration on page two and (ii) a completed declaration of custodian of records in compliance with Evidence Code sections 1560, 1561, 1562, and 1271. (1) Place a copy of the records in an envelope (or other wrapper). Enclose the original declaration of the custodian with the records. Seal the envelope. (2) Attach a copy of this subpoena to the envelope or write on the envelope the case name and number; your name; and the date, time, and place from item 1 in the box above. (3) Place this first envelope in an outer envelope, seal it, and mail it to the clerk of the court at the address in item 1. (4) Mail a copy of your declaration to the attorney or party listed at the top of this form.

5. **IF YOU HAVE BEEN SERVED WITH THIS SUBPOENA AS A CUSTODIAN OF CONSUMER OR EMPLOYEE RECORDS UNDER CODE OF CIVIL PROCEDURE SECTION 1985.3 OR 1985.6 AND A MOTION TO QUASH OR AN OBJECTION HAS BEEN SERVED ON YOU, A COURT ORDER OR AGREEMENT OF THE PARTIES, WITNESSES, *AND* CONSUMER OR EMPLOYEE AFFECTED MUST BE OBTAINED BEFORE YOU ARE REQUIRED TO PRODUCE CONSUMER OR EMPLOYEE RECORDS.**

   DISOBEDIENCE OF THIS SUBPOENA MAY BE PUNISHED AS CONTEMPT BY THIS COURT. YOU WILL ALSO BE LIABLE FOR THE SUM OF FIVE HUNDRED DOLLARS AND ALL DAMAGES RESULTING FROM YOUR FAILURE TO OBEY.

[SEAL]          Date issued:

Clerk, by _____, Deputy

*(See reverse for declaration in support of subpoena)*          **Page one of three**

Form Adopted for Mandatory Use
Judicial Council of California
SC-107 [Rev. January 1, 2000]

**SMALL CLAIMS SUBPOENA
AND DECLARATION**

Code of Civil Procedure,
§ 1985 et seq.

# Sample Small Claims Subpoena (continued)

| PLAINTIFF/PETITIONER: Public Library, 100 Allston Way, Berkeley | CASE NUMBER: |
|---|---|
| DEFENDANT/RESPONDENT: John O'Gara, 100 Scenic Dr., Berkeley | 123456 |

**DECLARATION IN SUPPORT OF
SMALL CLAIMS SUBPOENA FOR PERSONAL APPEARANCE
AND PRODUCTION OF DOCUMENT AND THINGS AT TRIAL OR HEARING
(Code Civil Procedure sections 1985, 1987.5)**

1. I, the undersigned, declare I am the ☐ plaintiff ☒ defendant ☐ judgment creditor
☐ other *(specify)*: in the above entitled action.

2. The witness has possession or control of the following documents or other things and shall produce them at the time and place specified on the *Small Claims Subpoena* on the first page of this form.

   a. ☒ For trial or hearing *(specify the exact documents or other things to be produced by the witness)*:

   Book inventory information collected by the main branch of the public library during the calendar year 20xx.

   ☐ Continued on Attachment 2a.

   b. ☐ After trial to enforce a judgment *(specify the exact documents or other things to be produced by the party who is the judgment debtor or other witness possessing records relating to the judgment debtor)*:

   (1) ☐ Payroll receipts, stubs, and other records concerning employment of the party. Receipts, invoices, documents, and other papers or records concerning any and all accounts receivable of the party.

   (2) ☐ Bank account statements, canceled checks, and check registers from any and all bank accounts in which the party has an interest.

   (3) ☐ Savings account passbooks and statements, savings and loan account passbooks and statements, and credit union share account passbooks and statements of the party.

   (4) ☐ Stock certificates, bonds, money market certificates, and any other records, documents, or papers concerning all investments of the party.

   (5) ☐ California registration certificates and ownership certificates for all vehicles registered to the party.

   (6) ☐ Deeds to any and all real property owned or being purchased by the party.

   (7) ☐ Other *(specify)*:

3. Good cause exists for the production of the documents or other things described in paragraph 2 for the following reasons:

   My contention is that I returned the books for which the library is suing me. The inventory should back me up on this.

   ☐ Continued on Attachment 3.

4. These documents are material to the issues involved in this case for the following reasons:

   The location of the books at issue is central to this case.

   ☐ Continued on Attachment 4.

I declare under penalty of perjury under the laws of the State of California that the foregoing is true and correct.

Date: May 20, 20xx

John O'Gara
(TYPE OR PRINT NAME)

▶ *John O'Gara*
(SIGNATURE OF PARTY)

(See proof of service on page three)

SC-107 [Rev. January 1, 2000]

**SMALL CLAIMS SUBPOENA
AND DECLARATION**

Page two of three

The judge has discretion as to whether or not to reimburse you for witness fees. Most judges are strict about this, making the loser pay the winner's witness fees only if they find that the subpoenaed witness was essential to the case. So if your case is so strong that you don't need a witness to appear in person, but you subpoena one anyway, you might have to pay the witness fee even though you won the case. (For more information on recovering costs associated with your small claims lawsuit, see Chapter 15.)

## How to Subpoena Police and Other Peace Officers

You use the standard subpoena form to subpoena a police officer, firefighter, or other peace officer to testify about anything observed or investigated in the course of duty. Fill the form out, take it to the court clerk for a seal and date stamp, then take it to the relevant police or fire department to comply with any of their additional procedures. (For example, the police department might require two copies of the subpoena instead of one.) Give the witnesses plenty of advance notice. You will have to pay the officer's salary for the time taken off work to appear in advance (usually about $200), payable to the agency employing the officer. The subpoena can be served on the officer personally or on the officer's superior.

Depending on the amount of the officer's time used, you might eventually get a refund of some of your deposit. Don't count on it, however. The law enforcement office might not have a procedure in place for issuing refunds.

## How to Subpoena Documents

Although rarely done in small claims court, you can also subpoena documents. An organization (such as a police department, phone company, hospital, or corporation) might have certain books, ledgers, papers, or other documents, including electronically stored information, that can help your case. Unless the organization volunteers to bring the documents to court, you'll need to prepare a court order, called a "subpoena duces tecum," that directs the person in the organization who is in charge of the records to send them directly to the court. This subpoena is very similar to the standard subpoena form, except for the added space where you describe the papers or other documents you want. Keep in mind that successfully bringing documents before the court does not guarantee that the judge will admit them into evidence. The judge must be convinced that the records are relevant to your case.

To get a subpoena duces tecum issued, you'll follow a procedure along the following lines: Attach to the completed subpoena form an affidavit stating "under penalty of perjury" why you need the written material. Prepare three copies of all papers and, after you get the clerk to issue the subpoena, serve it on the witness using personal service, as described in Chapter 11. As with a regular subpoena, the witness is entitled to ask for a fee. The Proof of Service is on the back of the subpoena form; it must be filled out and returned to the clerk.

CAUTION
**Rules for subpoenas vary from state to state.** Technical rules on filing and serving papers, as well as paying witness fees, vary considerably from one state to the next. Make sure you know what will be required. Also, before subpoenaing documents, be sure to ask whether the other side will simply give you photocopies in advance.

A subpoena duces tecum must be directed to the person in charge of the documents, books, or records you want produced in court. It might take a few phone calls to find out who this is. Be sure you get the correct information. If you list someone on the subpoena duces tecum who has nothing to do with the documents, you won't get them. When dealing with a large corporation, public utility, or municipal government, it is wise to list the person in charge of the department where the records are kept. If you want records having to do with library fines from a public library, or having to do with business license fees from the city tax and license department, you should not list the city manager or the mayor. Instead, list the head librarian or the director of the tax and license office.

**EXAMPLE:** The city is suing you on behalf of the public library for $800 for eight rare books they claim you failed to return. You know you returned the books but can't convince the library that you aren't a thief. You learn that the library inventories its books each April and think that the inventory information might help your case. Specifically, the inventory might show that a significant percentage of the library's books aren't accounted for, implying that they, not you, lost the books.

Your first step would be to ask the library to provide the inventory information to you voluntarily. If they refuse, you might want to subpoena it. Here's how:

1. Complete the subpoena form.
2. Prepare a declaration under penalty of perjury. Briefly describe the documents you need and why they are necessary to prove issues involved in the case. If you want the custodian of the records to show up in person, give a reason. Don't argue the merits of your case.
3. Have a subpoena issued by the small claims clerk. Then deliver the subpoena to the head librarian, and don't forget to properly fill out the proof of service (see Chapter 11) and return it to the clerk.

> **TIP**
>
> **Ask to examine documents prior to your court hearing.** The documents you have subpoenaed will be mailed or presented to the court—not to you. You will probably want an opportunity to examine them and should request that from the judge, who will likely let you look at them right there in the courtroom while other cases go ahead. Or, if necessary, the judge might postpone the case for a few days and arrange to have you examine the documents at the place of business where the records are kept.

## Witness Testimony by Letter

Most small claims courts don't have formal rules of evidence requiring a witness to testify in person. It is often preferable to have a witness appear in court, but this isn't always possible, and a judge will usually accept written statements from both eyewitnesses ("I was there and saw the filthy apartment") and expert witnesses ("I examined the transmission and found that a rebuilt part was installed improperly"). Check with the court's website and local rules for guidelines about presenting evidence.

When presenting a written witness statement, make sure the witness states the following facts:

**For an eyewitness:**
- who the witness is—name, age (or adult or minor status), county of residence, and relationship to the plaintiff or defendant
- the date of the event, and
- what that person saw, heard, smelled, felt, or tasted, and where and how it transpired.

**For an expert witness:**
- who the witness is—name and relationship to the plaintiff or defendant
- the witness's work and education credentials demonstrating the person's expertise in the applicable field (if these are lengthy, it's a good idea to attach the person's résumé or curriculum vitae)
- what the witness reviewed, examined, or tested before rendering the opinion ("I examined the paint on Mr. Jones's 35-foot Cabin Cruiser and subjected it to the following test…")
- when the witness did the work
- the conclusion ("The paint used was not suitable for saltwater immersion")
- if possible, an estimate of the cost to redo the work properly, and
- any other facts that have a bearing on the dispute.

TIP
**Make sure you establish your expert's experience and training.** It's a good idea to attach to an expert's letter a separate list of the expert's credentials. If your expert has a résumé or curriculum vitae listing credentials, attach it to the letter in which the witness states his or her findings. The more distinguished your expert, the more likely the judge is to respect the opinion.

**Sample Letter by Eyewitness**

Victor Van Cleve
37 Ogden Court
Kansas City, KS 12333
September 30, 20xx

Presiding Judge
Small Claims Court
Kansas City, KS 12333

Re: *John Swift v. Peter Petrakos*

Small Claims Case No. 11478

Your Honor:

On September 15, 20xx, at approximately 7:30 a.m, I was parked near the corner of South Dora and 7th Streets in Larchville. I was parked on South Dora, about three parking spaces south of the intersection. Just after 7:30 a.m., I witnessed an auto accident involving John Swift and Peter Petrakos.

I clearly saw Mr. Petrakos's yellow Toyota, which was heading north on South Dora, go through a red light and hit Mr. Swift's blue van, which was proceeding west on 7th, well inside the 25 MPH speed limit. I noticed that the traffic light facing Mr. Petrakos did not turn to green for ten seconds or so after the accident, so it is clear to me that Mr. Petrakos really did go through the light while it was fully red. In short, this was not a situation where Mr. Petrakos was just a tiny bit early getting into the intersection at a light change.

Sincerely,

*Victor Van Cleve*
Victor Van Cleve

## Sample Letter by Expert Witness

Gail McClosky
47 Penrod Street
Helena, MT 12344
September 30, 20xx

Judge
Small Claims Court
Helena, MT 12344

Re: *James Dills v. R & B Construction*
Small Claims Case No. 11478

Your Honor:

I am a fully licensed contractor with 20 years' experience here in Helena (Contractor's License 4021B). For the last ten years I've run my own five-person contracting company specializing in building enclosures and buildings to house horses and other large animals. I enclose a résumé outlining my specialized training and experience in this field.

On April 23, 20xx, I was asked by James Dills to inspect several new stalls he had contracted to be built in the main barn of his Lazy T Riding Stable by R&B Construction.

In my opinion these stalls are seriously below normal industry standards, for three reasons.

1. They are too small for the animals intended to be kept in them. [*Continue with details.*]
2. Walls and doors are built of plywood too thin to safely contain an agitated animal. [*Continue with details.*]
3. Construction is so rough and unfinished in several places as to pose a danger of injury to an animal intended to be kept there. [*Continue with details.*]

In conclusion, I believe the stalls are so poorly constructed they can't reasonably be upgraded to provide safe habitable housing for horses. Were they mine, I would rip them out and start over.

Sincerely,

*Gail McClosky*
Gail McClosky

# Judges as Witnesses

A small claims judge has the discretion to leave the bench to check out evidence. Asking a judge to examine items involved in your case can be a valuable technique in some situations. For example, in disputes involving damaged clothing, it is routine to bring the damaged or defective garment into court for the judge's examination. Indeed, it normally makes sense to bring physical evidence that meets these three criteria:

- showing it to the judge will help your case
- it will fit through the door, and
- bringing it into the courtroom is not dangerous or inappropriate, as would be the case with an animal, firearm, or extremely dirty or smelly items.

But sometimes your evidence is impossible to bring into the courtroom, such as a car with a poor paint job that isn't adequately captured in photographs. Judges have the flexibility and discretion to handle their cases as they see fit. So you could ask the judge to accompany you to the courthouse parking lot to examine the car personally. Many judges will agree do so if you make a convincing argument as to why it is necessary to understand the dispute—especially if it won't take too long. For instance, in one case the judge was disturbed when two eyewitnesses gave seriously contradictory testimony about a traffic accident. He questioned both in detail and took the case under submission. That evening, he drove over to the relevant corner.

Once there, it was clear that one of the witnesses couldn't possibly have seen the accident from the spot on which she claimed to be standing. The judge decided the case in favor of the other party.

CAUTION

**Don't waste a judge's time.** Never ask a judge to take time to leave court to view evidence if you can establish or prove the same point by other means, such as by presenting the testimony (or letter) of a witness or by showing the judge a photograph.

**JUDGE'S TIP**
**Small claims court judges might independently consult expert witnesses.**
Many small claims judges keep lists of "experts" they consult with from time to time regarding particular issues in medicine, dentistry, plumbing, auto repair, and other areas. A judge should tell the parties so they have some idea where the judge's information is coming from. If you think the judge is considering such a step, you can ask the judge to state the expert's name in the written judgment. The worst the judge can do is say no.

**JUDGE'S TIP**
**A judge might go on a "walkabout."** A colleague who was deciding a small claims neighborhood nuisance case went out and walked through the neighborhood in question, getting a stronger understanding of the problem than if he had remained in the courtroom. —The late Judge Roderic Duncan

## Testimony by Telephone

A surprising number of small claims court judges will take testimony over the phone if a witness cannot be present because the person is ill, disabled, out of state, or can't take time off from work. While procedures vary, some courts will do this by setting up a conference call so that the opposing party has the opportunity to hear what is being said and to respond.

However, don't assume that a judge will allow telephone testimony. If you think you'll need to have a witness testify by phone, explain your problem to the court clerk well in advance. If you get a negative response, don't give up—ask the judge when you get into the courtroom. Be sure you also present a letter from the witness stating what the person would testify to if present—for example, your opponent's car ran a red light and broadsided you—and explaining why it is impossible to be there.

This letter should look like the first sample letter in "Witness Testimony by Letter," above, except the witness should add:

Mr. Swift has asked me to testify on his behalf, and I would be happy to do so. However, I will be in New York City on business during the months of October, November, and December 20xx and cannot be present.

I have asked Mr. Swift to let me know the day and approximate time of the court hearing and have told him that I will give him a phone number where I can be reached. If you think it desirable, I will be pleased to give my testimony by phone.

# Your Day in Court

This chapter focuses on how to present your case to the judge. We'll go over what typically happens when you appear for your trial so you have a good understanding of what to expect. We'll also cover some basic courtroom etiquette—the dos and don'ts—so you can make the most of your day in court.

CAUTION

**Virtual appearances during the COVID-19 pandemic.** The procedures below apply to the in-person hearings typically held in small claims court. Your hearing could be held virtually. Check your court's website for instructions. Also, be aware that your court might require you to send in evidence before the trial date. Be sure to meet all deadlines provided to avoid losing the ability to use evidence to prove your case.

## If the Defendant Is a No-Show

If one party to a case doesn't appear in court on the trial date, the case is usually decided in favor of the other. Before doing so, the judge will verify that the defendant was properly served with court papers and that neither party requested a postponement.

TIP

**Don't rely on a second chance.** In some states, if neither party appears, the judge might take the case "off calendar" and delay the case until a future date. Don't count on it, however. Make every effort to show up or notify the court clerk if you can't make it.

If the plaintiff appears but the defendant doesn't show up, the plaintiff will likely win the case. But first, the judge in most states will ask the plaintiff to "prove up" the case by stating the facts and presenting necessary evidence, such as a copy of the contract. The reason for requiring proof before issuing a default judgment is to ensure the judgment is reasonable and supported by evidence.

JUDGE'S TIP
**Don't expect to win just because your opponent failed to appear.**
The law requires that you give enough evidence to show that the defendant owes you money.

If you're asked to prove up a case, do yourself a favor and keep it brief. You do not need to make an extended argument because, in the absence of your opponent, the judge will assume your version of what happened is accurate. Saying more than necessary is always risky because it opens up the possibility that you'll accidentally undermine your case. As any litigation attorney will tell you, witnesses undermine their own testimony with astonishing regularity without even realizing that they're doing so.

> EXAMPLE: "Your Honor, I own the Racafrax Auto Repair Shop. On January 11, 20xx, I repaired the defendant's 20xx Honda Prius. He paid me $1,500 and agreed to pay another $1,500 on March 1. He has not made the second payment. I have copies of the contract the defendant signed and the unpaid bills I sent him. I am asking for a judgment of $1,500 plus $125 for my court filing fee and the cost of having the papers served."

If you are the defendant and a small claims court judge entered a default judgment against you, and you have a good excuse for failing to appear at the hearing, you can ask the judge to retract the judgment. This is called "setting aside the judgment" or "vacating the judgment." Most courts won't set aside or vacate a default judgment unless you can show that you weren't served with the original papers and that you didn't know about the hearing. In some states, this can happen if someone signs your name for a certified letter and then doesn't give it to you. In all states, it can occur when a dishonest process server doesn't serve you, but tells the court otherwise. As soon as you find out that a default judgment has been entered against you, call the court clerk. It doesn't matter if the hearing was months before, as long as you move to set it aside immediately upon learning about it.

If a default judgment has been entered against you after you were properly served, you will face an uphill struggle to get it set aside. A few judges will accept excuses such as "I forgot," "I was sick," or "I got called out of town." Generally, however, judges assume that you could have at least called, or had a friend call, no matter what the emergency. In any event, the court won't vacate the judgment except for an extremely good cause.

To set aside a default, go to the small claims court clerk's office and ask for the proper form, which will be titled something like Notice of Motion to Vacate Judgment.

Sometimes the defendant files a motion to vacate a default judgment after a writ of execution to collect the small claims judgment has already been entered for the plaintiff. In most states, under these circumstances, the writ of execution will be recalled by the court until a decision on the motion to vacate the default judgment is made. If the plaintiff already served the writ of execution as part of an effort to collect, the defendant must file a motion to suspend the writ of execution (often called a "Motion to Stay or Quash the Writ of Execution"), pending the court's decision on whether or not to set aside the default judgment and reopen the case. For more information on how to do this, or to find out the exact rules for your state, consult your small claims court clerk.

In most states, you can't appeal a default judgment. Unless you get the default set aside, the judgment will be final.

If the small claims judge grants the defendant's motion to vacate a default judgment, then one of two things will happen. If all parties are present and agree, the small claims judge might hear the original case without rescheduling it. If, however, the plaintiff is not present for the hearing on the defendant's motion to vacate judgment, or if the parties do not agree to hear the case then and there (and they likely won't agree to it if witnesses are needed), the judge will reschedule the hearing, and the clerk will mail written notice of the new hearing date to the parties.

If the small claims judge decides not to set aside the default, defendants in most states can appeal the judge's refusal (but not the decision in the case itself) to a higher court. (See Chapter 23 for more on appeals.)

If the higher court judge agrees with the small claims court judge, then the case is over and the plaintiff wins. If, however, the appeals court judge disagrees with the small claims court judge and vacates the default judgment, and if both parties are present and agree, the appeals court judge in most states can hear and decide the case immediately. If both parties aren't present or do not agree, then the appeals court judge will order the small claims court to schedule another hearing.

## How to Handle a Motion to Vacate Judgment

Some judges will vacate defaults based on almost any hard-luck story. However, others will refuse to vacate a default judgment unless the defendant makes a written request for a postponement before the hearing or can show that a real emergency caused them to miss the hearing. An example of such an emergency might be a death in the family or never having received the original court papers, and therefore not knowing a hearing was scheduled.

Because the judge can decide whether to vacate a default, it's impossible to predict what the judge will do. For this reason, defendants should make their motion to vacate the judgment as soon as they realize they missed the original hearing.

Plaintiffs, who benefit from a default judgment and understandably would prefer it to stand, should emphasize that they played by the rules and showed up on the original hearing date. In contrast, the defendant failed to do so and, assuming it's true, failed to request a postponement. If the plaintiff's witnesses were ready to testify at the original hearing and would have difficulty coming back to court, the plaintiff should submit written statements explaining the situation.

TIP

**Always be ready to argue your side of the actual case.** If the judge decides to grant the defendant's motion to vacate judgment, the judge will ask the parties whether they are prepared to argue the underlying case. Or, if the defendant appeals to superior court and the judgment is set aside there, the superior court judge has the authority to decide the underlying small claims court case. For that reason, both parties should always be prepared to argue the case whenever they have a hearing. Also, if you need witness testimony, be ready to explain that requiring you to proceed would be prejudicial because you wouldn't be able to present the evidence needed to prove your case.

## If the Plaintiff Is a No-Show

Occasionally, though less frequently, the plaintiff fails to show up. If the plaintiff didn't request a postponement, the judge will either dismiss the case or decide it based on the defendant's evidence if the defendant filed a defendant's claim. The defendant usually will prefer to have the judge decide the case because if the case is dismissed without prejudice, the plaintiff can refile it before the statute of limitations expires. If the court dismisses your case without prejudice, you'll want to refile quickly (some states have a 30-day limit).

However, if the judge dismisses the case "with prejudice," the plaintiff can't refile the case without first asking the judge to cancel (vacate or set aside) the dismissal. Most courts won't dismiss a case with prejudice unless some other unusual event occurs, too. For instance, a judge would be more likely to dismiss a case with prejudice if the plaintiff failed to appear a second time on the same matter. A judge might also dismiss a case with prejudice if the defendant shows up in court, and the no-show plaintiff hadn't filed a written request for postponement before the court date.

The judge is most likely to grant your motion to set aside the dismissal if both of the following are true:

- The plaintiff moves to have the judgment vacated promptly upon learning of the mistake. "Promptly" usually means within 30 days after the day the dismissal was entered.
- The plaintiff has a good explanation for being unable to attend or call on the regularly scheduled date. A judge might accept something like this: "I had a flu with a high fever and lost track of a couple of days. By the time I recovered enough to reschedule the case, I found out the court had dismissed my case."

To get a dismissal vacated, ask the small claims court clerk for the rules and forms you should use.

If the judge enters a default judgment for the defendant, the plaintiff cannot appeal the judgment but can appeal the judge's decision to give the defendant a default judgment. Remember, the plaintiff is the one who initiated the case and established the hearing date, so no one is going to have a great deal of sympathy for a plaintiff's failure to show up. The plaintiff's reason for not appearing should be good and supported by written evidence. The procedure for vacating or setting aside a judgment is the same as the procedure discussed above for defendants.

## Your Day in Court

The big moment has arrived. You're in the courtroom, all parties are present, and your case is called by the clerk. What happens now? First, the judge will ask everyone's name and whether they're the plaintiff, defendant, or a witness. Second, the judge will ask the plaintiff for a brief statement of the case. The defendant will have the chance to present a statement immediately afterward, but can reserve it until after the plaintiff presents witnesses. After the plaintiff and the plaintiff's witnesses speak, the defendant will give a statement, if reserved, and present evidence and witnesses.

## Tips for Both Parties

Before we focus on the plaintiff's and defendant's presentations, here are a few tips both parties should find helpful. These are not absolute rules, just suggestions:

- **Consider standing when you make your presentation to the judge.** Standing gives some people a sense of presence and confidence when they might be a little nervous. It's fine to sit while your opponent is talking. If the judge interrupts your opponent's presentation to ask you a quick question that requires a short answer, stay seated, as well. If, however, you're more comfortable remaining seated during your presentation, do so. And if it appears the judge would prefer you to sit, or if it seems to be the norm in the courtroom, then, by all means, do what makes the most sense.

- **Be as brief as possible.** You want to stick to the issues and get to the point while making sure that you properly explain your case and present all of your evidence.

- **Start with the end of the story, not the beginning—sort of.** That is, describe your loss and how much you are asking for. Then go back to the beginning and tell your story chronologically.

- **Don't read your statement.** Reading in court won't result in the dynamic presentation you'd probably like to make. Instead, if you're comfortable doing so, create an outline you can use as a reminder in case you get nervous or forget something. If you decide to do this, create headings for the major parts of your presentation, such as "introductory statement," "witness one," and "closing argument." Under each heading, use bullets to list the points you want to make, the questions you must remember to ask, and the evidence you intend to present. Be sure your list is easy to read at a glance and that the topics are in the correct order. (See Chapter 13 for a sample list.)

- **During your or your witness's presentation, the judge is likely to interrupt to ask questions.** Never put the judge off by saying you'll get to the point later in your presentation. It's far better to answer any questions directly. Just be sure that you and your witnesses eventually get a chance to make all of your key points. If you feel rushed, say so. The judge will likely slow things down a little. Also, if you need a moment to organize your thoughts, take it. In fact, you might want to practice placing your index finger over your mouth in a "thinking" pose. It will let the court know that your pause is intentional, and everyone in the courtroom will wait. As long as you keep it brief and continue on course, no one will think twice.

 JUDGE'S TIP
**Really, don't interrupt.** When I presided over small claims cases, I would start each session by announcing, "Please do not interrupt the other side when they are speaking, no matter how outrageous you think any particular statement might be. I promise you'll have a turn to tell me your side of the case. I don't usually use a point system in deciding a case, but if you interrupt the other side while they are speaking and sing out with something like, 'That's a lie!,' I'd be tempted to subtract a point from any score I was keeping. And you never know, you might need that point later on." I'd smile at the audience, and they'd chuckle, but when the first person violated that rule, there'd be a big groan from the audience.  —The late Judge Roderic Duncan

- **Try to present any portion of your case that is difficult to explain verbally in another way.** This often means bringing your damaged clothing or other exhibits, such as photographs or canceled checks, and presenting them to the judge in an organized way. Short videos can be helpful, but call in advance to see whether they are allowed and what technology is used to show them.
- **Don't act like a lawyer when asking your witnesses to testify.** If possible, let your witnesses tell their story and only ask questions at the end if they've left out an important fact. However, it's a good idea to write out questions that will solicit the information you need to prove your case. When your witness gets off course and you're not sure how to get them back on track, prepared questions can be a lifesaver.
- **Use drawings if helpful.** If drawings will be helpful, as is almost always true in cases involving car accidents, be sure to ask the judge for permission to use the blackboard or dry erase board which should be available in the courtroom. You will want to draw clearly and legibly the first time, so it's wise to practice in advance or prepare a small version of the drawing ahead of time to copy from.

**Sample Legal Research Memo**

MEMO

August 10, 20xx

*Lee v. Yew*
Small Claims #127654

To: Small Claims Judge
From: Robert Yew, Defendant
Re: California law on boundary trees

This case involves Mr. Lee, my next-door neighbor, suing me because he claims my Monterey Pine tree drops debris on his roof and yard. Although he is asking for a judgment of $500 for cleanup costs, what he really wants is for me to pay several thousand dollars to remove the 80-foot tree.

There is only one problem with Mr. Lee's argument—because the tree touches our boundary line, the tree is half his. California law, as set forth in Civil Code Section 834, clearly states, "Trees whose trunks stand partly on the land of two or more coterminous owners, belong to them in common."

Mr. Lee will argue that the tree was planted 100% on my property by the person who owned my house before I bought it and that the tree is still 90% on my side of the property line. Both contentions are true, but as you can see under Civil Code Section 834, it makes no difference. As long as the tree touches the boundary line—which the photographs I have presented the court clearly prove—the tree belongs to both of us as co-owners (tenants in common). (*Anderson v. Weiland*, 12 Cal.2d 730 (1936).)

I have offered to try and mediate the dispute, but so far Mr. Lee says, "No." I hope he will change his mind.

Respectfully submitted,

*Robert Yew*
Robert Yew

- **If you are the defendant, don't repeat facts already presented by the plaintiff that you don't dispute** (for example, that the two of you had a fender bender at a certain corner in a certain city at a certain time during certain weather conditions). Instead, focus on the facts of your principal disagreement (whether the light facing you was green or red, for example) and introduce evidence to prove that point.

- **Ask for a continuance if necessary.** Plans occasionally go haywire. Perhaps a key witness doesn't show up, or maybe, despite careful preparation, you overlook some aspect of the case that the judge feels is crucial. If this occurs, you might want to ask the judge to reschedule for another day to give you time to address the problem. It is perfectly proper to make this sort of request. Whether or not it will be granted is up to the judge. If the judge feels that more evidence isn't likely to change the result, or that you are making the request as a stalling tactic, it will not be granted. If, despite the fact that you prepared conscientiously, there is a good reason for a delay, it will usually be allowed.

- **Recognize that a judge who is convinced that one side is morally right will try to find a legal reason to rule in that person's favor.** For example, if you lent a friend money in an emergency and he is now trying to wriggle out of his obligation based on a legal technicality (claims the loan was really a gift), make sure the judge understands the trouble your opponent's bad act has caused you (you can't afford to pay college tuition).

- **If you've done legal research and believe that a statute or court decision supports your position, call it to the attention of the judge as part of your oral presentation.** If possible, it's also a good idea to provide the judge with a brief written memo. (See "Sample Legal Research Memo," above.) Begin with the name and number of your case. Then list the official citation of the statute, ordinance, or court case you think helps your case and briefly explain why. (See Chapter 25 for an explanation of how to cite statutes and cases.) In court, give one copy of the memo to the clerk to hand to the judge and another to your opponent.

JUDGE'S TIP

**Less can be more when you're testifying.** If the judge asks you a question like, "Did you have a written lease with the landlord?" the better answer is either "Yes" or "No," as appropriate, not something like: "Well, Your Honor, before I answer that question I need to tell you the background of the case. I first met the landlord in 1967, and then. ..." You get the idea.

TIP

**Practice your presentation early and often.** As emphasized throughout this book, it pays to practice making your oral presentation ahead of time. Have a tough-minded friend or family member play the part of judge, ask questions, and try to poke holes in your best points. Run through your presentation several times until you get it right.

## From the Plaintiff's Side

If you are the plaintiff, you should clearly tell the judge what the dispute is about before you start describing the details of what happened.

If your case involves a car accident, you might start by saying:

*"This case involves a car accident at Cedar and Rose Streets in which my car suffered $872 worth of damage when the defendant ran a red light and hit my front fender."*

That introduction is much better than:

*"It all started when I was driving down Rose Street after having a bagel with cream cheese for breakfast."*

It's a rare case where the plaintiff's initial presentation should take longer than five minutes. As part of your statement, you should present and explain the relevance of any papers, photos, or other documentary evidence. You should hand these to the clerk, who will pass them on to the judge. You should also be sure to tell the judge if you have any witnesses to present.

Your witness will typically be given a chance to speak after you complete your presentation. The witness should be well prepared to explain key information in an organized way—for example, the witness inspected the apartment and found it clean. Too often, when witnesses testify, they either leave out important points or are so disorganized that their testimony loses impact. (For information on preparing your witnesses, see Chapter 14.)

TIP
**The judge will probably question your witnesses.** Don't count on being allowed to ask all of your witnesses questions or to cross-examine the other party or their witnesses fully. Most judges will want to do at least some of the questioning of witnesses. If one of your witnesses forgets an important point, wait until the judge finishes before requesting permission to ask the witness a few questions. Don't be intimidated by the judge. You're responsible for proving your case. The judge should recognize that you know the facts and that there might be a crucial point the judge doesn't know to ask. If the judge seems determined to ask all of the questions—which there could be good reason to do, such as keeping hostility in check—politely explain that a particular topic remains uncovered. For example, you might say, "Your Honor, Ms. Peterson hasn't said anything about the color of the traffic light. Would it be possible for you to ask her to cover that subject?" If your opponent or a witness skirts an important issue, try something similar, like, "Your Honor, the defendant hasn't said anything about how many beers he drank that night. Can you ask the defendant to tell the court about his alcohol consumption that evening?"

## From the Defendant's Side

It will be the defendant's turn after the plaintiff's case is presented. Defendants often get so angry at something the plaintiff has said that when they get to speak, they attack angrily. This is usually counterproductive. It's far better to calmly and clearly present your side of the dispute to the judge. Plus, doing so tells the judge that you're confident in your position.

Start with the key point of contention and then fill in the details of what happened from your point of view. If the plaintiff has made significant false or misleading statements, these should definitely be pointed out. But to show the judge how calm and fair-minded you are, wait until after you have made your key points before pointing out your opponent's misstatements.

> EXAMPLE: "Your Honor, it's true that the bumper of my truck hit the plaintiff's fender and pushed it in slightly. But the key thing I want you to understand is that this happened because the plaintiff's pickup entered the intersection before it was clear, so the accident was his fault. Here is what happened. I was driving south on Cedar and entered the intersection just as the light first turned yellow. I slowed briefly near the centerline behind a car that was turning left and then continued across, at which point the plaintiff's car darted in front of me."

## Recovering Costs

Both plaintiff and defendant are entitled to ask that a judgment in their favor include any recoverable costs, such as for filing and serving court papers or subpoenaing essential witnesses. Sometimes defendants have no costs at all. In most states, costs that are recoverable by the winner include:

- The plaintiff's court filing fee (defendants pay no fee to appear unless filing a defendant's claim).
- Service of process costs. A plaintiff must always pay this fee, which can vary from a few dollars for certified mail to considerably more if professional process service is required. A defendant will typically only have to pay to serve the defendant's claim (counterclaim).
- Subpoenaed witness fees, if approved by the judge. Both the plaintiff and defendant can incur this cost if a witness must be subpoenaed and claims a fee. Fees for subpoenaing witnesses and documents are likely to be approved only if the judge believes the presence of the witness in court was necessary to prove the case.
- The cost of obtaining necessary documents, such as verification of car ownership. (Both plaintiffs and defendants can have these costs.)

If you forget to get your costs added to the judgment in court, ask the small claims clerk what to do. Usually, you can file a written request for costs within a few days of the judgment. For information on recovering costs incurred after judgment when your opponent won't voluntarily pay the judgment, see "Property Liens" in Chapter 24.

> **CAUTION**
> **Some costs are not recoverable.** You can't recover for personal expenses such as taking time off from work to prepare for or attend court, paying a babysitter, parking your car, or making photocopies of evidence.

## A Sample Contested Case

Now let's look at how a contested case might be presented from both the plaintiff's and defendant's perspectives.

**Clerk:** *"The next case is John Andrews v. Robertson Realty. Will everyone please come forward?"* (Four people come forward and sit at the table facing the judge.)

**Judge:** *"Good morning. Which one of you is Mr. Andrews? Okay, will you begin, Mr. Andrews?"*

**John Andrews:** (stands) *"This is a case about my failure to get a $700 cleaning deposit returned, Your Honor. I rented a house from Robertson Realty at 1611 Spruce Street in Rockford in March 20xx on a month-to-month tenancy. On January 10, 20xx, I sent Mr. Robertson a written notice that I was planning to move on March 10. In fact, I moved out on March 8 and left the place extremely clean. I know it was clean because I spent eight hours, a lot of them on my hands and knees, cleaning it. Also, all of my rent was properly paid. A few days after I moved out, I asked Mr. Robertson to return my $700 deposit. He wrote me a letter stating that the place was dirty and he was keeping my deposit.*

*"I have with me a copy of a letter I wrote to Mr. Robertson on March 15 setting out my position in more detail. I also have some photographs that my friend, Carol Spann, who is here as a witness, took on the day I moved out. I believe the pictures show that I did a thorough cleanup."* (John Andrews hands the letter and pictures to the clerk, who hands them to the judge.)

*"Your Honor, I am asking not only for the $700 deposit, but also for $1,400 in punitive damages, which the law of this state allows a tenant when a landlord improperly refuses to return a deposit."*

**Judge:** *"Mr. Andrews, will you introduce your witness?"*

**Andrews:** *"Yes, this is Carol Spann. She helped me clean up and move on March 7 and 8."*

**Judge:** (looking at the pictures) *"Ms. Spann, were you in the house the day John Andrews moved out?"*

**Carol Spann:** (standing) *"Yes, your Honor, I was—and the day before, too. I helped clean up, and I can say that we did a good job. Not only did we do the normal washing and scrubbing, but we waxed the kitchen floor, cleaned the bathroom tile, and shampooed the rugs."*

**Judge:** (turning to Mr. Robertson) *"Okay, now it's your turn to tell me why the deposit wasn't returned."*

**Harry Robertson:** (standing) *"I don't know how they could have cleaned the place up, your Honor, because it was filthy when I inspected it on March 9. Let me give you a few specifics. There was mildew and mold around the bathtub, the windows were filthy, the refrigerator hadn't been defrosted, and there was dog—how shall I say it—dog manure in the basement. Your Honor, I have brought along Clem Houndstooth as a witness. Mr. Houndstooth is the tenant who moved in three days after Mr. Andrews moved out. Incidentally, your Honor, the place was so dirty that I only charged Mr. Houndstooth a $200 cleaning deposit, because he agreed to clean it up himself."*

**Judge:** (looking at Clem Houndstooth) *"Do you wish to say something?"*

**Clem Houndstooth:** (standing) *"Yes, I do. Mr. Robertson asked me to come down and back him up and I am glad to do it because I put in two full days cleaning that place up. I like a clean house, your Honor, not a halfway clean, halfway dirty house. I just don't think that a house is clean if the oven is full of gunk, there is mold in the bathroom, and the insides of the cupboards are grimy. All these conditions existed at 1611 Spruce Street when I moved in. I just don't believe that anyone could think that that place was clean."*

**Judge:** *"Mr. Andrews, do you have anything to add?"*

**John Andrews:** (standing up) *"Yes, I sure do. First, as to the mildew problem. The house is 40 years old, and there is some dampness in the wall of the bathroom. Maybe there is a leaky pipe someplace behind the tile. I cleaned it several times, but it always came back. I talked to Mr. Fisk in Mr. Robertson's office about the problem about a month after I moved in, and he told me that I would have to do the best I could because they couldn't afford to tear the wall apart. As to the cupboards and stove, they are both old. The cabinets haven't been painted in ten years, so, of course, they aren't perfect, and that old stove was a lot dirtier when I moved in than it is now, because I can tell you I personally worked on it with oven cleaner for over an hour."*

**Judge:** *"What about the refrigerator, Mr. Andrews? Was that defrosted?"*

**John Andrews:** *"No, your Honor, it wasn't, but it had been defrosted about three weeks before I moved out, and I thought that it was good enough the way it was."*

**Judge:** *"Okay, if no one else has anything to add, I want to return your pictures and letters. You will receive my decision by mail in a few days."*

The case presented is patterned on a real small claims case. Here's what a judge had to say about a similar case.

> *"This is a typical case in which both sides have some right on their side. What is clean to one person might be dirty to another. Based on what I heard, I would have to guess that the old tenant made a fairly conscientious effort to clean up and probably left the place about as clean as it was when he moved in, but that the new tenant, Houndstooth, had much higher standards and convinced the landlord that it was filthy. The landlord may not have needed too much convincing since he probably would just as well keep the deposit. But I did hear enough to convince me that Andrews, the old tenant, didn't do a perfect job cleaning up. My decision will be that Andrews gets a judgment for the return of $450 of the $700 deposit, with no punitive damages. I believe that $250 is more than enough to compensate the landlord for any damages he suffered as a result of the house 'being a little dirty.'"*

When asked about the presentation in the case this mock scenario was patterned after, the judge had this to say:

*"Better than average. I think I got a pretty good idea of what the problems were. The witnesses were helpful and the pictures gave me a pretty good idea that the place wasn't a total mess. Both sides could have done better, however. Andrews could have presented a witness to testify to the condition of the house when he moved in if, in fact, it was truly a lot dirtier than when he left. Another witness to testify to the fact that the house was clean when he moved out would have been good, too. His friend, Carol Spann, seemed to be a very close friend, and I wasn't sure that she was objective when it came to judging whether or not the place was clean. The landlord, Robertson, could also have done better. He could have presented a more disinterested witness, although I must say that Houndstooth's testimony was pretty convincing. Also, he could have had pictures documenting the dirty conditions and an estimate from a cleaning company for how much they would have charged to clean the place up. Without going to too much trouble, I think both sides could have probably done somewhat better with more thorough preparation."*

# Motor Vehicle Repair Cases

magine that you go to the auto repair shop to pick up your beloved car after a complete engine overhaul. The bill, which you agreed to pay in advance, is $10,500. While this seemed a little steep, the mechanic talked you into it by claiming he would do a great job and that the overhauled engine should last another 50,000 miles. You write a check and leave. As you head up the first hill, you hear a funny noise that quickly gets louder. Realizing that your car is worse off than before, you recognize that you have no choice but to turn around and take it back to the garage. The garage assures you that they'll look it over, but when you call the next day, you find out nothing has been done.

You call the bank to stop payment on the check, but the garage already cashed it. The next day the garage owner tells you the problem is in a part of the engine they didn't work on and asks for another $1,500. Refusing to pay more, you get your mechanical friend to help you drive it home—slowly. Furious, you decide to pursue every legal remedy, no matter what the trouble. But where do you start? First, sleep on it. Good decisions aren't made when you're mad. Then, read this chapter and decide whether it makes sense to take action.

## Do You Have a Case?

Following the approach presented throughout this book, you'll want to start by asking yourself these two key questions:

- Have you suffered a loss?
- Can you prove the defendant's negligence caused your loss?

The first question is easy. You suffered a loss. Your car was in worse shape after paying a lot of money to have it fixed.

The second question isn't as easy. You're convinced that a lousy repair job caused your problem. But the garage owner will claim the car needed more work, and for all the judge will know, it could be true. In short, to win the case, you'd have to prove that the repair work was not up to a reasonable standard of competence. If you can't put on evidence to that effect, you'll lose.

## Collect Available Evidence

Gather all the relevant evidence as soon as you can. If possible, you'll want to get your used parts (a good idea any time you have major work done). If the garage refuses to return them, confirm it in writing, ask again in the letter, and keep a copy for your file. If you get the parts, fine—if you don't, you have evidence that the garage is poorly run or has something to hide.

## Have Your Car Checked by an Expert

Before driving any appreciable distance, have your car checked by an experienced mechanic. While you might get a free estimate from a repair shop, you'd probably be better off paying someone to look at the engine thoroughly. Plus, you can arrange for the mechanic to testify on your behalf in small claims court beforehand—or at the very least, write a letter stating what's wrong with the engine. Before getting any work done, keep in mind that a few states require that you present three written estimates in small claims court. Even if it isn't necessary in your state, it's a good idea to have them.

## Try to Settle

Once you know what the first garage did wrong, call and ask them to redo the job or refund part or all of your money. The repair shop might agree to do the work to avoid a hassle. If so, insist on a written agreement detailing what they will do and how long it will take. Also, talk to the mechanic to be sure you both understand the scope of the work. It's a good idea to take someone with you who can testify about the conversation if the mechanic or shop changes the story later.

You might be worried about taking your car back to the garage that just screwed it up. However, unless they have proven themselves outrageously incompetent, this is probably your best approach because it's usually easier to get work redone than it is to get a big refund. Also, if you sue and the garage owner shows up in court and says he offered to work on the car again, but that you refused, it could weaken your case.

## Write a Demand Letter

If the garage isn't cooperative, the next step is writing a formal demand letter. Review the discussion in Chapter 6 for help. Your letter should be short but complete, polite, and written with an eye to a judge reading it. (See sample letter, below.)

> **TIP**
> **Be sure to emphasize any promise made by the garage.** Most small independent garages don't make a written warranty or guarantee on their work. However, if you were given any promises in writing, mention them in your letter. Also, if you were promised things orally about the quality of the work and you relied on these statements when authorizing the repairs, make sure the letter describes this "express oral warranty." (See Chapter 2.)

## File Your Court Papers

If you still don't get a satisfactory response from the garage, file your papers at the small claims court clerk's office in the county where the garage is located.

# Prepare for Court

If you want the judge to understand your case, you must understand it yourself. Sounds obvious, right? Of course it does—until you realize that *feeling* wronged and *verbally explaining* how you've been wronged are two different things.

This is an important point. Trying to argue a small claims case that you can't explain clearly will likely result in a loss. Here's a way to test the theory: Stand in front of the mirror and explain your case from start to finish. Don't be surprised if you don't do well. Next, consider the added stress of presenting your case in open court, and you'll start to understand how things can go wrong fast without proper preparation.

## Sample Car Repair Demand Letter

Haig Mackey
15 Orange Street
Hamden, CT 12344
October 1, 20xx

Happy Days Motors
100 Speedway
New Haven, CT 12333

Dear People:

On August 13, 20xx, I brought my 2015 Ford to your garage. The car worked well but was a little short on power. You agreed to do a complete engine rebuild job for $12,000 while assuring me, "Your car will be purring like a kitten when we're through with it." However, when I picked it up two days later, it barely moved at all. The engine was so noisy I was afraid to drive it home.

I've had two mechanics inspect it, and both say you did the work improperly. Not only did you install used instead of new parts—which I didn't agree to—but the mechanic did the engine ring repair particularly poorly.

I repeatedly asked you to fix the car or refund my money. After receiving no response from you, I had the repairs done for $9,000, and my car now works well. Please issue a refund for $9,000. If I don't receive the refund within ten days, I will file a complaint with the Better Business Bureau and a dispute in small claims court. I hope to hear from you promptly.

Sincerely,


Sincerely,

*Haig Mackey*
Haig Mackey

cc:  Connecticut Dept. of Consumer Affairs
     Bureau of Automotive Repair
     Hartford, CT 12333

The fact of the matter is that convincing a judge that the mechanic failed to properly repair your car (or any other issue) will require you to do some homework. After all, the representatives from the garage will likely show up in court claiming they did a stellar job rebuilding the pistons, bearings, and camshaft.

In court, you want to know what went wrong, so you have no trouble explaining to the judge that the mechanic did a substandard job. A 15-minute conversation with a knowledgeable mechanic might be all you need to understand what the first mechanic did wrong. (Also, your local library might have car manuals with diagrams.) But ultimately, the judge will rely heavily on expert testimony, which we discuss more below.

> **TIP**
> **Remember, the judge is probably not a mechanic.** It's important to pay attention to the person who will be deciding your case. It's no secret that many, if not most, small claims judges don't understand the insides of cars any better than you do. So be prepared to make a simple, concise, and convincing presentation to someone who probably doesn't understand the difference between the driveshaft and the axle.

## Appearing in Court

When you show up in court, you'll want to be well organized. Bring all the letters you have written or received about your car problem, any written warranty that applies, photographs if they are helpful, and your used parts if they help make your case. If you have a witness who can testify to oral statements made by the garage, be sure to bring them with you. Or at least ask the person to write a letter explaining what was heard. Also, you'll want to present any letters written by independent experts who examine your car. Judges rely on experts regularly, so this type of evidence will likely be the strongest. Even one persuasive letter from an experienced mechanic explaining that the garage performed substandard work could be enough to win the case.

Keep in mind that judges drive cars and have to get them fixed, and they tend to be sympathetic with this type of consumer complaint. Presenting your story (see Chapter 15), your documentation, and your witnesses with confidence, knowing that the judge will understand, will go far. If you are well prepared and the facts are on your side, you should easily win this type of case.

TIP

**A good drawing can help.** In cases involving machinery, presenting a large picture illustrating the mistake or problem can work well. This approach is most effective when your expert appears in court and uses the drawing to explain the issue. Contact the court for information about the technology available for presentations.

# Motor Vehicle Purchase Cases

O ccasionally, someone buys a vehicle and drives it a short way, only to have it fall apart. And too frequently the seller of the defective vehicle won't stand behind the product. What can you do if you are the victim of this kind of problem? There are major differences in how you should approach your problem depending on whether you purchased a new or used vehicle, so let's look at each situation separately.

## New Vehicles

It can be especially frustrating to buy a new car and have it break down much sooner than it should. Most states have a "lemon law" that requires the car dealer or manufacturer to give you a new car or a refund if your new car:

- has a substantial defect covered by the warranty that occurred within a certain period of time or number of miles after you bought the car (the specifics vary by state), and
- is not fixed after a reasonable number of repair attempts.

Unfortunately, because most new vehicles cost more than the small claims maximum, it is unlikely that you will be able to bring a small claims lawsuit against a car dealer or manufacturer for violating the lemon law.

RESOURCE
**Making lemonade out of your lemon.** For more information on lemon laws, see the following websites:

- www.ftc.gov/news-events/media-resources/consumer-finance/auto-marketplace (addresses consumer protection issues in the auto marketplace)
- www.consumerfinance.gov/consumer-tools/auto-loans (learn about auto loan rights)
- www.consumeradvocates.org/for-consumers/automobiles (includes auto fraud information)
- www.autopedia.com (includes individual summaries of each state's lemon laws)
- www.autosafety.org (includes state-specific tips)

What if your car breaks down just outside the warranty period? Luckily, you might still have a winnable case: When a relatively new vehicle falls apart for no good reason, many small claims court judges bend over backward to look for a legal way to give you protection over and above the actual written warranty that comes with the vehicle. For example, you still might be able to recover some money under one of the following approaches.

**Prove that the defects arose while your car was still under warranty.** Often a newish car that suffers serious mechanical problems soon after the warranty period runs out suffered similar problems during the warranty period. If so, you will want to argue that the dealer made inadequate repairs in the first instance and should still be responsible for the subsequent problems.

> **TIP**
>
> **Document your attempts to have your car repaired.** Make sure the judge knows about all the trips you have made to the dealer's repair shop. One way to establish this is by presenting copies of work orders you signed. If you don't have these or other records, request copies from the dealer (see Chapter 14 for instructions on subpoenaing documents), or sit down with a calendar and reconstruct the dates you brought your car in for repair. In court, give the copies or your list to the judge. If you have only your list, explain that it's your best estimate. The judge should accept it as being true unless the car dealer disputes it.

**Investigate the possibility of a "secret warranty."** After a model has been in production for awhile, a pattern of problems or failures may develop. Manufacturers are extremely sensitive to complaints in "high problem" areas—if for no other reason than to head off a possible federal safety recall. As a result, the manufacturer might have issued a "service bulletin" and created an adjustment program that extends the warranty or offers to pay for the repair of conditions that substantially affect the vehicle's durability, reliability, or performance. Here's how you can find out about service bulletins and adjustment programs:

- Dealers must post a notice in the showroom or other areas with information on obtaining service bulletins.
- You can search the National Highway Traffic Safety Administration's database of technical service bulletins at www.safercar.gov (click on "Vehicle Owners").
- If you go to the dealer to repair a condition covered by an adjustment program, the dealer must inform you of the program's terms.
- The manufacturer must notify eligible owners about an adjustment program within 90 days after adopting it.

If your vehicle has a serious problem, but the manufacturer hasn't issued a service bulletin or adopted an adjustment program (or you can't find out about either), talk to people at independent garages that specialize in repairing your model. If they tell you the problem is widespread and that the manufacturer has fixed it without charge for some persistent customers, your next step is to write a demand letter to the car dealer and manufacturer. (See Chapter 6.) Mention that if your problem is not taken care of, you will take further action. This might well cause the manufacturer to settle with you. If not, sue in small claims court and you will subpoena all records having to do with this defect.

> EXAMPLE: Bruno bought an expensive car that repeatedly had engine problems while under the manufacturer's written warranty. Each time, Bruno brought it into the dealer's repair shop and adjustments were made that seemed to fix the problem. A few months after the written warranty ran out, the engine died. Even though the car was only a little over a year old and had gone less than 50,000 miles, both the dealer and the parent car company refused to repair or replace it. Their refusals continued even though the owner repeatedly wrote to them, demanding action. How does Bruno deal with his problem?
>
> First, because he needed his car, he had the repairs made. Second, although the repairs cost slightly more than the small claims limit, he decided he would scale down his claim and sue for the small claims maximum to save the extra expense and hassle of finding a lawyer and suing in regular court.
>
> At the hearing, both Bruno and his wife testified about their trials and tribulations with the car. They gave the judge copies of the several letters they had written to the dealer, one of which was a list of the dates they had taken the car to the dealer's shop while it was still under warranty. They also produced a letter from the owner of the independent garage that finally fixed the engine, stating that when he took the engine apart, he discovered a defect in its original assembly. The new car dealer testified that his mechanics had done their best to fix the car when it was under the written warranty. He then contended that, once the written warranty had run out, he was no longer responsible. The dealer made no effort to challenge the car owner's story, nor did he bring his own mechanics to court to testify to how they had repaired the car while it was still under warranty. Bruno won and the court ordered the dealer to reimburse him for the repair costs.

> **TIP**
> **Find out about dispute resolution services provided by your state.**
> Many states provide help to consumers experiencing new vehicle problems. Your state might offer mediation or arbitration services to new car dealers and consumers at no cost. To find out, call your department of motor vehicles and ask whether they have a "new motor vehicle" division. Or you can search online. Include your state name along with terms such as "new motor vehicle," "mediation," "arbitration," "board," and "program."

## Used Vehicles From Dealers

Successfully suing used vehicle dealers can be tricky. Unlike new vehicle dealers, who are usually somewhat dependent upon their reputation in the community for honesty, a fair percentage of used vehicle dealers don't have a good reputation to start with and survive by becoming experts at self-protection.

> **TIP**
> **Used car dealers have a weakness—they don't want to talk to the judge.**
> Don't get discouraged by the fact that used car dealers plan out how to get away with certain acts. No matter how good it might sound, the dealer knows a judge will likely see right through it. Because these tactics can be sneaky, your job is to figure out exactly where the deception occurred and be confident that a judge would see the fraud just as clearly as you do. Next, meet with the dealer. Calmly explain your position and your desire to settle amicably. Expect the dealer to argue with you, but don't respond in kind. Instead, tell the dealer that you'll try again by sending another offer to settle in writing (a formal demand letter) and that if you can't reach an agreement, that you'll explore other options.

The main self-protection device employed by used vehicle dealers is the "as is" designation in the written sales contract. The salesperson might praise a car to the sky, but when you read the contract, you will see it clearly stated that the seller takes no responsibility for the condition of the vehicle and that it is sold "as is."

To successfully sue a used car dealer, you must be able to prove both of the following:

- you suffered a financial loss (this is not hard if you had to pay for repairs), and
- the dealer is legally responsible for your damages.

This second point is often harder to prove. Almost surely, the used car dealer will testify that there was no way of knowing how long a ten-year old Ford would last, which is why the dealer sold the car "as is." The dealer will present the written contract containing the "as is" designation and the provision stating "this written contract is the entire agreement between the parties and no oral statements or representations made by the dealer or any salesperson are part of the contract."

How can you fight this approach? It's difficult to do after the fact. The time for self-protection is before you buy a vehicle, when you have the opportunity to have it checked by an expert and to get a vehicle history report. There are a lot of online resources for checking a vehicle's history, particularly if you have the Vehicle Identification Number (VIN). Also, you have the opportunity to refuse to close the deal unless the salesperson's claims about the great condition of the car are put in the contract. Of course, after the damage has been done, good advice such as this isn't worth much. Here are some suggestions you can employ at this stage.

**Your state's lemon law might apply to used vehicles.** In some states, the lemon law applies to used as well as new cars. Check to see if your situation is covered.

**Argue fraud.** If the car broke almost immediately after you took it out of the used car lot, you can file in small claims court and argue that the dealer defrauded you. Your theory is that, no matter what the written contract said, there was a clear implication that you purchased a car, not a junk heap. When the dealer produces the "as is" contract you signed, argue that it is no defense to fraud. The fraud argument will apply to most other problems that arise when purchasing a used car, too. For instance, the dealer might fraudulently lead you to believe that you'll pay a particular price, but prepare the paperwork in such a way that you end up paying more. Review the paperwork closely to find the dealer's "mistake." (For more discussion of fraud, see Chapter 2.)

**Did the dealer make promises?** A dealer who makes promises about the vehicle's good condition, either in writing or orally, might be required to live up to them. Why? Because, as noted in Chapter 2, statements about a product that you rely on as part of deciding whether to purchase the product constitute an express warranty that the dealer breaches if the promise turns out to be a lie. This is true even if the seller had you sign a contract with an "as is" statement that disclaims all warranties because an "as is" statement does not disclaim an express warranty after one is made. The key to winning this sort of case is to produce a witness to the dealer's laudatory statements about the vehicle, copies of ads that state the car is in good shape, and anything else that will back up your story. A companion who heard the statements can appear as a witness, too.

**There also might be an implied warranty.** There are two types of implied warranties. One type—the implied warranty of fitness—means that the vehicle is warranted to work for a particular purpose (say, consistency). The more common implied warranty is for merchantability. Here, you would argue that the car you bought was so defective that it didn't meet the reasonable standards expected of even a used car. (See Chapter 2 for more on warranties.)

**A radical remedy: Give the car back and stop payment.** You might consider having the vehicle towed back to the lot and then refusing to make future payments. Although you should consider this option only in an extreme situation, it does shift the burden of taking legal action to the other side, at which point you can defend based on fraud (see above). If you take this approach, be sure you have excellent documentation that the car was below any reasonable expectations. And be sure to write a letter detailing the circumstances surrounding your extreme difficulties with the dealer, along with a convincing statement that the dealer's conduct amounts to consumer fraud. Send copies to the dealer and the bank or finance company to whom you pay your loan. Of course, you will probably have already made a down payment, so you might want to initiate action in small claims court to recover it.

CAUTION

**Your credit rating will suffer.** If you stop making payments, it will appear as a default on your credit report and significantly affect your credit score, so think carefully before choosing this course of action.

TIP

**How to find signs of fraud.** If you suspect fraud, have your car checked by an experienced mechanic who will be willing to write a letter explaining the findings. If the mechanic can find affirmative evidence that you were cheated, you will significantly improve your small claims case. The mechanic might, for example, find that the speedometer had been tampered with in violation of state law, or that a heavy grade of truck oil had been put in the crankcase so that the car wouldn't belch smoke. Also, this is the sort of case where subpoenaing documents might help. Specifically, you might wish to subpoena the car dealer's records, including any that indicate the dealer's purchase price, the condition of the car when purchased, and any repairs the dealer had made, including the smog records. It might also be helpful to learn the name of the car's former owner so you can contact that person. You can also check the car's history through an online service (search online for "vehicle history"), which can tell you whether the car had been stolen or salvaged, or was used as a rental or a taxi. (See Chapter 2 for more on fraud.)

**Consider other remedies besides small claims court.** These can include checking with your state department of consumer affairs or the local department of motor vehicles to see if used car lots are regulated. In many states, the department of motor vehicles licenses used car dealers. It can help get disputes resolved, particularly where your complaint is one of many against the same dealer for similar practices. Also, contact your district attorney's office. Most now have a consumer fraud division, which can be of great help. If you can convince someone that the dealer wronged you and is likely defrauding others, too, or if your complaint is against someone already identified, they might be willing to look into the situation further. Of course, the D.A.'s only job is to bring a criminal action, so this approach will likely help others more than yourself.

# Used Vehicles From Private Parties

It can be easier to win a case against a private party than against a used vehicle dealer. Why? Because a nondealer is usually less sophisticated in legal self protection than someone in the car business. Indeed, in most private party sales, the seller does no more than sign over the title slip in exchange for the agreed-upon price without any formal contract.

Too often, trouble develops soon after you purchase the vehicle and you must pay money for unexpected repairs. Just as with a used vehicle purchased from a dealer, you won't have a problem proving that you suffered a loss. Instead, the issue will be proving to the judge that the seller is responsible for making your loss good. To do this, you'll have to prove that the seller claimed that the vehicle was in better shape than it really was, and that you relied on these promises when you purchased it. The seller will almost certainly claim that the car was sold "as is." Remember, however, that an "as is" statement does not invalidate an express promise made about the car's condition.

> **EXAMPLE:** Brianna, a 20-year-old college student, bought a used BMW motorcycle from John. She sued John for $2,150 in repair costs, claiming that the motorcycle was in far worse shape than he had advertised. In court, she explained her conversations with John, testifying that he repeatedly told her that the motorcycle was "hardly used." She hadn't gotten any of John's promises in writing, but she did a good job presenting what evidence she had, including:
>   - a copy of her letter to John outlining her position (see letter below)
>   - copies of repair estimates and bills dated within two weeks of her purchase, the lowest of which came to $2,150
>   - a copy of John's newspaper ad, which read: "BMW motorcycle, almost new—hardly used—excellent condition—$7,500."
>   - a letter from the mechanic who worked on the motorcycle for Brianna (below).
>
> In court, Brianna presented her evidence, and explained she had saved for six months to get the money to buy the motorcycle. Although testimony about financial hardship isn't relevant, a quick tug on the judge's heartstrings never hurts.
>
> Next, John had his turn. His testimony consisted of asking, "How could I know when it would break?" When the judge asked him specific questions about the age, condition, and previous history, he didn't have answers. When the judge asked him if he had made specific guarantees about the motorcycle's condition, John's response was to say when selling things, you "puff them up a little." The judge decided in Brianna's favor based on her clear presentation and the documents she presented supporting her case.

**Demand Letter**

14 Stockton Street

Moline, IL 12233

January 27, 20xx

John Malinosky

321 South Zaporah

Moline, IL 12233

Dear Mr. Malinosky:

This letter is a follow-up to our recent phone conversation in which you refused to discuss the fact that the 2010 BMW motorcycle I purchased from you on January 15 is not in the "excellent condition" that you claimed.

To review: On January 12, I saw your ad for a motorcycle that was "almost new—hardly used—excellent condition" in the local flea market newspaper.

I called you, and you told me that the motorcycle was a terrific bargain and that you would never sell it except that you needed money for school. I told you that I didn't know much about machinery.

The next day, you took me for a ride on the motorcycle. You told me specifically that:

1. The motorcycle had just been tuned up.

2. The motorcycle had been driven less than 30,000 miles.

3. The motorcycle had never been raced or used roughly.

4. If anything went wrong with the motorcycle in the next month or two, you would see that it was fixed.

Relying on these statements, I bought the motorcycle from you for $7,500.

I had the motorcycle less than a week when the brakes went out. When I had them checked, the mechanic told me that the transmission also needed work (I confirmed this with another mechanic—see attached estimate). The mechanic also told me that the motorcycle had been driven at least 75,000 miles (perhaps a lot more) and that it needed a tune-up. In addition, he showed me caked mud and scratches under the motorcycle frame that indicated to him that it had been driven extensively off the road in rough terrain and had probably been raced on dirt tracks.

## Demand Letter (continued)

The lowest estimate to do the repairs was $2,150. Before having the work done, I called you to explain the situation and to give you a chance to arrange for the repairs to be made, or to make them yourself. You laughed at me and said, "Sister, do what you need to do—you're not getting one dime from me."

Again I respectfully request that you make good on the promises you made to me on January 15. I relied on the truth of your statements when I decided to buy the bike. I enclose a copy of the mechanic's bill for $2,150, along with copies of several higher estimates that I received from other repair shops.

Sincerely,

*Brianna Parker*

Brianna Parker

## Witness Letter

February 3, 20xx

To Whom It May Concern:

It's hard for me to get off work, but if you need me, please ask the judge to delay the case a few days. I have been in the motorcycle-repair business for 20 years, and have repaired hundreds of BMWs. The BMW that Brianna Parker brought to me was in fair shape at best. It's impossible to be exact, but given that the brakes and transmission were completely shot, I would conservatively guess it had been driven at least 75,000 miles. And given the damage to the underside of the bike, it was definitely driven a lot of those miles on dirt.

Respectfully submitted,

*Benjamin Green*

Benjamin Green

In used car transactions, it's often one person's word against another's, particularly if there's no written warranty or advertisement. Any shred of tangible evidence that the seller did make an express oral warranty of condition and that the seller relied on it to make the purchase can be enough to shift the balance to your side. Of course, if you have a friend who witnessed or heard any part of the transaction, the testimony will be extremely valuable. Getting a mechanic to check over a vehicle and then testify for you is also a good strategy. Sometimes you can get some help from publications that list wholesale and retail prices for used cars. Some people bring these publications into court to back up their assertion that they paid above the "Blue Book" price for a used car "because the car was represented to be in extra good shape." This type of evidence doesn't constitute much in the way of actual proof that you were taken advantage of, but it is helpful to at least show the judge that you paid a premium price for unsound goods.

# Bad Debts: Initiating and Defending Cases

M any small claims cases involve bad debts—a claim that the defendant owes the plaintiff money. Usually, a bill for goods or services hasn't been paid, but a bad debt also can involve failure to pay a promissory note—for example, a loan from a friend or relative—or even a civil fine for something as simple as the failure to return a library book. The plaintiff wins the vast majority of these cases, often because the defendant defaults by failing to show up to defend the case. This illustrates how effective small claims court can be as part of any business's collection strategy. Individuals also use small claims court to sue over goods or services that are shoddy, not as promised or ordered, or not delivered at all.

**TIP**
**Even bad checks for small amounts might be worth pursuing.** A bad check could be worth three times its face value. Every merchant is stuck with a bad check now and then, although not as often as in the past. In many states, special laws allow a person receiving a bad check to obtain a judgment for a significant amount of money in damages in addition to the check's face value, sometimes up to three times its amount.

But small claims court can also work for a defendant who doesn't owe money or when the plaintiff asks for too much. Because, unlike formal court, small claims defendants don't need to file complicated paperwork or jump through other legal hoops to present their side of the story. Indeed, all a defendant has to do is show up on the appointed day and make a convincing, well-documented presentation.

Some professionals, like doctors, dentists, lawyers, and other business people, don't use small claims court to collect unpaid bills because they think it takes too much time. They must either write off the loss or turn the bill over to a collection agency. But small claims court actions can be handled with little time and expense once you understand the process. And in many states, businesses can delegate the job of actually appearing in court.

TIP
**Unincorporated businesses can often send a representative to small claims court.** Oftentimes, a bookkeeper, financial manager, or other employee of a sole proprietorship or partnership can appear and present a case in small claims court if you can prove your case with a business record—for instance, by showing nonpayment of a bill—and no other issues of fact are involved. And, in many states, a corporation or limited liability company can send an authorized employee, officer, or director. A partnership can also send a partner to court.

## Who Should Appear in Court?

Small claims courts vary from state to state in terms of who can sue to collect unpaid bills. As listed in the state-by-state appendix, some states:

- allow bill collectors (called "assignees") to use small claims court
- ban bill collectors, but let lawyers carry out much the same task by representing multiple creditors, or
- ban both bill collectors and lawyers, only allowing businesses to sue on their behalf.

There are essential differences even among the states where businesses can't hire third parties but must represent themselves to sue on bad debt claims. For example, a few states entirely prohibit corporations from suing in small claims court. In contrast, others make it difficult for unincorporated businesses to send anyone but an owner or partner to court. However, most states allow corporations to sue and make it reasonably easy for incorporated and unincorporated businesses to designate a bookkeeper or another employee to handle court appearances. (See Chapter 7 for more on who can sue in small claims court.)

After first checking the rules in Appendix A and on your state's website, contact your small claims court clerk and find out which laws govern bill collection activities in your state. If you are a business, talk to other businesspeople or business associations, such as the chamber of commerce to learn practical strategies to cope with these rules. Also, if you are in a state where bill collectors or lawyers do small claims collection work, you will want to find out how much they charge and how efficient they are and then compare this information to the time and energy it would take for you to do it yourself. Because bill collectors and lawyers typically charge from 20%–50% of any money they collect, you might conclude that you want to do this work yourself.

In many states, a business owner can send an employee to court. A bookkeeper or financial manager will be a good choice when the defendant owes money because the person can testify that a valid contract existed and that the defendant did not pay the promised amount. However, if the defendant shows up and claims that the goods or services were defective, delivered late, or otherwise not acceptable, the bookkeeper probably wouldn't have firsthand knowledge of anything except that the check was not in the mail. For example, if you own a graphics business and sue on an unpaid bill expecting the defendant to claim you did lousy work, you will need someone in court who knows the details of the particular job. Typically, this should be the employee who dealt with the customer and did the work.

## From the Plaintiff's Point of View

The job of the plaintiff who sues for nonpayment of a debt is often easy. That's because in the majority of cases, the debtor doesn't show up. In the absence of a defendant, the plaintiff needs only to introduce evidence that a valid debt exists and wasn't paid. To accomplish this, present written proof of the debt in the form of a contract, work order, promissory note, or purchase order signed by the defendant. Even if a debt is based on an oral contract, it's usually easy to get a judgment because the defendant isn't present to contradict the plaintiff's version of events.

Here are a few suggestions for plaintiffs who plan to sue to collect a debt.

## When It Doesn't Pay to Sue

Although using small claims court to collect a bad debt often makes sense, there are exceptions. Here are the principal ones:

**When there isn't enough money at stake.** For disputes involving a few hundred dollars or less, for businesses, the costs of filing, preparing, and presenting a small claims case are likely to be high relative to what they are likely to recover. Of course, this is doubly true if you doubt that a court judgment will be collectible.

**When you won't be able to collect the judgment.** As discussed in more detail in Chapters 3 and 24, when the defendant has a job, bank account, investments, or real estate, a court judgment is relatively easy to collect. However, some people are broke and unemployed and are likely to stay that way. One thing is sure—you don't want to spend your time and energy suing someone who is not likely to have enough money to pay the resulting judgment. Better to write off the debt and tighten up your credit-granting procedures.

**When you want or need to get along with the person in the future.** Any court action, even a small claims lawsuit, tends to aggravate a dispute and cause more anger between the parties. This isn't a big problem when dealing with people or businesses you don't plan to deal with in the future. But in other circumstances, such as when a relative or local business owes you money, your ongoing relationship will likely be more important than collecting the amount owed. It might make sense to minimize any conflict through mediation or by writing it off altogether. (See Chapter 6.)

## Ask for Your Money Before You Sue

Writing an effective letter demanding payment might prompt the debtor to pay or at least open up settlement negotiations. You should always send a demand letter before filing in small claims court (and your letter might be helpful in explaining your case to the judge). Unfortunately, instead of doing this, many businesses rely on fill-in-the-blank past-due notices and letters purchased from commercial sources. While sending one of these is better than nothing, it's far more effective to write your own, more personal letter (see the sample demand letter in Chapter 6)—or at least to customize a form letter enough that it's clear it's intended for the debtor. But be aware that if you regularly demand payment of business debts, you'll have to comply with laws to protect the debtor from overzealous collection techniques, guard the debtor's privacy, govern communications with the debtor, and more. For the legal dos and don'ts of collecting bills, see *Legal Guide for Starting & Running a Small Business,* by Fred S. Steingold (Nolo).

**TIP**

**Plan in advance to counter any claim that your bill wasn't paid for a good reason.** If you provide goods or services, it's wise to include a statement on all your bills and collection letters requesting that the debtor notify you if goods are defective or services are substandard. Bring copies of these notices to court. Then if the debtor shows up and claims nonpayment because the goods or services were defective, you will be prepared to counter this claim. Do this by first showing the judge your many notices asking that any problem be brought to your attention and then testifying that the defendant never made a complaint. This should go far toward convincing the judge that the defendant is fabricating, or at least exaggerating, the current complaint in an effort to avoid paying you.

## Bring Your Case Promptly

For maximum success collecting bad debts, file suit as soon as you conclude that informal collection methods are unlikely to work. You'll be pleasantly surprised that a small but significant number of debtors will quickly pay up—or call you to work out a payment plan—to avoid having a court judgment appear in their credit records. Fast action is also advisable for other reasons, the most important being that people who owe you money are likely to have other debts as well and might be considering bankruptcy. The quicker you act, the faster you'll get a judgment and be eligible to start collection activities, like a wage garnishment or property attachment.

Also, if you file promptly, you will avoid worrying whether you are within the legal filing deadline, the statute of limitations. Depending on the state and the type of debt, the limitations period is usually from one to four years. (There is a discussion of the statutes of limitations applicable to different sorts of debts in Chapter 5.)

## Installment Debts

If you lend money or sell an item with payments to be made in installments, and a payment or two is missed, you usually are entitled to sue only for the amount of the missed payments, not the whole debt. Before you can sue for the entire amount, you must wait until all payments are missed. However, there is a major exception to this rule: You can immediately sue for 100% of the debt—plus any interest—if your contract contains an acceleration clause. This is a statement that if one payment is missed, the whole debt becomes due. To see whether this type of provision is present, carefully read your installment sales contract and consider rewriting it to include such a clause.

## Written Contracts

Most debts are based on written contracts. The contract might be a purchase order, credit agreement, lease, or formal contract. It normally makes no difference what your document is called, as long as you have something in writing with the defendant's signature.

Always bring your written documentation to court when your case is heard and be ready to show it to the judge. Also, bring any ledger sheets, computer printouts, or other business records documenting the payments that have been made or missed. Bring an extra copy for the judge and defendant.

It's essential to be organized; you don't want to show up with botched records or become flustered when closely questioned by the judge. The courtroom is not the place to straighten out a poor accounting system.

## Oral Contracts

Generally, a debt based on an oral contract is legal as long as the contract was (or could have been) carried out in one year and is not for the sale or mortgage of real estate or the sale of goods (personal property) worth more than $500. (See Chapter 22 for more on written documentation requirements for the sale of goods.) Of course, it might be hard to prove the debt exists if the defendant flat out denies borrowing the money or buying the goods or services. Your best bet is to attempt to come up with some written documentation that your version of what occurred is true. For example, even if there is no written agreement, the defendant might have provided you with a down payment check or a letter asking for more time to pay. Either would be a huge help in convincing the judge that a debt exists. Or, when you write a letter demanding payment before you sue (see Chapter 6), include a description of the oral agreement and existing debt along with a phrase like "If my understanding is incorrect in any way, please contact me in writing or by phone by [date]." If the debtor doesn't dispute your version of events, then bring a copy of your letter to court and tell the judge you never got a reply, if that's truly the case.

If you can't come up with anything in writing, try to think of a person who has firsthand knowledge of the debt and who is willing to testify. For example, if you asked for your money and the defendant said in the presence of a friend, "I know I owe you $1,000. I'll pay you next month," or "Too bad you will never get your money back," or anything similar that indicates that the loan existed, bring your witness to court. If that's not possible, the witness should write a letter explaining what was heard. You'll want to show the letter to the judge.

If you don't have a witness, consider whether you can establish the debt's existence by looking at the debtor's actions. It is often easy to do this when you haven't been paid for services you provided in a commercial context. After all, if the other party accepted your labor, there is almost always an implication that payment is expected.

EXAMPLE: Jane, a commercial illustrator, freelances for ad agencies, publishers, and other clients. One day she gets a call from Harold, a dress designer, asking her to draw his new eveningwear line. Jane completes the drawings and submits her bill for $2,000. Harold refuses to pay, claiming the payment was conditional on a fashion magazine publishing the drawings and that even if a contract did exist, Jane charged too much. Jane files in small claims court. The judge has no trouble finding an oral contract based on Harold's admission that he asked Jane to do the work. However, the judge only awards Jane $1,400 because she can't document an agreed-upon pay rate of $100 an hour, and Harold made a convincing argument that illustrators with similar qualifications customarily charge no more than $70 per hour.

 RELATED TOPIC
**More on contract cases.** See "Breach of Contract Cases" in Chapter 2 for more on oral and implied contracts.

## From the Debtor's Point of View

If you are being sued for nonpayment of a debt, don't assume you'll auto-matically lose your case. If you show up with well-thought-out, convincing defenses, the judge might reduce the amount the plaintiff asked for, or even find that no debt exists.

Here are some examples of cases in which the defendant succeeded in whole or part:

EXAMPLE 1: A local hospital sued a man for failing to pay an emergency room copay in the amount of $678. It seemed like an open and shut case—the hospital's representative presented the proper records demonstrating that the defendant hadn't paid. But the defendant had a defense. He explained that after waiting four hours to be treated for a superficial but painful gunshot wound, the hospital did nothing more than bandage him up before sending him home.

He provided medical records and receipts proving that after leaving, he suffered complications that could have been avoided if the attending physician had treated him promptly and with more care. He said he didn't mind paying a fair amount, but he didn't believe the $678 copay was warranted, especially when the hospital received more than $5,000 from his health insurance provider. The judge agreed and gave judgment to the hospital for $250, plus court and service of process costs. After the defendant explained that his employer laid him off due to COVID-19 and that his only income was unemployment benefits, the judge granted his request to pay the judgment at the rate of $25 per month.

EXAMPLE 2: A large local tire retailer sued a woman for not paying the balance on a tire bill. She had purchased eight light truck tires manufactured by a major tire company and still owed $612. The tire company representative presented the judge with the original copy of a written contract along with the woman's payment record, and then waited for judgment. The woman, who ran a small neighborhood gardening and landscaping business, produced several advertising flyers from the tire company that strongly implied that the tires would last at least 40,000 miles. She then testified and presented a witness to the fact that the tires had lasted less than 25,000 miles before wearing out. The defendant also had copies of four letters she had written over the past year to the headquarters of the tire company in the Midwest complaining about the tires. Both in the letters, and in court, she repeatedly stated that the salesperson at the tire company told her several times that the tires were guaranteed for 40,000 miles. Putting this all together, the judge declared the total price of the tires should be prorated on the basis of 25,000 miles and, after figuring what the defendant had already paid, gave the tire company a judgment for only $350, instead of the $612 requested. The woman wrote a check on the spot and departed feeling vindicated.

EXAMPLE 3: A rug company sued a customer for $1,486 and produced all the necessary documentation to show that the carpet had been installed and that no payment had been received. The defendant testified that the rug had been poorly installed, with a seam running down the center of the room. He brought pictures that left little doubt that the rug installer was either incompetent or completely thoughtless. The defendant also presented drawings that illustrated that there were several better ways to cut the carpet to fit the room. The rug company received nothing.

Of course, the real point of these examples is not to be found in their individual fact situations—yours will surely differ. Rather, they illustrate that if you can convince the judge that goods or services were substandard, chances are you'll win at least a partial victory.

## Common Defenses

As discussed in more detail in Chapter 2, below are some defenses in cases where you are sued for nonpayment.

**Breach of contract.** The other party failed to live up to (perform) the terms of the contract within the correct period, with the result that you are no longer obligated to keep your payment obligation. For example, you contracted to have your kitchen counter replaced with a Carrara marble slab but ended up with a cheaper quartz look-alike. Or, you ordered a cake from a website that arrived looking nothing like the picture.

> **CAUTION**
>
> **Trivial defects won't void a contract.** To succeed with a breach of contract defense, you must show that the other party's breach was significant enough to prevent you from receiving all or at least a substantial amount of the benefits that you wanted from the contract. For example, suppose you order light yellow flowers for a wedding and refuse to pay the bill after the florist delivers cream-colored flowers. You can be pretty sure the judge will decide in favor of the flower vendor, especially if you used the flowers. By contrast, if you order yellow flowers but receive dark purple—a color no one can deny clashes with your theme—your chances of winning would be much better.

**Fraud.** The other party intentionally lied to you about a key fact in a transaction. For example, you purchased a used car with 75,000 miles on the odometer. Later, you meet the vehicle's first owner who says it really had gone 125,000 miles and that the odometer said so when he sold it to the used car dealer who sold it to you.

**Breach of warranty.** An express or implied warranty (assurance) made by the seller of goods is breached. For example, a roofer claims in writing that your new roof will last 20 years. In fact, it leaks in the first big storm.

**Violation of statute.** Many federal and state laws require the seller of a particular type of goods or services to comply with specific rules. For example, federal regulations provide that a door-to-door seller of goods and services that cost more than $25 must give you notice of your right to cancel the purchase within three business days, along with a cancellation form. (There are a few exceptions.) If he fails to do so, your right to cancel continues indefinitely. For example, if you buy an expensive vacuum cleaner from a door-to-door salesperson and ask (in writing) to cancel the deal the next day, you have a good defense if the vacuum cleaner company sues you for nonpayment.

> EXAMPLE: B. Best Models, a New York modeling agency, sued Morgana, claiming she hadn't paid the agency's $1,000 fee for a portfolio of "professional quality photographs" designed to help Morgana obtain modeling employment. In her defense, Morgana claimed that B. Best had violated New York State's employment agency licensing law (N.Y. Gen. Bus. Law §§ 170 and following) by falsely claiming it would help her find modeling jobs when in fact, the agency made no effort to do so. After concluding that B. Best was primarily a scheme designed to get consumers to overpay for photographs and had not attempted to find Morgana modeling work, the court ruled that Morgana owed B. Best nothing.

## Evidence to Defend Your Case

To successfully defend a suit claiming you owe money, you'll typically need to document a very good reason why the goods or services you received were inadequate or some other reason why you are not legally required to pay. This means you'll need to do more than tell the judge a sad story. If shoddy goods are involved, show them to the judge or bring a picture or written report from an expert. (See Chapter 14.) If you received truly bad service, bring a witness or other supporting evidence to court. For example, suppose the new paint on your recently refinished boat immediately began to chip and peel and, as a result, you notified the boat yard that you would not pay for the job. In case you are later sued, you will want to take pictures clearly showing the problem and get a written opinion from another boat refinisher stating the work was substandard as well as an estimate to fix or redo the job. If a company misrepresented a product or service to you, it is very helpful if you can find others who were also victims who will either go to court with you to tell the judge a similar story to yours, or give you a letter you can take to court, describing the false statements they were given.

## Appearing in Court

You might have a tactical advantage at the hearing if the person who appears in court on behalf of the creditor is not the same person with whom you dealt. For example, if you state that a salesperson told you X, Y, and Z, the salesperson probably won't be present to state otherwise. This could tilt a close case in your favor. It is perfectly appropriate for you to point out to the judge that your opponent has only books and ledgers, not firsthand knowledge of the situation. The judge might postpone the case until another day to allow the creditor to present the testimony of the employee you dealt with, but often this is impossible if the employee has moved on to another job.

TIP
**You can ask for a little more time to pay.** In some states, the judge has considerable discretion to order that a judgment be paid in installments. If you are financially pressed, installment payments can be extremely helpful. If you meet the payment schedule, the creditor can't initiate a wage levy (garnishment) or other collection activity. So don't be shy about asking the judge to establish time payments—the judge won't know that you want them if you don't ask. Even if you don't make your request in court, it might not be too late. Some courts allow you to file a request to pay a judgment in installments after the hearing.

# Vehicle Accident Cases

t is a rare small claims session that does not include at least one fender bender. Unfortunately, plaintiffs often prepare and present these cases poorly, leaving the judge to decide the case at least partially by guesswork.

> **TIP**
> **File personal injury cases in formal court.** Unless it's very minor, personal injuries don't belong in small claims court because most involve claims for far more money than the small claims maximum. And in states that have no-fault insurance, personal injury cases might not be allowed in court at all unless you've first complied with the requirements of your state's no-fault insurance law.

The average vehicle accident case that ends up in small claims court doesn't involve personal injury but is about damage to one or both parties' vehicles. And, unless the drivers' respective car insurance companies are battling it out (which would be unlikely in small claims court), the claimants are typically the drivers themselves. Whether they are uninsured, carry insufficient coverage, or their policies don't apply to the accident case for some other reason, most drivers will find themselves personally on the financial hook if they lose their small claims case. That's one reason why these cases are extremely hard fought. Plus, it's common for both drivers to believe the other driver was at fault.

Chapter 2 explains the legal concept of negligence. You'll want to reread the material because before recovering in a motor vehicle accident case, you must prove the other person was negligent (careless) and you were driving safely or, if both of you were negligent, that you were less so. Usually, dealing with concepts of negligence in a vehicle accident is a matter of common sense; you probably have a reasonably good idea of the rules of the road and whether you or the other driver was at fault. One key is whether a police officer cited you or the other party for breaking a highway safety law. (See "Determining Fault," below.) When someone violates a safety-related law, negligence is usually presumed.

⊘ CAUTION
**Check rules in no-fault states.** States with no-fault insurance laws generally require that people involved in auto accident disputes—especially those involving less severe injuries—submit the case to the no-fault administrative system, not resolve the matter in the court. Check your state's rules.

You can still win a negligent case, at least partially, even if you were not entirely in the right. Under the doctrine known as "comparative negligence," if the other person was significantly more at fault than you were, you might still have a good case. (See Chapter 2 for more on comparative negligence.)

## Who Can Sue Whom?

The vehicle owner should file a claim for vehicle damage even if the owner wasn't driving when the accident occurred. You'd bring the suit against the negligent driver and the registered owner if they aren't the same person. You can find out who owns a car by contacting the state Department of Motor Vehicles as long as you have the vehicle license number. (See "Motor Vehicle Accident Cases" in Chapter 8.)

## Was There a Witness?

Because the judge has no way of knowing what happened unless one or more people tell the story, a good witness can make or break your case. It is better to have a disinterested witness than a close friend or family member, but any witness is far better than none. If the other person is likely to have a witness who supports their point of view (even though it's wrong) and you have none, you will have to work extra hard to develop other evidence. Reread Chapter 14 for more information on witnesses. If you can't get your eyewitness to show up in court voluntarily, try to get that person to give you a written statement outlining what they observed and present the statement as evidence.

## Traffic Collision Reports

When you have an accident and believe the other person was more at fault, it's wise to call the police and ask an officer to prepare a traffic collision report. (In some areas, an officer will come out only if someone claims to be injured. Check whether you can report the accident online.) A traffic collision report might be admissible as evidence in small claims court; however, the court might not allow it under the evidentiary theory of hearsay. You'll stand a better chance if you can bring in the officer who prepared the report and any supporting witnesses if it's possible to do so.

If an officer prepared a traffic collision report, purchasing it will be a good investment. If it supports you, try to bring in the actual parties involved. If you can't, bring the traffic collision report to court. If it doesn't support you, be prepared to refute what it says and argue that it's hearsay and shouldn't be admitted. If both an eyewitness and a traffic collision report are against you, you might want to rethink filing a lawsuit unless you can present solid evidence of your opponent's negligence.

## Determining Fault

Chapter 2 explains what you must prove in a negligence case. It's the law that applies in motor vehicle cases. Negligence can also be established by showing that the other driver caused the accident due to safety-related violations of driving laws. For instance, if Elijah runs a red light and hits a car crossing the intersection, Elijah will be presumed negligent unless he can offer a sufficient excuse for his action. On the other hand, if Elijah is driving without his seatbelt and has an accident, the seatbelt violation cannot be said to have caused the accident and can't be used to presume negligence.

If there is a traffic collision report, the reporting officer will have noted any driving law violations that occurred during the accident. The report might even conclude that a driving violation caused the accident. The fact that the officer cited the other driver would be something you'd want to show to the judge. If there is no report, you might want to do some research on your own.

You should be able to find your state's vehicle code online by visiting your state legislature's website. Vehicle codes can also be found in large public libraries, and all law libraries. Scan the table of contents for driving rules that the other driver might have violated. Call any law violation that might have caused the accident to the judge's attention. (For more tips on legal research, see Chapter 25.)

CAUTION
**Beware! Professional drivers have an incentive to bend the truth.** If you're opposing a bus or truck driver, or even someone with an Uber-type side gig, watch out. Many of these people risk job-related consequences if they are at fault in an accident. As a result, they have an incentive to deny fault automatically. Judges who know this might take the testimony of a professional driver with a grain of salt. Still, it never hurts to ask the driver in court whether a demerit system or some other work-related penalty exists if the court finds the driver at fault in an accident.

## Diagrams

You shouldn't assume the judge will be able to visualize a busy intersection or multilane thoroughfare without help. Instead, consider incorporating a diagram of the scene into your court presentation. It will be easier for the judge to grasp the involvement of each vehicle and determine fault.

For example, suppose you're involved in an intersection accident—you collide with another car coming from the right. You'd want to draw the intersecting streets, showing the lane separators and any stop signs or signals, and use arrows to indicate the lines of travel. Draw any obstructions, such as trees and other vehicles.

If you're comfortable drawing your diagram on the spot, a whiteboard might be available for courtroom use. Also, some courts can display your computer screen on a larger monitor (call to find out your options). If neither is available, recreate the scene on paper and bring it with you. Just be sure to practice using your diagram beforehand.

## Photos

Photographs are very helpful in auto accident cases, especially if they back up your story about how an accident occurred. For example, if you claim you were sideswiped while parked, a photo showing a long series of scratches down the side of your car will likely be convincing. Assuming they help tell a compelling story, showing the judge pictures of the defendant's car and accident scene can also be effective.

## Estimates

Whenever you attempt to recover money for damage done to your vehicle, you must prove how much it will cost to fix the car. If you forget this step, you'll end up with nothing. Showing the judge several estimates for the cost of repairs—usually three—works well. If you have already had the work done, bring your canceled check or receipt from the repair shop along with the other estimates. Be sure to get your estimates from reputable shops. If, for some reason, you get an estimate from someone you later think isn't competent, don't use it and get another. Also, you don't have a legal responsibility to get your car fixed by a shop recommended by the person who caused the damage. Indeed, common sense often dictates that you don't.

Unfortunately, you can't recover money to cover the time you put in to get estimates, take your car to the repair shop, or appear in court. However, you can recover money for the fair market value of anything in your car that was destroyed. You must be prepared to establish that the accident caused the damage and the dollar amount of the loss. (See Chapter 4 for a discussion of how to do this.) You can also recover the cost to rent a car for the time it reasonably should have taken to get your car fixed. If it usually would take two days to fix a fender, you would be entitled to rental car reimbursement for two days, not more.

(!) CAUTION
**Defendants should be on their guard against plaintiffs who try to pad their repair bill.** Sometimes, plaintiffs will try to fix existing damage to their car as part of getting legitimate accident work done. If you think the plaintiff is asking for too much money, try to develop evidence to support your belief. For example, if you can present evidence that the plaintiff's car was damaged at the time of your accident, but that the plaintiff is suing you for 100% of all repair costs, the judge should award less—maybe a lot less—than the amount they are demanding. Also, remember that the plaintiff is only entitled to get repairs worth up to the car's total value before the accident. If the car was worth only $1,500 and the repairs would cost $2,500, the plaintiff is only entitled to $1,500. (See Chapter 4.)

## Your Demand Letter

As in almost every other type of small claims court case, you should write a letter to your opponent that proposes settlement, keeping in mind that the judge might read it. See the sample letters in Chapter 6. A Sample Demand Letter After Auto Accident is shown below.

## Appearing in Court

Here's how you can present a motor vehicle accident case in court:

**Clerk:** *"Next case,* McClatchy v. Rugg. *Please come forward."*

**Judge:** *"Please tell me what happened, Ms. McClatchy."*

**Jenna McClatchy:** *"Good morning. This dispute involves an auto accident that occurred at Rose and Sacramento Streets on the afternoon of August 15, 20xx. I was coming uphill on Rose (that's east) and stopped at the corner. There is a four-way stop sign at the corner. I turned right, or south, on Sacramento Street, and as I was doing so, Mr. Rugg ran the stop sign on Sacramento and crashed into my front fender. Your Honor, may I use the whiteboard to make a quick diagram?"*

**Sample Demand Letter After Auto Accident**

18 Channing Way
Eugene, OR 12345

August 27, 20xx

Kenneth Rugg
27 Miramar Crescent
Eugene, OR 12345

Dear Mr. Rugg:

I am writing to settle the case arising from the accident that occurred on August 15, 20xx. Shortly before the accident, I was traveling eastbound on Rose Street in Eugene, Oregon. It was a sunny afternoon at about 3:30 p.m. I stopped at the stop sign at the corner of Rose and Sacramento and proceeded to turn right (south) on Sacramento.

While making my turn, I saw your car going southbound on Sacramento about 20 feet north of the corner of Rose. However, instead of stopping at the stop sign, you proceeded across the intersection and struck my car on the front left fender. By the time I realized that you were coming through the stop sign, there was nothing I could do to get out of your way. After the accident, the Eugene police cited you for failure to stop at a stop sign, and the traffic collision report confirms these facts.

I have obtained three estimates to repair the damage with the lowest being $3,612. I need my car for work, so I am proceeding with the repairs. Please send a check reimbursing me for $3,612 or call 541-486-xxxx to discuss further.

Sincerely,

*Jenna McClatchy*
Jenna McClatchy

**Judge:** *"Please do, I was about to ask you if you would."*

**Jenna McClatchy:** (makes a drawing as suggested in "Diagrams," above, points out the movement of the cars in detail, and answers several questions from the judge): *"Your Honor, before I sit down, I would like to give you several items of evidence. First, I have a copy of the police accident report from the Eugene police, which states that Mr. Rugg got a citation for failing to stop at the stop sign in question. Second, I have photos showing the damage to the front fender of my car. Third, I have the letter I wrote to Mr. Rugg trying to settle this case. Finally, I have several repair estimates showing how much it would cost to fix the damage to my car. As you can see from my receipt, I took the lowest one* (hands the bailiff a copy of each piece of evidence for the judge and Mr. Rugg)."

**Judge:** *"Thank you, Ms. McClatchy. Now, Mr. Rugg, it's your turn."*

**Kenneth Rugg:** *"Your Honor, my case rests on one basic fact. Ms. McClatchy was negligent because she made a wide turn into Sacramento Street. Instead of going from the right-hand lane of Rose to the right-hand or outside lane on Sacramento Street, she turned into the center lane on Sacramento Street. (*Mr. Rugg moves to the whiteboard and points out what he says happened.) Now it might be true that I made a rolling stop at the corner—but I would never have hit her if she had kept to her side of the road. Also, your Honor, she darted out; instead of easing out slow like she should have, she jumped out like a rabbit chased by a red fox."*

**Judge:** *"Do you have anything else to say, Ms. McClatchy?"*

**Jenna McClatchy:** *"I am not going to argue about Mr. Rugg's rolling stop because the police officer cited him for running the stop sign. But I do want to address his allegation that I was driving inappropriately. It's true that I made a slightly wider turn than usual. If you look at my diagram, you'll see I had to drive a little farther into Sacramento than usual to avoid a parked car located at the corner of Sacramento and Rose. However, I didn't turn into the center lane. As I made the turn, my outside fender crossed into the center lane slightly, and that's when Mr. Rugg hit me. I wasn't negligent. I had the right of way and did what I had to do to make the turn."*

**Judge:** *"Thank you both—you will get my decision in the mail."*

(The judge decided in favor of Jenna McClatchy and awarded her $3,612 plus court costs.)

# Landlord-Tenant Cases

B y using small claims court, tenants in most states can sue for money damages over a whole host of landlord violations—failure to return a cleaning or damage deposit, invasion of the tenant's privacy, violation of the duty to provide safe and habitable premises, and rent control violations, to name but a few. In addition, a group of tenants or neighbors can individually (but simultaneously) sue a landlord who tolerates an illegal or even legal but highly annoying situation on the rental property. For example, if ten tenants sue a landlord who tolerates drug dealing for $7,500 each, the landlord would face $75,000 worth of lawsuits.

Although tenants initiate many cases, landlords can also use small claims court—for example, to sue a former tenant for damages done to the rental property. In fact, in states like California, landlords can collect overdue rent amounts exceeding the small claims limits. In some states, it's even possible for a landlord to use small claims court to evict a tenant. (See Appendix A for state-by-state information.) It's notable because it's an exception to the general rule that only money damage cases can be heard in small claims court—but it's an exception landlords might find hard to take advantage of, as discussed in "Evictions for Nonpayment of Rent," below.

---

### Further Reading on Landlord-Tenant Law

If it looks like you're heading toward small claims court, you'll want to consider using some of Nolo's other respected titles. Each recommended book provides detailed state-specific information on landlord-tenant law. You'll also find checklists and forms that will help you avoid disputes involving security deposits, housing code violations, late rent and rent withholding, inspections (tenants' privacy rights), discrimination, illicit tenant activity, and more.

- For tenants: *Every Tenant's Legal Guide*, by Marcia Stewart and Attorneys Janet Portman and Ann O'Connell.
- For property owners and managers: *Every Landlord's Legal Guide*, by Marcia Stewart and Attorneys Janet Portman and Ann O'Connell.
- Also, at www.nolo.com/legal-encyclopedia/landlords, you'll find charts with state laws, security deposit limits, rent rules, and articles on topics such as evictions.

!  CAUTION
**Check whether COVID-19 laws are in effect.** Many of the laws discussed below were altered during the coronavirus pandemic. Verify that all moratoriums have been lifted before relying on the information below. For the latest information, read "Emergency Bans on Evictions and Other Tenant Protections Related to Coronavirus" at www.nolo.com/evictions-ban.

## Security Deposit Cases

Disagreements in this area account for a large percentage of the landlord-tenant disputes in small claims court. Problems involving security deposits often arise like this:

- the tenant moves out, making what the tenant considers to be a reasonable effort to clean the unit
- the landlord keeps all or part of the deposit, stating that the unit was left damaged or dirty, and
- the tenant is furious, claiming the landlord is illegally withholding the deposit.

If the tenant and landlord can't reach a compromise, the tenant's best remedy is to sue the landlord for the money withheld, leaving it up to the small claims court judge to decide who is telling the truth.

Whether you're a tenant filing a case or a landlord defending one, it's important to understand state law on security deposits.

## State Deposit Laws

State law often dictates how large a deposit a landlord can require, how the landlord can use it, when the landlord must return it, and more. In some states, landlords must offer a "pre–move-out inspection" that informs the tenant of any damage or uncleanliness the landlord expects fixed. Inspecting the premises before the tenant leaves gives the tenant time to address any problems and avoid a deduction.

In most states, it is up to the landlord to prove that dirty or damaged conditions justify keeping all or part of a deposit. Often, state law also provides that if a deposit is not returned within a specified time after the tenant moves out (usually somewhere between 14 and 30 days, depending on the state), the tenant is entitled to receive the entire deposit back.

If the landlord acts in bad faith by unjustifiably withholding a deposit in violation of the law, and despite requests to return it, the tenant might be entitled to extra "punitive" damages over and above the withheld amount. Whether the tenant gets the punitive damages would be up to the judge. Each state's rule should specifically describe the conduct needed to support a request for punitive damages. Go to www.nolo.com/legal-encyclopedia/state-landlord-tenant-laws for more information.

## Deposit Cases From the Tenant's Point of View

How should a tenant prepare a case involving a landlord's failure to return a deposit? Ideally, preparation should start when you move in. Any damaged or dirty conditions should be noted in the lease or rental agreement or an inventory or checklist signed by you and the landlord (some states require an inventory by law). You should also take photographs or videos of substandard conditions and have neighbors or friends look the unit over. When you move out and clean up, you should do much the same thing— take photos or videos, have friends (or another tenant in the building) check the unit, keep receipts for cleaning materials, and, once the home is cleaned up, try and get the landlord to agree in writing that it is in satisfactory condition or that the earlier noted areas of damage are all there is.

Now let's assume that you are a tenant, and your former landlord has not returned your $900 security deposit even though you moved out more than three weeks ago, having paid all your rent, given proper notice, and "passed" the move-out inspection. Start by writing the landlord a letter like the one shown below.

**Sample Letter Demanding Security Deposit**

October 25, 20xx

Adam Anderson
Anderson Realty Co.
10 Rose Street
Anytown, [state] 12345

Dear Mr. Anderson:

As you know, until September 30, 20xx, I resided in Apartment #4 at 1700 Walnut Street and regularly paid my rent to your office. When I moved out, I left the unit cleaner than it was when I moved in. During the move-out inspection, you told me the rental unit looked fine.

I have not received my $900 security deposit or accounting of funds to date. I'm confident that you're aware of [*insert state law § xxxx*] requiring you to return my deposit or provide an accounting within [insert period] and that knowingly failing to do so constitutes bad faith. Please be aware that if you don't comply within one week, I will take action to recover the $900 deposit plus interest and any penalties allowed by law.

Sincerely,

*Latoya Shields*
Latoya Shields
456 Main Street
Anytown, [state] 12345

CAUTION
**Be specific when requesting the return of a deposit.** If your landlord has returned only part of your security deposit, deducting more for cleaning or damages than you thought was reasonable, your demand letter should detail why you believe the deductions were improper. For example, if the landlord says a door was damaged and cost $200 to fix, you might be able to prove that the work could have been done competently for $75. If you don't get a satisfactory response from your landlord, consider filing your case.

## Who Should Tenants Sue in Security Deposit Cases?

A tenant who knows who owns the building should sue this person or business. However, sometimes it is hard to know whom to sue because the tenant often pays rent to a manager or an agent instead of the owner. Multiple occupancy buildings must post ownership information on the premises in most states or list the owner's name and agent for service of process on the lease or rental agreement. If you don't know who owns your unit, you are probably safe suing the person you pay your rent to.

On court day, a well-prepared tenant should show up in court with as many of the following pieces of evidence as possible:

- Date-stamped photos or a video of the apartment showing how it looked when you moved in, including any dirt or damage that already existed. If you don't have these, it's not fatal, but it will help if you do.
- A copy of the pre–move-out inspection report, if completed.
- Date-stamped photos or video showing clean conditions when you moved out.
- A copy of an inventory of conditions upon moving in and moving out, signed by the landlord and tenant.
- Receipts or canceled checks for any cleaning supplies used in the final cleanup.

- A copy of your written lease or rental agreement.
- A copy of a demand letter to the landlord showing that you made the required demand before suing.
- Witnesses familiar with the property who will testify that it was in good shape when you left. Testimony or written statements of people who scrubbed an oven or toilet will be helpful, as will a witness who saw the unit wasn't in perfect order when you moved in or that damage already existed.

## The Landlord's Perspective: Defending Deposit Cases

Your best protection against spending hours haggling over security deposits is to follow the law precisely when a tenant moves out. It is your responsibility to return the deposit within the number of days legally required or explain why you are withholding some or all of it. But no matter how meticulous you are about accounting for your tenants' deposits, you might be sued by a tenant who disagrees with your assessment of the cost of cleaning or repairs. This section explains how landlords can defend themselves in tenant-initiated small claims court cases.

Within the time limit set by your state's law, after inspecting the premises and documenting any dirty or damaged conditions, send the tenant a written itemization of deductions for repairs, cleaning, and unpaid rent. Include details on the costs of any cleaning or damage repair, including a reasonable hourly charge if you or your employees do any necessary cleaning or repainting, and an itemization if work is done by an outside firm. Keep receipts for costs of repairs such as new carpets or repainting. If you use an outside cleaning service, ask the service whether they will testify in small claims court, if necessary, or at least write a letter describing what they did in detail in case the tenant contests your deposit deductions.

Before your court hearing, you should gather all the evidence you have demonstrating that the premises needed cleaning or was damaged. It's important to understand that you, the landlord, have the legal burden of proving these facts. If you fail to do that, the tenant will win. In other words, all a former tenant must prove is that a residential tenancy existed, that they paid you a deposit, and that you didn't return all of it.

To make a winning case, a landlord should show up in court with as much evidence as possible, including any of the following when available:

- Date-stamped photos or a video of the premises before the tenant moved in showing the unit was clean and undamaged.
- Photos or a video showing a mess or damage at the pre–move-out inspection and after the tenant left.
- Copies of inventory sheets signed by the landlord and tenant detailing the rental unit condition when the tenant moved in and out. (These are particularly valuable if they show that an item that is now broken was in good shape when the tenant moved in.)
- A copy of your written lease or rental agreement.
- An itemization of hours spent by you, or your repair or cleaning people, working on the unit, complete with the hourly costs for the work.
- A copy of the written security deposit itemization(s) (pre–move-out and post–move-out) you sent the tenant, with details about the deductions.
- Any damaged items that can be brought into the courtroom (for example, a curtain with a cigarette burn).
- Receipts for professional cleaning or repair services.
- One or more witnesses who saw the property just after the tenant left, and who will testify that the unit was dirty or that items were damaged. People who helped in the subsequent cleaning or repair, or the new tenant who saw the unit before cleaning could be helpful witnesses. Written statements or declarations under penalty of perjury can be used, but they aren't as effective as live testimony. A sample written statement is shown below.

## The Landlord's Perspective: Suing When the Deposit Is Depleted

Most of the security deposit cases in small claims court involve tenants arguing for their return, and landlords defending their use of the money. Occasionally, landlords go to small claims court as plaintiffs when the tenant has left damage or dirty conditions that the security deposit doesn't cover. For example, if your tenant leaves you with $2,000 worth of damage and cleaning, but the deposit comes to only $1,500, you'll be out of pocket $500 unless you sue.

**Sample Declaration**

---

**Declaration of Paul Stallone**

I, Paul Stallone, declare:

1. I am employed at A & B Maintenance Company, a contract cleaning and maintenance service located at 123 Abrego Street, Tucson, Arizona. Gina Cabarga, the owner of an apartment complex at 456 Seventh Street, Tucson, Arizona, is one of our accounts.

2. On May 1, 20xx, Gina asked me to go to the premises at 456 Seventh Street, Apartment 8, to shampoo the carpets. When I entered the premises, I noticed a strong odor, part of which seemed like stale cigarette smoke. An odor also seemed to come from the carpet.

3. When I began using a steam carpet cleaner on the living room carpet, I noticed a strong smell of urine. I stopped the steam cleaner, moved to a dry corner of the carpet, and pulled it from the floor. I then saw a yellow color on the normally white foam-rubber pad beneath the carpet. I also smelled a strong urine odor, apparently caused by a pet (probably a cat) having urinated on the carpet. On further examination of the carpet, I noticed similar stains and odors throughout the carpet and pad.

4. In my opinion, the living room carpet and foam-rubber pad underneath need to be removed and replaced and the floor should be sanded and sealed.

5. I declare under penalty of perjury under the laws of the State of Arizona that the foregoing is true and correct.

Dated: June 15, 20xx

Signature: _____
              Paul Stallone

Few landlords pursue tenants in small claims court over relatively small amounts for three good reasons:

- they can't find the tenant
- the amount at issue isn't worth their time and trouble, or
- they know the tenant is "judgment proof" and won't be able to pay.

But if you know where to find the tenant, the tenant has a job or another source of money, and you're out a significant amount, you might want to file.

A plaintiff will prepare a case much the same way as you would prepare a defense to deposit withholding, described in the section above. You'll need the same kind of evidence—proof of damage caused by this tenant along with invoices from a repairperson or cleaning establishment documenting the money you had to spend to deal with the mess. You'll also need to prove that you collected a specific sum as a security deposit. Suppose the security deposit available to you, minus proper deductions, does not cover the legitimate expenses you incurred in cleaning or repairing, and you wrote the tenant a demand letter requesting those additional expenses. In that case, you'll have met your burden. In that case, it will be up to the judge to determine whether your expenses were needed or were part of the regular refurbishing required due to tenants' normal wear and tear.

## Unpaid Rent and Former Tenants

Landlords sometimes go to small claims court to sue former tenants—those who have already moved out—for unpaid rent when the security deposit isn't sufficient to cover the amount. These cases arise when one of the following is true:

- the tenancy is month-to-month, and the tenant has left without giving the required 30 days' notice, or
- the tenant has a lease, but has broken it by leaving before its term is up.

CAUTION

**Take care of your reputation.** If you are a landlord with many rental units and regularly use a local small claims court, make sure that every case you bring is a good one. You do not want to lose your credibility with the court by appearing unfair or poorly prepared.

## Unpaid Rent and Month-to-Month Tenants

Month-to-month tenants must give at least the legally required number of days' notice of their intent to move out and must pay rent during those days. For example, if the notice period is 30 days, and the landlord receives notice on the 20th, that tenancy will end 30 days later. If the tenant pays rent on the first of the month, they will owe prorated rent for 20 days of the following month. If the tenant doesn't pay and simply moves out, the landlord could sue for those 20 days' worth of rent, assuming the security deposit is too small or already depleted due to needed repairs or cleaning.

Landlords in these situations rarely find it sensible to go to court over a month's (or less) rent unless their total losses are augmented by having to deal with significant damage as well. If you are a landlord and find yourself in this position, follow the advice above for preparing a case when you sue over damage or uncleanliness. You'll need to also prove that the rent was not paid, by showing that your rent ledger, for example, does not include an entry for that month.

## When the Tenant Has No Defense

Often the tenant has moved away and doesn't bother to show up in court. If this happens, the landlord briefly states their case and will win by default if credible. (See Chapter 15.) Sometimes the tenant does show up but fails to present a defense—hoping, perhaps, to pay the judgment in installments. (See Chapter 24.) Again, the landlord should easily prevail.

The landlord should bring the lease or rental agreement to court and state the periods when rent was due but not paid. Nothing else is required unless the tenant presents a defense, as discussed below.

## Unpaid Rent and Tenants With Leases

Tenants who leave without legal justification before the expiration of a fixed-term lease and refuse to pay the remaining rent due have "broken the lease." The tenant is liable for the rent for the entire lease term (except where the landlord breaches an important lease provision first). However, most states limit the tenant's responsibility by imposing a duty on the landlord to "mitigate damages." Stated in plain English, the landlord has a legal duty to limit financial loss by finding a new tenant as soon as reasonably possible.

What all this adds up to is that a landlord whose tenant breaks a lease with no legally recognized reason is entitled to:

- the remaining rent due under the lease, minus
- any portion of that amount that the landlord can reasonably obtain by rerenting the unit, plus
- any reasonable advertising expenses incurred in finding a new tenant, plus
- charges for necessary repair and cleaning after the tenant moves out.

A landlord can deduct the total cost of these items from the tenant's security deposit (see "Security Deposit Cases," above) and sue for the remainder in small claims court. (See Chapter 4 for a discussion of the "mitigation of damages" concept.)

## Former Tenants' Defenses to Unpaid Rent

Lease-breaking tenants might have a defense to a landlord's suit for unpaid rent—rent the landlord would have collected had the tenant stayed in the rental. Landlords file these lawsuits when there's considerable time left on the lease, and their reasonable efforts, if legally required (see the section above), have failed to produce a new tenant (perhaps because the market is soft or the rental just isn't that attractive). As explained above, landlords usually don't bother filing suit unless they can find the tenant, have some reason to think they can collect if they win, and are confident that the tenant has no legal defense for failing to stay through the end of the lease.

Tenants might have legal justification for breaking a lease and leaving early—for example, if the tenant is the victim of domestic violence or is entering active military service. The most common defense to breaking a lease is the tenant's claim that the rental was uninhabitable under state law. Landlords must offer and maintain "fit and habitable" premises, and if they fail to do so, their failure justifies the tenant's lease breaking. To successfully raise this defense, the tenants must prove that they did not cause the problem themselves, the defects were serious enough to threaten health or safety or constituted a lack of basic services, and the landlord had been given a reasonable amount of time to fix the problem.

## Tenants Suing Cotenants for Unpaid Rent

Cotenants are two or more people who rent property together and sign the same rental agreement or lease. Each cotenant shares the same rights and responsibilities under the lease or rental agreement. For example, each cotenant, regardless of agreements the tenants make among themselves, is liable to the landlord for the entire amount of the rent. But being cotenants together does not establish one cotenant's legal right to sue the other cotenant for his share of the rent. The cotenants must have a separate agreement between them that specifies how much each will contribute to the total rent. A cotenant who doesn't pay the amount agreed to can be sued by another cotenant in small claims court.

> EXAMPLE: James and Helen sign a month-to-month rental agreement for an $800 apartment. They agree to each pay half of the rent. After three months, James moves out without notifying Helen or the owner, Laura. As one of the two cotenants, Helen is still legally obligated to pay all the rent but might be able to recover James's share by suing him in small claims court. Laura, the owner, can serve Helen, the tenant, with a notice to pay the whole rent or leave (or face eviction).

## Rent Control Cases

Renters who live in New York and California cities with rent control laws can sue a landlord who charges illegally high rent for the excess rent charged, and a punitive amount as well (often several times the overcharge).

# Drug Dealing and Other Crimes

Landlords have some degree of legal responsibility to provide secure housing. This means they must take reasonable steps to:

- protect tenants from would-be assailants, thieves, and other criminals
- protect tenants from the criminal acts of fellow tenants
- warn tenants about dangerous situations they are aware of but cannot eliminate, and
- protect the neighborhood from their tenants' illegal activities, such as drug dealing.

Landlords who don't live up to this responsibility can be liable for any injuries or losses that befall tenants as a result.

Also, a tenant or neighbor can sue the landlord for maintaining or allowing a "nuisance"—a serious and persistent condition that adversely affects the tenant's (or neighbor's) enjoyment of the property—even if no physical injury occurs. For example, a tenant plagued by the stench of a pile of garbage because the landlord hasn't provided enough garbage cans for the apartment building can sue the landlord for the annoyance and inconvenience of putting up with the smell.

# Tenants Band Together

Increasingly, tenants have gotten together to hold landlords accountable for failing to fulfill their legal responsibility to maintain rental property in a habitable condition. For example, tenants and homeowners have extended this group action approach to sue landlords for failing to protect tenants and neighbors from drug dealers, neighborhood gangs, or other tenants creating excessive noise, running an illegal business, or throwing trash in common areas. Similarly, homeowners have filed multiple suits to collect damages from neighbors who allow their teenage children to create disturbances that keep the neighborhood awake all night.

As noted in "Class Actions (Group Lawsuits)" in Chapter 7, this technique of using small claims court for groups of individual actions became popular after a neighborhood group successfully banded together to bring hundreds of small claims suits against the City of San Francisco to recover damages for the nuisance created in their neighborhood by the noise from the city airport. (*City & Co. of S.F. v. Small Claims Division, San Mateo Co.*, 190 Cal.Rptr. 340 (1983).)

Despite the fact that this approach is legal and effective, some judges have greeted the filing of many simultaneous lawsuits with verbal disapproval. Nonetheless, some claimants in such cases have been successful in obtaining a quick and inexpensive resolution of their neighborhood disputes when other channels for solving their problems had failed.

One problem that often arises in this type of case is how much to sue for. Assuming the annoyance is serious and persistent and the landlord does not take reasonable steps to reduce or eliminate it after receiving a written demand to do so, it often makes sense for each claimant to sue for the small claims maximum and let the judge scale it back if the court feels that a lower amount is appropriate.

## The Obnoxious Landlord

Typically, tenants have problems with landlords who are overly involved with their property. Smaller landlords tend to develop this problem to a greater extent than do the larger, more commercial ones. Nosy landlords are always hanging around or coming by, trying to invite themselves in to look around and generally being pests. Also, a tenant might run into a manager or an owner who sexually harasses tenants or has bullying tendencies.

A landlord or manager who is difficult or unpleasant to deal with can make a tenant's life miserable. There are no laws that protect a tenant from a landlord's disagreeable personality, and when tenants have no lease, they are especially unprotected from all but the most outrageous invasions of privacy, sexual harassment, or trespass (discussed just below). However, if the landlord or manager's conduct is truly obnoxious, courts in some states recognize that tenants have a right to sue for the intentional infliction of emotional distress. (See Chapter 4 for advice on determining the dollar amount of a suit for emotional or mental distress.)

# The Landlord's Right of Entry and the Tenant's Right of Privacy

Tenants are easily and understandably upset when they feel their privacy is invaded. Landlords, on the other hand, have a legal right to enter their rental units in certain situations. Sometimes a tenant's need to be left alone and a landlord's need to enter can cause conflict. When it does, it is important that both parties understand their rights.

About half the states have access laws specifying when and under what circumstances landlords can enter tenants' premises. Typically, there are only four broad situations in which a landlord can legally enter while a tenant is still in residence. They are:

- to deal with an emergency
- to make needed repairs (or assess the need for them)
- to show the property to prospective new tenants or purchasers, or
- when the tenant gives permission (for example, invites the landlord to enter).

In most instances (emergencies and invitations by tenant excepted), a landlord can enter only during "normal business hours" (usually considered to be 9 a.m. to 5 p.m. Monday through Friday) and then only after "reasonable notice," which is presumed to be 24 hours.

If a landlord does not follow these rules, a tenant's first step is to politely ask the landlord to do so. If violations persist, a follow-up letter is in order. If this doesn't help, it is possible to sue in small claims court if the landlord's conduct persists. The specific claims that a tenant might make against a landlord in such a situation include: invasion of privacy, trespass, harassment, violation of the tenant's right to enjoy their home free from the landlord's unreasonable interference, or intentional or negligent infliction of emotional distress.

A tenant who sues a landlord for entering the tenant's unit without permission might have a hard time proving much in the way of money damages. (A judge will want to know why the landlord's improper entry justifies a good-sized monetary award.) However, if a tenant can show a repeated pattern of trespass (and the fact that the tenant asked the landlord to stop it) or even one clear example of outrageous conduct, the tenant might be able to get a substantial monetary recovery.

As a tenant who feels you've been trespassed upon, how much do you sue for? There is no easy answer, but one approach is to keep or reconstruct a list (or diary) of each incident, complete with a fair amount of detail about the distress it caused you. Then read it over and assign a reasonable dollar value to each hour of distress. For example, if a landlord's repeated illegal entries into your house caused you 75 hours of serious upset, and you value your time at $25 per hour, you would sue for $1,875.

If you are a landlord being sued, but believe that your entry or conduct was legal, you should be able to document this. For example, if a tenant claims that you entered their apartment without 24-hour notice, then you should be able to show a copy of a formal 24-hour notice to enter to make needed repairs that you sent to your tenant (notes you took documenting related phone conversations would also be useful). You could also ask a repairperson or cleaning service to testify (either in person or in writing; see Chapter 14) as to the date and time that person entered the rental unit, which should be at least the legally required amount of time after you delivered the notice. Or, you might be able to explain that the urgent nature of the repair required you to enter sooner.

But what if you are a landlord whose tenant repeatedly refuses to let you or your employees enter during normal business hours for one of the legitimate reasons cited above? In such a situation, you can legally enter anyway, provided you do so in a peaceful manner. Bring someone along who can later act as a witness in case the tenant claims some personal property is missing.

## Discrimination

Federal laws make it illegal for a landlord to refuse to rent to a tenant or to engage in any other kind of discrimination (such as requiring higher rent or more significant deposits) on the basis of any group characteristic such as race, color, religion, national origin, familial status (includes families with children younger than 18 and pregnant women), disability, and gender (includes sexual harassment). In some states and localities, additional characteristics, such as gender identity and sexual orientation, are protected. A landlord who attempts to or actually terminates someone's tenancy for a discriminatory reason, or discriminates in providing services such as the use of the pool or another common area, is also acting illegally.

The discriminated-against tenant can use the landlord's behavior as a defense to an eviction lawsuit as well as a basis for suing the landlord for monetary compensation and an order directing the landlord to stop the discriminatory behavior. Even an innocent owner whose agent or manager discriminates without the owner's knowledge can be sued and found liable. A landlord who unlawfully discriminates against a tenant or prospective tenant could end up in federal or state court, including small claims court, or before a state or federal housing agency, facing a tenant's allegations of discrimination.

Most of these cases involve amounts in excess of the small claims maximum. If you've experienced discrimination, your most effective remedy is to file an administrative claim through the Department of Housing and Urban Development (HUD), or to sue the offending landlord in formal court. For more information on how to spot and prove discrimination, see *Every Tenant's Legal Guide*, by Marcia Stewart and Attorneys Janet Portman and Ann O'Connell (Nolo). To find a lawyer who handles this type of lawsuit, contact a tenants' rights or civil rights organization in your area.

## Evictions for Nonpayment of Rent

In some states, it is legal to do some types of evictions (known technically as "unlawful detainer," "summary dispossess," or "forcible entry and detainer," depending on the state) in small claims court. A few larger cities even have separate landlord-tenant courts that amount to small claims courts for this specific purpose.

Landlords should have a cheap and straightforward way to free themselves of tenants who don't pay their rent. But in states that don't have special landlord-tenant courts, the only practical method is to file an unlawful detainer action in formal court. Traditionally, this has required the expense of a lawyer, though more and more landlords are learning to handle their eviction actions.

Formal court, though less friendly to nonlawyers than small claims court, might be preferable when you have a choice. The small claims court rules, even in those states where evictions are allowed, tend to limit a landlord's rights when it comes to getting the tenant out in the minimum time and getting a judgment for the maximum amount of rent and other damages. In a few states' small claims courts, a losing tenant even has an automatic right to appeal the eviction judgment and to stay in the rental unit while the appeal is pending, despite the fact that the tenant isn't paying rent and hasn't posted bond.

So before you bring an eviction action in small claims court, find the answers to the following questions by reviewing your state's small claims court rules (see Chapter 25 for tips on painless legal research):

- If you win an eviction order, can you get the sheriff or marshal to enforce it immediately?
- Can a defendant who appeals stay in the dwelling while the appeal is pending?
- Can you sue for enough damages to fully or at least mostly cover your legitimate claim for back rent and damages to the premises?
- If the defendant can stay in the dwelling during an appeal, must money in the form of a bond be posted that will go to you to cover lost rent if the appeal fails?

If you decide to go ahead with an eviction in small claims court, you must prove that the rent was not paid and that a pay-or-quit notice was properly served. Bring a copy of this notice to court along with an appropriately completed Proof of Service form. The fact that a tenant is suffering from some hardship, such as illness, poverty, or birth of a child is not a defense to failure to pay rent. Possible tenant defenses are discussed above. In most states, the tenant can claim that the rental property was uninhabitable. But remember, a tenant cannot legally raise the existence of a defect for the first time on the day of the court hearing. The landlord must be given reasonable notice that a defect exists before the tenant withholds rent or makes repairs.

# Miscellaneous Cases

B y now you should have a pretty clear idea of how a small claims case should be researched and presented. The facts of each situation will vary, but the general approach will not. This chapter will briefly discuss a few of the common types of cases not covered in the previous few chapters. Unfortunately, given the variety of fact situations that can result in small claims disputes, it still might not cover your problem in detail. You'll want to adapt the approaches outlined in Chapters 13–20 as necessary.

## Clothing (Alteration and Cleaning)

It's surprising how often you'll encounter people in small claims court clutching an injured garment. All too often, people react with a level of indignation out of proportion to the monetary loss when a favorite item is damaged. Unfortunately—no matter how much we love a favorite coat, dress, or sweater—winning a significant amount of money in a case involving clothing is challenging. That's because—as also discussed in Chapter 4—while it's often relatively easy to prove that the defendant ruined your garment, most used clothing simply isn't worth much. Remember: You're only legally entitled to the fair market value of the item of clothing just before it was damaged or destroyed, not to its replacement value. You'll need luck and an unusually sympathetic judge to get more.

Here are some ways to handle a clothing case:

- Bring the damaged clothing to court. It's hard for a tailor to say much in their own defense when confronted with a coat two sizes too big or featuring three sleeves.
- Be ready to prove the original purchase price with a receipt, canceled check, advertisement, or credit card statement. If the item was purchased at a pricey store, let the judge know where.
- If you only wore the damaged or destroyed item a few times, tell the judge. For example, if you paid $500 for a good-quality suit jacket you planned to wear to work 50 to 100 times over the next three years, and a dry cleaner screwed it up after just five wearings, try to get the judge to value it at close to $500.

- Be sure that the person you are suing (cleaners or alteration service) really caused the problem. As noted in the example of the suede coat in Chapter 2, some problems that develop during cleaning or alterations might be the responsibility of the manufacturer.

💡 **TIP**

**Don't let the cleaners take you to the laundry!** Cleaners are particularly apt to offer "proof" from "independent testing laboratories" that the damage caused to your garment during cleaning was really the fault of the manufacturer. Because these labs work almost exclusively for the dry-cleaning industry, the idea that they are independent is a joke. If you are faced with one of these reports, ask the defendant:

- "How much did you pay the testing lab for the report?"
- "How many times have you used the same testing lab before?"
- "How did you know about the testing lab (for example, does it place ads in dry cleaners' trade journals that say, 'Let us help you win in court')?"

## Dog-Related Cases

No question, dogs can be frustrating, especially to people who don't own dogs. As a result, lots of dog-related cases end up in small claims court. Because many of these involve neighbors who will benefit by maintaining or establishing a pleasant relationship, trying to work out the dispute through mediation is almost always a good first step. (See Chapter 6.) Also, before heading to court, check whether the dog-related incident is covered by the dog owner's homeowners' or other insurance policy.

## Dog Bites

Many states have dog-bite statutes that make dog owners liable for injuries their dogs cause—no ifs, ands, or buts. Some statutes cover only injuries occurring off the owner's property. Also, some statutes cover only bites, whereas others apply to any injury (for example, the dog jumps on you, scratches you, or knocks you over) or property damage (for example, the dog digs up your rose garden). Do a little research online to find out whether your state has a dog-bite statute. If it does, your task in court could be a lot easier.

If your state doesn't have a dog-bite statute, the old common law rule probably applies. You'll have to prove that the owner was aware of, or should have been aware of, the fact that the dog was likely to injure someone or damage property. So, if a dog bites you and you show that the owner knew the dog had snarled, snapped, and lunged at people before but let the dog run free anyway, the owner is probably liable for the damage caused by the dog (unless you provoked it).

Also, be ready to prove the extent of the injury, where it occurred, and the amount of your losses. As discussed in Chapter 4, this consists of the value of any uncompensated time you took off from work, out-of-pocket medical expenses, property damage (for example, a ripped coat), and the value of your pain and suffering.

## Barking Dogs

City or county ordinances often regulate the problem of barking dogs. A general noise ordinance covers dogs in many places, but sometimes there is a separate ordinance for animals. Look up the city or county law to determine the specifics and whether your government will help enforce it. Also, the owner of a barking dog that interferes with your ability to enjoy your home has committed a civil wrong (tort) called a "nuisance." As with any other tort, the dog's owner is responsible for compensating people harmed by the nuisance. (For more information about suing someone for causing a nuisance, see Chapter 2.)

If you can't work something out through negotiation or mediation and you file in small claims court, you will face two main challenges:

**Establishing that the barking dog has damaged your ability to enjoy your property.** One good way to do this is to get several neighbors to write letters or, better yet, testify in court to the fact that the dog is a noisy menace. (Don't forget to bring a copy of the local dog-barking ordinance to establish that the owner is also a lawbreaker.) Also, if your city has cited the dog's owner for violating the noise ordinance, make sure the judge knows about it.

**Proving money damages.** Establishing financial losses caused by a noisy dog is a subjective task. One approach is to try to put a monetary value on each hour of your lost sleep. For example, if you can convince the judge that each hour you lie awake is worth a certain amount (perhaps $10 or even $20), your damages will quickly add up. As a backup to your oral testimony about how miserable it is to be denied sleep by a howling canine, keep a log of the dates and times you are awakened and present it to the judge. In one case, six neighbors kept a log for 30 days detailing how often a particular dog barked after 10 p.m. The number, more than 300, was influential in convincing the judge to give the plaintiffs a good-sized judgment.

# Damage to Real Estate (Land and Buildings)

If you own real property (land and structures) that has been damaged by another person or by a force of nature, the chances are that you won't turn first to small claims court to cover your loss. That's because virtually all landowners have property insurance, primarily because most owners have a mortgage or a loan secured by the land. Mortgagors and lenders will not finance a purchase of real property or make a loan secured by land unless the borrower obtains and maintains sufficient property insurance. Even those owners without mortgages or loans have property insurance to protect their investment.

Property insurance comes in three basic types: basic coverage, covering just a few perils or causes; broad coverage, which covers more perils; and all-risk coverage, which covers all risks except specified ones. All three types exclude damage from nuclear hazards, earthquakes, and floods, though you can sometimes buy separate policies to cover some excluded perils. All property insurance comes with a deductible—the higher your deductible, the lower your premium. And all policies include a policy limit—the most that the insurance company will pay for a loss.

Even though you have property insurance that will cover the damage your property has suffered, you might still have small claims court in your future. Here's how that can happen: Suppose the first floor of your commercial building is damaged when your neighbor's sewer line ruptures. Most property policies will cover damages in this situation even if they don't cover a flood, which is, in insurance lingo, the result of a "sudden inundation" of water from the sky. In this case, let's assume that your property insurance covers the $10,000 worth of damage to the walls, floors, and basement, but you've had to pay your $1,500 deductible.

Your insurance company has the right to go after the neighbor to recoup the money it's paid you. With a large claim, they'll do just that—and fortunately, they will also demand your deductible. If they collect, they will reimburse the $1,500 deductible.

But not all claims are worth pursuing. The smaller the claim, the less willing the insurance company will be to go after the responsible party. For instance, suppose the damage amounted to only $2,500. Your company would be out-of-pocket only $1,000 ($2,500 minus your $1,500 deductible). It might not be worth the insurance company's time to pursue your neighbor over such a small sum. If you need the $1,500 for repairs, you might want to try to recoup it in small claims court.

To recover from your neighbor, you'd have to convince the judge that the neighbor carelessly or negligently maintained his sewer pipes. Did he know that they were already leaking? Did he know that they were at risk of breaking at any time? Or were they relatively new and failed because they were installed improperly—in other words, the neighbor had no reason to suspect they'd break? The more you can show that your neighbor knew or should have known that this was an accident waiting to happen, the more likely you'd prevail.

## Defamation

Many states have placed an outright ban on bringing libel and slander cases in small claims court. However, even in states where you can bring a defamation case in small claims court, judges don't always take them seriously because most untrue statements don't result in serious damage.

To prevail, you need to show that the statement made about you was false, that others saw or heard it and understood that it was about you. Most importantly, you must demonstrate that the statement significantly harmed your reputation. If you are a public figure (politician, actor, media celebrity), you not only need to show that the statement was false, but also that the defendant either knew it was false or made it in reckless disregard of whether or not it was true.

In short, the fact that the defendant's statement was just plain wrong isn't enough to make you a winner if you are a public figure.

> **EXAMPLE:** Your neighbor tells everyone in the neighborhood that you are an idiot. You wonder if you have grounds to sue. Probably not, because chances are you haven't been harmed—after all, everyone in the neighborhood knows your neighbor is odd, so it's probable that no one has taken his comments seriously. However, if he writes and distributes a leaflet all over town that falsely accuses you of having sex with minors, your chances of winning are much better. There are several reasons why: Being accused of a sex crime is much more likely to damage your reputation than being called an "idiot"; the fact that the defamatory statement is printed on a flyer makes it easier to prove; and the wider distribution of the printed fliers makes it more likely that at least some people who receive the flyer won't know that the writer isn't very reliable and might take it seriously.

> RESOURCE
> **There are many intricacies to defamation law.** To learn more, start with online resources such as the Legal Information Institute–Cornell Law School website (www.law.cornell.edu). You'll also find more information in a public law library— ask the librarian for help.

## Online Transactions

Not only does everyone love the Internet, but technology has changed how we live, work, and communicate. We shop at home and have packages delivered to the front door. We create websites for our small businesses and communicate with friends and family through social media. And some of us do much of our work online.

But what about when something goes wrong? The package doesn't arrive or is different than advertised. Or perhaps you agree via email to write a restaurant review for a local magazine, and you email the article to the editor but never receive payment. Are these types of problems any different from the face-to-face disputes we've discussed in the rest of this book? Can you use small claims court to get compensation from a person or business you've dealt with only over the Internet?

The answer is, maybe. As with face-to-face disputes, your ability to sue in small claims court for a wrong you suffered through an online transaction depends on where the person or business you want to sue is located. As you recall from Chapter 9, you cannot automatically sue someone in small claims court when you have suffered an economic loss. The court must have power over that particular party, which depends on where the person or business lives, works, or has an office. If your web-related dispute is with a person or business located in your state, then you shouldn't have a problem. However, only under specific circumstances can you sue a nonresident in your state's small claims court.

If the person or business does not regularly do business with state residents online (in other words, if the transaction at issue is a one-time event), then you will not be able to sue in your local small claims court, because that person does not live, work, or regularly do business in-state. It is therefore fundamentally unfair to ask that party to travel to your state to defend itself from a lawsuit. If, however, the person or business regularly transacts with online customers in your state, you should be able to bring your lawsuit in your local small claims court.

When it comes to transacting business online, what does it mean to "regularly do business" in a state? The courts are actively discussing this issue, and different judges have different opinions, but here are some basic guidelines:

- Does the website conduct direct sales online (versus referring customers to offline distributors, retail stores, or other resellers)?
- At the time of the transaction, did the person or business know what state you were a resident of—for example, did you fill out a form with your address or have a package shipped to you?
- Does the person or business do a lot of business with state residents?

- Does the person or business have any offices or employees in-state, even though its main "location" is on the Internet?
- Does the person or business send employees or agents into your state to conduct business?
- Does the person or business advertise or solicit business in your state?
- Does the person or business have a registered agent for service of process in your state? (See Chapter 11 for instructions on finding out if a business has a registered agent.)

If your answer to all or most of these questions is yes, then you will probably be successful in bringing your case against the party in your local small claims court. The only other issue is whether, as a condition of your transaction, you entered into a "Terms and Conditions" agreement with the website owner that establishes where you can bring a dispute.

> **EXAMPLE:** Mary Mallone lives in Vermont and sells handmade jewelry to customers worldwide through her website. She designed the website herself, and stores the computer files on a Web hosting company located in Colorado. She signed a contract for this service and regularly uploads new files from her computer in Vermont. The contract also requires that parties must resolve all disputes by arbitration in Colorado. When customers visit her website, they can make purchases online, and that information is temporarily stored on the Web hosting computers until it is transmitted to Mary. One day, due to the carelessness of a Web hosting employee, the office floods, ruins the servers, and Mary loses 15 jewelry orders. Can Mary sue the Web hosting company in Vermont for losing $2,000 worth of jewelry orders even though its offices are in Colorado?
>
> No. The contract establishes where all disputes must be brought. Mary will have to take her case to an arbitrator in Colorado.

An online business can also be subject to jurisdiction for purposefully causing an injury in the state. If someone uses the Internet to cause an injury in one state, the person causing the damage can be hauled into court in the state where the injury occurred. In cases where the connection between the activity and the injury is not completely clear, courts also look for evidence that the activity was "purposefully directed" at the resident of the forum state or that the person causing the injury had contacts with the state.

**EXAMPLE:** James lives in California. He buys new gears for his brand new $3,000 bicycle from a bicycle parts distributor on eBay, Will Wheely. Will, who is based in Nevada, sells almost all his inventory via eBay. The gears are defective, and James crashes, ruining the bicycle. James finds out that Will Wheely bought the gears from Big Gear, Inc., a bicycle parts manufacturer in Florida that does occasional business in California. James later learns that both Will and Big Gear were aware that the gears had a defect. Can James sue either Will Wheely or Big Gear in California small claims court to get compensation for his busted bike?

Yes. James can sue both Will and Big Gear in California. Even though neither potential defendant is a California resident, they each purposefully caused an injury in the state by placing the gears in commerce in California.

CAUTION

**Nonresidents will fight your attempt to sue them in your state's small claims court.** It's a tremendous hassle for a nonresident to travel to defend a lawsuit, which is why the courts have strict rules stating that a person must already do regular business in a state in order to be sued there. (See Chapter 9 for information on how a nonresident defendant might challenge such a lawsuit.)

---

### Consumer Complaints About Internet Transactions

If an online transaction goes wrong, you might consider filing an official complaint against the person or business, either in addition to or instead of filing a lawsuit. The Federal Trade Commission accepts complaints about consumer Internet transactions. Visit www.ftc.gov and go to "File a Consumer Complaint."

# Disputes Between Small Businesses

More small business owners are turning to small claims court to settle disputes between businesses. Small claims court offers speed and cost efficiency, especially in business-friendly states.

A surprising variety of businesspeople use small claims court for small business disputes. They include:

- A dentist dissatisfied with a dental equipment wholesaler who passed off slightly used equipment as new.
- An architect who wasn't paid for drawing preliminary plans for a small retail complex when the development failed to get financing.
- A landscape designer who tried to enforce an oral agreement for the additional fees incurred when a client made changes to the final plans.
- An author who claimed that her publisher had taken too long to publish her book.
- A client who claimed that his lawyer's incompetence was a prime reason he had to pay too much to settle a case.

In this chapter you'll learn more about using small claims court for disputes between businesses. Typically, these matters involve work done poorly, late, or not at all. Cases involving the failure to pay a bill are covered in Chapter 18.

## Remember: You Didn't Always Hate the Other Guy

Although the disputes listed above seem very different, they all have one thing in common: In each situation, the disputing parties previously enjoyed a friendly business or personal relationship. And in each case, at least part of the reason the plaintiff brought the dispute to court was that the plaintiff was just plain mad at the defendant.

Disappointment is a significant factor driving many small business disputes. But feeling let down by the other party doesn't help you evaluate whether you have a good case. Nor does it help you prepare for court or collect your money should you win. Because disappointment can get in the way of clear thinking, your first job is to cool your emotions. If you are having trouble doing this, enlist help from someone whose decision-making skills you respect. After explaining both sides of the dispute, ask for an honest evaluation of the case's merits and whether it makes sense to take the case to court.

TIP
**Mediation might offer the best way to settle your dispute.** Assuming you do have a good case and the defendant is solvent, going to small claims court is a quick and cost-effective way to put dollars in your pocket. But like all courts, small claims court tends to polarize disputes and deepen enmities. In some circumstances —especially where business people will benefit from working together, or from at least being civil to each other in the future—attempting to arrive at a compromise settlement through mediation is a better initial choice. Keep in mind, however, that it is still an adversarial-type situation and that mediating a case does more to save litigation costs than relationships. (See Chapter 6 for more on mediation.)

## Organizing Your Case

When it comes to preparing for court, small business owners have two advantages over other litigants. First, as a matter of course, business people maintain sound filing systems for bids, contracts, customer correspondence, and a bookkeeping system that tracks payables and receivables—all of which are helpful when proving up a small claims case.

The second advantage is many businesspeople have natural organizational skills, which will be helpful when it comes to organizing facts into a coherent and convincing narrative. Of course, when one businessperson sues another, those advantages often cancel out, meaning that both sides are likely to be well organized and prepared.

Other sections of this book explain how to decide whether you have a good case (Chapter 2) and, assuming you do, how to prepare and present it in court (Chapters 13–21). Rather than repeat this information, the rest of this chapter will supplement it with material of particular interest to small businesses.

## Contracts—The Most Common Case

In the majority of business cases one business claims that the other has broken a contract. (See Chapter 2 for more on contract law.) If you're facing this issue, take a close look at any contract involved in your case. Specifically, ask yourself what were your obligations and expected benefits from the deal? What was the other person supposed to do and how was that person going to benefit?

Usual business practices and customs in a particular field are commonly viewed as being part of a contract and can be introduced as evidence in small claims court to support or thwart your case. You'll want to provide expert testimony that speaks to expectations unique to your industry if that's part of your case.

Also, keep in mind that contracts can be changed many times as negotiations go back and forth and circumstances change. As you're likely aware, the important agreement is the most recent one.

---

### The Sale of Goods

The Uniform Commercial Code (UCC), adopted by all states, contains special rules affecting contracts for the sale of goods. It requires you to produce something in writing if you want to enforce a contract for a sale of goods and the price is $500 or more, but it also provides that this writing can be very brief— briefer than a normal written contract. Under the UCC, the writing need only:

- indicate that the parties have agreed on the sale of the goods, and
- state the quantity of goods being sold.

If terms such as price, time and place of delivery, or quality of goods are missing, the UCC fills them in based on customs and practices in the particular industry. And where specially manufactured goods are ordered, the UCC doesn't require any writing at all once a party makes a significant effort toward carrying out the contract terms.

> EXAMPLE: A restaurant calls and orders 200 sets of dishes from a restaurant supply company. The dishes are to feature the restaurant's logo. If the supply company makes a substantial beginning on manufacturing the dishes and applying the logo, the restaurant can't avoid liability on the contract simply because it was oral.

## Oral Contracts Are Usually Legal

Most oral contracts—except those for the sale of real estate or goods (tangible property) worth $500 or more, or those that can't be carried out in one year—are legal and enforceable if they can be proven. But when nothing has been written down, proving that a contract existed can sometimes be difficult. An exception to this rule applies when you did work for someone and weren't paid (for example, you are a commercial photographer and spend a day taking pictures of a hat designer's new creations), because the judge is likely to agree with your contention that, by implication, the designer must have noticed what you were doing, and you wouldn't have done the work unless the person had promised to pay you.

## Presenting Your Evidence in Court

In business disputes, litigants might undermine a case by having *too much* evidence, rather than too little. Your job is to separate the material that is essential to proving your claim from that which is irrelevant. Organize both your oral presentation and evidence around the heart of the dispute. Use background information only as necessary.

EXAMPLE: Alicia, the owner of Ames Country Inn, hires Ted, an interior designer, to freshen up the decor of her bed and breakfast. Ted submits an estimate, which Alicia verbally accepts by telephone. Later, Alicia stops by Ted's office to drop off a set of detailed architectural drawings. Ted works for three days on the new decor plan before Alicia suddenly calls and cancels the deal because, "on second thought, I don't like the colors you are proposing." After Alicia fails to pay Ted's bills and ignores his demand letter, Ted files in small claims court, asking for three days' pay plus the money he spent on supplies. In court, Ted very sensibly begins his presentation like this: "Your Honor, the defendant hired me to prepare a detailed plan to redecorate the Ames Country Inn. I worked for three days and bought $200 worth of supplies before she canceled our contract. Today, I'm asking for a judgment for my usual pay rate of $80 per hour for the 24 hours I worked, plus the $200 for supplies. The total is $2,120."

Of course, there is more to Ted's story, and he'll want to make these points:

- He and Alicia had worked together before, his work had always been acceptable, and Alicia paid all previous bills.
- He can document the 24 hours claimed by showing the judge his work product of drawings and worksheets
- He can produce canceled checks covering an itemized list of supplies he purchased for the job.

This should be enough for Ted to win the case. But as is true of all small claims litigants, Ted should also try to anticipate Alicia's key points. For example, if Ted thinks Alicia will claim she canceled because Ted used a design theme and colors she had explicitly ruled out, he should clarify that the contract contained no such restrictions.

Many businesspeople have employees, partners, or business associates who know about the facts of the dispute and bring them to court as witnesses. A witness who is knowledgeable about the transaction is just as valuable as a stack of documentary evidence.

> **EXAMPLE:** Assume Ted's assistant Doris was at the meeting when Ted asked Alicia for a list of suggestions. Also assume Doris can truthfully testify that when the subject of color came up, Alicia just waved her hand and said, "You know I don't like purple too much, but it's really up to you—you're the designer." Doris's testimony will help Ted win the case if Alicia claims his use of purple violated their agreement.

As discussed above, in some situations, having a witness testify as to the standard business practices in an industry or field can also be helpful. Suppose that in your industry, goods are typically shipped within five to 15 days after an order is received in the absence of a written notice of a delay. If the opposing party claims you must pay for goods shipped 90 days after your order was received, you'd want to present an expert witness—or a letter from someone knowledgeable about relevant business practices—who could testify that in your industry, unfilled orders are never good for more than 30 days.

# A Case Study—Proving a Contract Exists

Don Dimaggio is an architect and industrial designer who heads a small company specializing in designing small manufacturing buildings. He prides himself on doing highly innovative and creative work. Recently Don did some preliminary design work for an outfit that wanted to build a candle factory. When they didn't pay, he was out $8,500. In Don's view, the dispute developed like this:

> *"Ben McDonald, who makes custom candles, had a good year and wanted to expand. He called me and asked me to rough out a preliminary design. McDonald claims now that we never had a contract, but that's simply not true. What really happened is that McDonald authorized me to do some preliminary work before his company got their financing locked down. When interest rates went through the roof, the whole deal collapsed. I had already completed my work, but they refused to pay. My next step was to get Stephanie Carlin, a lawyer who has done some work for me, to write McDonald a letter demanding payment. When that didn't do any good, I took Stephanie's advice and filed a small claims court suit against McDonald. True, I had to scale my claim back to $7,500, the small claims maximum. But I obviously couldn't afford to pay Stephanie $200 an hour to file in formal court, so it seemed like the best approach."*

Don's most immediate problem was that he had never used small claims court before. He wasn't sure how he needed to prepare, but knew, at the very least, he had to develop a coherent plan—if for no other reason than to overcome his anxiety. Here is how the attorney he hired coached him to do this:

**RW:** *"Your first job is to establish why McDonald owes you money. Presumably, it's because he violated an agreement that he would pay you for your work."*

**DD:** *"True, but unfortunately, nothing was written down."*

**RW:** *"Oral contracts to provide services are perfectly legal if they can be proven, and judges typically bend over backward to see that freelancers get paid. But don't be so sure you have nothing in writing. Tell me, how did McDonald contact you?"*

**DD:** *"Mutual friends recommended me to him. He phoned me and we talked a couple of times. There was some back and forth about how much I would charge for the whole job and how much for parts of it. After a little garden-variety confusion, we decided that I would start with the preliminary drawings and be paid $8,500. If the whole job came through and we felt good about one another, I would do the entire thing. On big jobs, I always insist on a written contract, but this one was tiny and I couldn't see wasting the time. McDonald just stopped by with someone else from his business, and we hashed out the whole thing in person."*

**RW:** *"Did you make notes?"*

**DD:** *"Sure. In fact, I made a few sketches, and they gave me specifications and sketches they had already made."*

**RW:** *"Do you still have those?"*

**DD:** *"Of course, in a file along with a couple of letters they sent later thanking me for my good ideas and making a few suggestions for changes. And of course, I have copies of the detailed drawings I made and sent them."*

**RW:** *"Well, that's it."*

**DD:** *"What do you mean, that's it?"*

**RW:** *"You've just told me that you can prove a contract exists. The combination of the sketches McDonald provided and the letters someone at his company wrote to you pretty convincingly prove they asked you to do the work. Of course, it helps your case that the law presumes that when a person is asked to do work in a situation where compensation is normally expected, he must be paid when the work is completed."* (In legalese, this presumption is called "quantum meruit." See Chapter 2.)

**DD:** *"That's all there is to it? I just tell the judge what happened and I win?"*

**RW:** *"Not so fast. First, let me ask if you are sure you can present your case coherently. After you make your opening statement, you need to back it up with the key facts that show that McDonald hired you, that you did the work, and that he broke the contract by failing to pay you.* (As discussed throughout this book, because so many people do a poor job making their oral presentation, make sure that you practice ahead of time.) *Ask a savvy friend to serve as your pretend judge. Then present your case as if you were in court. Encourage your friend to interrupt and ask questions, since that's what a judge will likely do. Finally, be sure you have organized all your evidence, especially the plans and letters, so you are ready to present them to the judge at the appropriate time."*

**DD:** *"What about McDonald? Is he likely to show up?"*

**RW:** *"Many cases involving money being owed result in defaults, meaning the person being sued ignores the whole proceeding. (See Chapter 15.) But you know that McDonald claims he doesn't owe you the money, so it's my guess he will probably show up and claim no contract existed. Therefore, you should be prepared to counter the points he is likely to make."*

**DD:** *"You're right. Although it's a total crock, he will probably claim I agreed to do the work on speculation that he would get financing and that since the job fell through, he doesn't owe me anything."*

**RW:** *"And if your case is typical, McDonald will also probably try to claim your work was substandard. That way, even if you prove that a contract existed, the judge might award you less than you asked for."*

**DD:** *"But they wrote me that my design was of excellent quality."*

**RW:** *"Great, but don't wait until they raise the issue. Because you are pretty sure this point will come up, emphasize in your opening statement how pleased McDonald was with your work and present the letter to the judge. Now, what about McDonald's argument that there was no deal in the first place? Do you ever do preliminary work without expecting to be paid unless the deal goes through? And is that a common way to operate in your business?"*

**DD:** *"Me? Never! I don't have to. I suppose some designers do, or at least prepare fairly detailed bid proposals without pay, but I have so much work coming my way these days, I'm turning jobs down right and left, so when I do submit a bid, I make it clear to all potential clients that I charge for preliminary drawings. In this situation, as I said, we agreed on the price in advance."*

**RW:** *"What about witnesses to that conversation?"*

**DD:** *"Well, Jim, my partner, sat in on one of the early discussions. We hadn't agreed on the final price yet, but we weren't too far apart."*

**RW:** *"Was it clear to Jim that you intended to charge for your work and that McDonald knew you did?"*

**DD:** *"Yes, absolutely."*

**RW:** *"Great, bring Jim to court with you as a witness. Here is how I would proceed. Organize your statement as to what happened so it takes you no longer than five minutes to present it to the judge. Bring your sketches, and most importantly, the sketch that McDonald made, along with the letters they sent you, and show them to the judge. (See Chapter 15.) Then introduce your partner and have him state that he was present when money was discussed."*

This little scenario is a simplified version of a real case. What happened? The small claims court judge awarded Don the entire amount he requested, and McDonald paid it.

## A Case Study—Personal Services Contract

Tiffany, a graphic artist, never prepares her own tax returns. For the past several years, she has turned all of her tax affairs over to Phillip, a local C.P.A. They discussed price the first year, but after that Tiffany just paid Phillip's bill when the job was done.

One spring, things went wrong. As usual, Tiffany's records weren't in great shape, and she was late in getting them to Phillip. By this time, Phillip, who was overly busy, put Tiffany's tax return together quickly without discussing it with her in detail. When Tiffany saw the return, she was shocked by the bottom line and felt she was paying way too much.

She called Phillip and reminded him of several deductions that she felt he had overlooked. There was some discussion of whether Phillip should have known about these items or not. Things began to get a little edgy when Phillip complained about Tiffany's sloppy records and her delay in making them available. Tiffany countered by accusing Phillip of doing a hurried and substandard job. But after discussion, Phillip agreed to make the necessary corrections. A week later, Phillip sent the revised return to Tiffany.

While her tax liability was reduced, Tiffany was still annoyed, feeling that Phillip hadn't corrected all of the oversights. Tiffany called Phillip again, and they quickly got into a shouting match. When Phillip reluctantly agreed to look at the return a third time, Tiffany replied, "Hell no, I'm taking my business to an accountant who can add."

True to her word, Tiffany did hire another accountant, who made several modifications to her return, resulting in a slightly lower tax liability. The second accountant claimed that because he needed to check all of Phillip's work to satisfy himself that it was correct, he ended up doing almost as much work as if he had started from scratch. As a result, he billed Tiffany for $2,300, saying that this was only $500 less than if he had not had the benefit of Phillip's work.

Phillip billed Tiffany $3,000. Tiffany, still furious, refused to pay. Phillip then sent Tiffany a demand letter asking to be paid and stating that most of the problems were created by Tiffany's bad records. He added that he had already made many requested changes and had offered to make relatively minor final changes at no additional charge. Phillip also suggested in his letter that he was willing to try to mediate the claim using a local community mediation center that charged very low fees.

When Tiffany didn't answer the letter, Phillip filed suit. Here is how Phillip should prepare the case:

## Phillip's Case

**Step 1.** Phillip has already written a clear demand letter (see Chapter 6 for a discussion of how to do this) and suggested mediation—a good idea, as both he and Tiffany work in the same small city, and Phillip doesn't want to turn Tiffany into a vocal enemy. Unfortunately, Tiffany didn't bite on Phillip's suggestion of mediation.

**Step 2.** Phillip knows that Tiffany's business makes money, so he is pretty sure he can collect if he wins, which of course, should be a primary consideration in deciding whether to file any small claims case. (See Chapter 3.)

**Step 3.** In court, Phillip's main job will be to prove that he did a job worth $3,000 and to refute Tiffany's likely contention that his work was so bad it amounted to a breach of their contract. Bringing copies of the tax returns he prepared for Tiffany and his worksheets is probably the simplest way for Phillip to accomplish this. He should not present the returns to the judge page by page, but as a package. The purpose is to indicate that a lot of work has been done without going into details.

**Step 4.** Phillip should then testify as to his hourly rate and how many hours he worked. He should emphasize that the extra hours were required because Tiffany did not have her records well organized. To illustrate his point, Phillip should present to the judge any raw data Tiffany gave him that he still has (for example, a shoebox full of messy receipts). If he no longer has Tiffany's material, he might create something that looks like it, carefully pointing out to the judge that this is a simulation of Tiffany's data, not the real thing.

**Step 5.** By testifying that he was hired to do a job, that he did it, and that he wasn't paid, Phillip has presented facts necessary to establish a breach of contract case. However, he would be wise to go beyond this and anticipate at least some of Tiffany's defenses, which will almost surely involve the claim that Phillip broke the contract by doing poor quality work and doing it late. In addition, Phillip should anticipate Tiffany's backup claim that he charged too much and that the judge should award him less than $3,000. Phillip could attempt to take the sting out of Tiffany's likely presentation by saying something along these lines:

*"Your Honor, when I finished my work, my client pointed out that several deductions had been overlooked. I believed then and believe now that this was because the data she provided me with was disorganized and inadequate, but I did rework the return and correct several items that were left out. When my client told me that she felt the revised draft needed additional changes, I again told her that I would work with her to make any necessary modifications. It was at this point that she refused to let me see the returns and hired another accountant. In my professional opinion at this stage, very little work remained to be done—certainly nothing that couldn't be accomplished in an hour or two.*

*"Now, as to the amount charged—it took me ten hours to reconstruct what went on in the defendant's business from the mess of incomplete and incoherent records I was given. At $90 per hour, this means that $900 of my bill involved work that had to be done before actually preparing the return. Taking into consideration the difficult circumstances, I believe I charged fairly for the work I did and that I did my work well."*

## Tiffany's Case

Now let's see how Tiffany, the upset graphic artist, might deal with the situation.

**Step 1.** For starters, Tiffany made a mistake by refusing to negotiate or mediate with Phillip. Work quality disputes are the type a judge will likely compromise by splitting the baby between the two litigants, so it would have saved time and anxiety for both parties to arrive at a compromise outside of court. (See Chapter 6.)

**Step 2.** Once Tiffany has decided not to settle the case, she should write a letter rebutting Phillip's demand letter point by point. (See Chapter 6.) She should bring a copy of this letter to court and give it to the judge as part of her presentation. The judge doesn't have to accept Tiffany's letter because it's not evidence of anything but the fact that she rejected Phillip's request for payment. But more often than not, the judge will look at both parties' letters as a quick way of understanding the facts.

**Step 3.** Next, Tiffany should testify that she refused to pay the bill because she felt that Phillip's work was so poor that she didn't trust Phillip to finish the job. To make this point effectively, Tiffany should testify about the tax issues Phillip overlooked. For example, the fact that Tiffany provided Phillip with receipts for expensive equipment she purchased but Phillip didn't claim depreciation would be convincing evidence of poor work. But Tiffany should be careful to make her points about tax law in a relatively brief and understandable way. She won't gain anything by a long and boring rehash of her entire return. One good approach might be for Tiffany to submit pertinent sections of IRS publications or a privately published tax guide outlining the rules that require equipment to be depreciated.

**Step 4.** Tiffany should next present more detailed evidence that supports her claim that Phillip did poor work. The tax return that was correctly prepared by the new accountant would be of some help. But it would be even better to have the second accountant come to court to testify about the details of Phillip's substandard work. Unfortunately for Tiffany, professionals are commonly reluctant to testify against one another, so this might be difficult to arrange. But Tiffany should at the very least be able to get a letter from the new accountant outlining the things that he found it necessary to do to change the return as prepared by Phillip.

**Step 5.** Tiffany should also present to the court her canceled checks, establishing the amounts she paid Phillip for the last several years' returns—assuming, of course, that Phillip's previous bills were substantially less. For example, if Tiffany had been billed $1,700 and $1,900 in the two previous years, it would raise some questions as to whether Phillip's bill of $3,000 for the current year was reasonable.

TIP

**Both Tiffany and Phillip should be prepared to answer the judge's questions.** Especially in a case like this one involving a technical subject, the judge is almost sure to interrupt both Tiffany's and Phillip's presentations and ask for details. So in addition to preparing and practicing presenting their cases before a critical friend, both Phillip and Tiffany should be prepared to answer likely questions and then smoothly return to presenting their cases.

This story is based on a real case. Here's what happened. The judge gave Phillip a judgment for $1,800. The judge didn't explain his reasoning but apparently felt that there was some right on each side. He split the difference with a little edge to Phillip; probably because Tiffany hired Phillip in the first place and had worked with him for several years, she was on somewhat shaky ground claiming he was incompetent. This sort of compromise decision, where each side is given something, is common in small claims court and again illustrates the wisdom of the parties' negotiating or mediating their own compromise. Even if Tiffany and Phillip had arrived at a solution where one or the other gave up a little more than the judge ordered, there would have been a savings in both time and aggravation that probably would have more than made up the difference.

# Judgment and Appeal

# The Judgment

In most states, the trial decision will be mailed to the address on record with the clerk any time from a few days to a few weeks after your case. The exception to this rule is when one side doesn't show up and the other wins by default. Default judgments usually are announced right in the courtroom.

 **RELATED TOPIC**
**See Chapter 15 for information on how to set aside a default.** For information on how to get a court judgment after a mediated settlement isn't carried out, see Chapter 6.

The truth is that in the vast majority of contested cases, the judge decides the matter immediately and jots down the decision before the parties leave the courtroom. Decisions are sent by mail because the court doesn't want to deal with angry, unhappy losers in court, especially those few who might get violent. However, even though an occasional person might get upset, some judges are willing to announce and explain their decisions in court so that both sides understand why the judge reached a particular conclusion. One judge explained his policy as follows: "The only time I don't announce my decision in court is when I have phoning or research to do before finalizing it, or if I feel that the losing party will be unnecessarily embarrassed in front of the audience."

**JUDGE'S TIP**
**Don't get perplexed if the judge takes everything under submission and sends the results by mail.** If, when you receive the decision, you have questions about it, consider writing to the judge (send a copy to your opponent) a polite request for a further explanation of the judge's reasoning. Most judges will respond.

> ⊙ **TIP**
> **Legal jargon note.** Once the court clerk enters a judgment, the person who wins the case (gets the judgment) becomes the "judgment creditor," and the loser is known as the "judgment debtor." Also, a court judgment awarding money is called a "money judgment."

Often after entry of judgment, the losing party feels that the judge would have made a different decision if the judge hadn't overlooked a crucial fact or failed to understand an argument. However, in the vast majority of cases, this is not true. Even if you argued the entire case again, it's unlikely it would change the judge's mind. Chances are good the judge understood the arguments but disagreed with your position. (See "The Appeal," below, for information about your appeal rights.)

If you sued more than one person, the judgment should indicate who the judgment is against and for how much. Some defendants might not owe anything, or their financial liability might be limited to a stated amount. If so, this is the maximum you can collect from them. However, in most instances where a judgment is against two or more defendants, they will be jointly and severally liable, with each defendant 100% responsible for the entire amount. For example, suppose you receive a $1,000 judgment against two defendants. In that case, you could collect it in any proportion from either defendant (for example, you could collect $800 from one defendant and $200 from another). If you collect too much from one defendant, that person must straighten things out with the codefendant. In this example, the defendant who paid the $800 might sue the other for $300.

> ⊙ **TIP**
> **The words "joint and several liability" may not appear on the judgment.** A judgment against two or more defendants will often simply list the names of the judgment debtors. This means they are jointly and severally liable for the entire amount. In cases where one defendant's judgment debt liability is limited (say to $200), the judgment will make that clear.

# Paying the Judgment

In most states, the judge can order the loser to pay the winner in installments over time rather than all at once. The judge usually won't make this sort of order unless you request it. Be sure the judge knows that if you lose, you wish to pay in installments. You might put your request this way:

- "In closing, I would like to say that I believe I have proven my case and should be awarded the judgment, but in the event that you rule for my opponent, I would like payments of no more than [*an amount convenient to you*] per month."

Or, if you have no real defense:

- "Your Honor, I request that you enter the judgment against me for no more than [*an amount convenient to you*] per month."

If you forget to ask for time payments in court and wish to make this request after receiving the judgment, first contact the other party to see whether the person will voluntarily agree to accept the money on a schedule you can afford to pay. If the other party consents, consider memorializing your agreement in writing for each to sign. Or check whether your court has a form you can fill out.

If your opponent refuses payments, contact the court clerk and ask if you can bring the case before the judge to set up a payment schedule. If the clerk can't arrange it, write a letter like the one below to the judge. (See "Sample Letter to Judge Requesting Installment Payments," below.)

In some states, the judgment debtor can pay the judgment to the small claims court directly. This procedure is helpful for a judgment debtor who doesn't want to deal directly with the prevailing party or doesn't know the person's current address. Contact your small claims clerk about a direct payment procedure or check for payment options on your local small claims court website.

### Sample Letter to Judge Requesting Installment Payments

October 17, 20xx

Honorable Felix Hamburg

Judge of the Small Claims Court

111 Center Street

New York, NY 12345

Re: *Elliot v. Toller*

Index No. _____

Dear Judge Hamburg:

I recently appeared before you in the case of *Elliot v. Toller* (Index No. _____).
Mr. Elliot was awarded a judgment in the amount of $1,526. Paying this amount
all at once would be nearly impossible because of [*state reason, such as lack of
employment or illness*]. I can pay $75 per month.

Please change the order to allow for a $75 per month payment. If I must make
this request in court, please let me know the procedure involved or when I
should be present.

Sincerely,

*John Toller*

John Toller

> **TIP**
> **Notify the court when you move.** It's essential to keep your current address on file if you've won a lawsuit but haven't yet been paid. That way, you'll receive the money the losing party pays directly to the court.

## Satisfaction of Judgment

Once a judgment debtor (the person who lost the case) pays the judgment, the judgment creditor (the person who won the case) must acknowledge payment by filing a form with the court clerk. It will be called a "Satisfaction of Judgment" form or something similar. Filing the form tells the world (especially credit rating agencies) that the judgment debtor paid the obligation. (See sample form, below.)

Judgment creditors who record a lien on real property (see Chapter 24), must remove the lien, as well. If you don't know how to do this, contact the recorder's office where you filed the lien for help. If a judgment creditor fails to file a Satisfaction of Judgment form, the judgment debtor should send the judgment creditor a written demand to do so. A first-class letter is adequate. If the judgment creditor still doesn't file the form within the time required (usually between 15 and 30 days—check your local rules) and without just cause, many states allow the judgment debtor to recover the actual damages suffered as a result of the failure. Also, some states will impose a penalty payment on the judgment creditor.

Below is a copy of California's form known as an "Acknowledgment of Satisfaction of Judgment." You can send it to the judgment creditor to sign and file with the court clerk after you pay the judgment so you don't have to track down the judgment creditor later.

> **TIP**
> **It's easy to get a copy of a Satisfaction of Judgment form.** If either party ever needs it (for example, to correct an out-of-date credit report), the court clerk will provide a certified copy of a filed Satisfaction of Judgment form. This form proves that the judgment was paid.

# Sample Acknowledgment of Satisfaction of Judgment

EJ-100

ATTORNEY OR PARTY WITHOUT ATTORNEY *(Name, address, and State Bar number):*
After recording, return to:

Andrew Printer, Judgment Creditor
1800 Marilee Street
Fremont, CA 94536

TEL NO.:      FAX NO. (optional):

E-MAIL ADDRESS *(Optional):*

☐ ATTORNEY FOR    ☐ JUDGMENT CREDITOR    ☐ ASSIGNEE OF RECORD

SUPERIOR COURT OF CALIFORNIA, COUNTY OF    Alameda

STREET ADDRESS:   600 Washington Street, 3rd Floor

MAILING ADDRESS:

CITY AND ZIP CODE: Oakland, CA 94607

BRANCH NAME:

*FOR RECORDER'S OR SECRETARY OF STATE'S USE ONLY*

| | |
|---|---|
| PLAINTIFF:   Andrew Printer<br>DEFENDANT:   Acme Illusions, Inc. | CASE NUMBER:<br>002006 |
| **ACKNOWLEDGMENT OF SATISFACTION OF JUDGMENT**<br>[X] FULL   ☐ PARTIAL   ☐ MATURED INSTALLMENT | *FOR COURT USE ONLY* |

1. Satisfaction of the judgment is acknowledged as follows:
   a. ☐ Full satisfaction
      (1) [X] Judgment is satisfied in full.
      (2) ☐ The judgment creditor has accepted payment or performance other than that specified in the judgment in full satisfaction of the judgment.
   b. ☐ Partial satisfaction
      The amount received in partial satisfaction of the judgment is $
   c. ☐ Matured installment
      All matured installments under the installment judgment have been satisfied as of *(date):*

2. Full name and address of judgment creditor:*
   Andrew Printer
   1800 Marilee Street, Fremont, CA 94536
3. Full name and address of assignee of record, if any:

   N/A

4. Full name and address of judgment debtor being fully or partially released:*

   Acme Illusions, Inc., 100 Primrose Path, Oakland, CA 94602

5. a. Judgment entered on *(date):* 7/21/20xx
   b. ☐ Renewal entered on *(date):*

6. [X] An   [X] abstract of judgment   ☐ certified copy of the judgment has been recorded as follows *(complete all information for each county where recorded):*

| COUNTY | DATE OF RECORDING | INSTRUMENT NUMBER |
|---|---|---|
| Alameda County | 8/14/20xx | 21 |

7. ☐ A notice of judgment lien has been filed in the office of the Secretary of State as file number *(specify):*

**NOTICE TO JUDGMENT DEBTOR:** If this is an acknowledgment of full satisfaction of judgment, it will have to be recorded in each county shown in item 6 above, if any, in order to release the judgment lien, and will have to be filed in the office of the Secretary of State to terminate any judgment lien on personal property.

Date:   8/14/20xx      ▶   *Andrew Printer*

               (SIGNATURE OF JUDGMENT CREDITOR OR ASSIGNEE OF CREDITOR OR ATTORNEY**)

*The names of the judgment creditor and judgment debtor must be stated as shown in any Abstract of Judgment which was recorded and is being released by this satisfaction. ** A separate notary acknowledgment must be attached for each signature.

Form Approved for Optional Use
Judicial Council of California
EJ-100 [Rev. July 1, 2014]

**ACKNOWLEDGMENT OF SATISFACTION OF JUDGMENT**

Page 1 of 1
Code of Civil Procedure, §§ 724.060, 724.120, 724.250

Sometimes judgment debtors forget to get the judgment creditor to sign the Satisfaction of Judgment form when they pay a judgment, only to find that they can't locate the judgment creditor later. If this happens and you need the form to clean up your credit record or for some other reason, you can get it if you present the court clerk with proof the judgment was paid. The following documents will help:

- A canceled check or money order written by you after the date of the judgment, for the full amount of the judgment, or a cash receipt for the full amount of the judgment signed by the judgment creditor after the date the court awarded judgment.
- A statement (see the sample below) signed by you under penalty of perjury stating all of the following:
  - The judgment creditor has been paid the full amount of the judgment and costs.
  - The judgment creditor has been asked to file an Acknowledgment of Satisfaction of Judgment form and refuses to do so or can't be located.
  - The document attached (for example, the check or money order) constitutes evidence of the judgment creditor's receipt of the payment.

## The Appeal

Unlike small claims court itself, where rules and procedures are remarkably the same throughout the United States, the rules that cover appeals from small claims court judgments vary greatly from one state to the next, and a few don't allow appeal. New York allows an appeal of a judge's decision but not an arbitration award. California, Massachusetts, and a few other states allow a losing defendant to appeal but do not permit the person who brought the suit (the plaintiff) to do so, except to appeal from a counterclaim initiated by the defendant. In Appendix A, you will find brief summaries of the appeal procedures of every state. You must follow your court's procedures exactly, and it is easy to make a mistake, especially when calculating the time to file the appeal. Be sure to protect yourself by reading your court's rules and, when needed, verifying the specifics with the court clerk, your local court's self-help department, or a local lawyer.

## Sample Statement of Debtor Regarding Full Payment of Judgment

My name is John Elliot. On January 11, 20xx, a judgment was awarded against me in small claims court in Ithaca, New York (Case # 1234). On March 20, 20xx, I paid Beatrice Small, the prevailing party, $1,200, the full amount of this judgment [*or, if payments were made in installments—"I paid Beatrice Small, the prevailing party in this action, installments of the following amounts on the following dates:* _____ *, concluding with a final payment of $_____ on March 20, 20xx."*]

I attach to this statement a canceled check [*or other proof that the judgment was paid*] for the full amount of the judgment endorsed by Beatrice Small. [*If payment was made by money order or cash (with a receipt), modify this statement as needed. If payment was made in installments, modify this statement as needed and enclose copies of all canceled checks.*]

Beatrice Small did not voluntarily file a Satisfaction of Judgment. When I tried to contact her, I learned that she had moved and had left no forwarding address. [*If the judgment creditor refuses to sign a Satisfaction of Judgment form, or is otherwise not available to do so, modify this statement as necessary.*]

I declare under penalty of perjury under the laws of the State of _____ _____ that the foregoing is true and correct.


DATED: June 4, 20xx.


_____
John Elliot

CAUTION
**You can't appeal if you didn't show up in small claims court.** Appeal rights are almost always restricted to those who showed up in small claims court, argued their case, and lost. If you defaulted (didn't show up), you usually can't appeal unless and until you get the default set aside. You must file appeal paperwork almost immediately, or the small claims judgment will become final and unappealable. (See Chapter 15.) Filing a request to set aside a default judgment typically does not extend the time allowed to appeal—check your local small claims court rules.

You may have heard that some higher court judges consider small claims appeals to be a nuisance and try to discourage them by routinely upholding the original judgment. There's very little truth to this. Most judges will give you a fair hearing on appeal if you are well prepared and able to present a convincing case. Therefore, if your case involves enough money to make a further investment of time and energy worthwhile, appeal if your state's rules allow it.

Determining whether you are eligible to appeal is important, but it is only part of the information you need. It is just as important to determine what kind of appeal is permitted in your state. Some states allow an appeal only on questions of law, while others allow the whole case to be replayed from scratch. Let's pause for a moment and look at some of the differences.

## New Trial

In several states, either party can appeal and have the case heard over from the beginning. In other states, only the defendant can appeal (in most cases), but if the defendant does file an appeal, the whole case is presented again by both sides as if the first trial hadn't occurred.

When a whole new trial is allowed on appeal (it's called a "trial de novo"), you simply argue the case over, presenting all necessary witnesses, documents, and testimony. Starting again is required because records often aren't kept at small claims court hearings. However, in some courts, judges record hearings, and these recordings are available to the appellate judge as part of the reargument of the case.

## Questions of Law

In many states, appeals can be based only on questions of law, not on the facts of the case. (See Appendix A.) What's the difference between law and facts? It's best illustrated with a couple of examples.

> EXAMPLE 1: You sue your mechanic in small claims court, claiming that he messed up a repair job on your car. After listening to both sides, the judge rules for the mechanic, concluding that the repairs were made properly and something else was wrong with your car. You disagree, contending that the repairperson really did mess up the job. You are not eligible to appeal, because the cause of the mechanical problem is a factual dispute.

> EXAMPLE 2: You are a tenant suing for the return of a cleaning deposit withheld by the landlord. The court agrees with you and awards you the amount of the deposit plus $500 in punitive damages. The landlord appeals, claiming that under the law of your state, the judge only has the power to award $250 in punitive damages. Because this appeal claims a mistake was made in applying the law, it is proper and will be considered.

In most states, appeals made based on a mistake of law must be supported by a written outline of the claimed mistakes. This can put nonlawyers unfamiliar with legal research and writing techniques at a disadvantage. Start by contacting the court clerk and requesting all forms and rules governing appeals. Take these seriously and do your best to comply. The good news is that most appellate judges will consider any well-reasoned written statement you submit claiming the small claims judge made a legal error.

RELATED TOPIC

**Some legal research tips.** Check out Chapter 25 for pointers on how to learn about the laws that apply to your appeal.

Here is a brief example of a statement that might be used in an appeal (use the form or format required by your state):

**Sample Appeals Statement**

Appeal from Small Claims Judgment #_____ ,
Based on Legal Error

Under the laws of the state of _____ , a small claims judgment may be set aside if it is based on a legal error or mistake. In my personal injury case, the court incorrectly applied the statute of limitations, because it did not take into consideration the fact that I was a minor when the accident occurred.

My case is based on a personal injury I suffered on January 23, 2019, when I was 17 years and two months old. The small claims judge dismissed my case because it was not filed within one year after my injury, as is required by the statute of limitations. This was an incorrect application of the law.

It's true that under the terms of Code of Civil Procedure, Section 340, a personal injury case must normally be filed within one year of the date of the injury, which in my case occurred on January 23, 2019. However, Sec. 352 of the Code of Civil Procedure also states: "If a person entitled to bring an action, mentioned in Chapter 3 of this title, be, at the time the cause of action occurred, ... under the age of majority ... the time of such disability is not a part of the time limited for the commencement of the action."

Because I was still a minor until November 23, 2020 (when I turned 18), under the terms of Code of Civil Procedure, Section 352, it was from this date (not from January 23, 2019) that the court should have begun counting the one-year statute of limitations for personal injury actions. Therefore, I was entitled to file my case until November 22, 2021. In fact, because I filed on June 27, 2021, I was well within the allowed time.

In conclusion, I request that the judgment in this case be vacated and that I be granted a new small claims court hearing.

## Filing and Presenting Your Appeal

It's essential that you obtain and study a copy of your state's small claims appeal rules. They vary considerably, especially between those states where you can only appeal questions of law and those where you are entitled to a completely new trial.

### File Promptly

In all states, appeals must be filed promptly (usually within ten to 30 days), so wherever you are, don't delay. In many states, you must file a notice of appeal shortly after the court clerk mails the judgment to the parties (or hands it over, if a decision is made in the courtroom).

> CAUTION
> **Don't oversleep in Washington, D.C., or Rhode Island!** You'll have only two days to appeal your small claims court decision in Rhode Island, and three days in Washington, D.C. Luckily, weekends and holidays don't count.

You'll need to consult your state statute to find out when to start counting your time to appeal. Many states start counting from the date the judgment was mailed, but not all, so be sure to read your court rules carefully when determining the appellate filing deadline. For instance, the last day to file will differ depending on whether your court rules say you must start counting from the date the clerk enters the judgment, from the date the clerk mails the judgment, or from the date you receive the judgment. If you run into problems, call the small claims clerk immediately and request help getting an extension of time to file your appeal, if necessary.

Appeals must usually be filed using a form supplied by the small claims court.

### Appeal Fees

The appeal fee is often higher than the original filing fee. If you ultimately win your appeal (that is, get the original decision reversed in your favor), you can add these court costs to the judgment. In many states, the party filing an appeal must post a cash bond (or written guarantee by financially solvent adults) when filing the appeal to cover the amount of the judgment in case of a loss. Courts impose this requirement to discourage the filing of frivolous appeals.

### Doing It Without a Lawyer

You are entitled to have an attorney in the appeals court. By definition, your small claims case likely isn't worth much, so you will probably decide it is not cost-efficient to hire one. Indeed, there should be little practical reason for an attorney, as you probably have an excellent grasp of the issues by this time.

 **JUDGE'S TIP**
**It doesn't take a lawyer to make a good impression in an appeal.**
A prepared, respectful, and self-represented litigant can often make just as impressive a showing at a small claims appeal as a lawyer would.

But what if your opponent hires a lawyer? Aren't you at a disadvantage if you represent yourself? Not necessarily. As noted in "Presenting Your Appeal," below, in many states the appeals court must follow informal rules similar to those used in small claims court. This puts you on a relatively equal footing, even if your opponent has a lawyer. If you have prepared carefully, you may even have an advantage: You carry with you the honest conviction that you are right. If you still feel a little intimidated, the best cure is to watch a few small claims appeals. Ask the court clerk for the schedule. Watching the process should reassure you that you are perfectly capable of handling your appeal.

### Presenting Your Appeal

On appeal, both sides should give careful thought to how to improve their presentation. This suggestion is particularly valid for the person who lost. Ask yourself: Did the judge decide against me because I presented my case poorly or because I didn't support my statements with evidence? Or did the judge simply misapply the law? To answer these questions, you may have to do some additional legal research. (See Chapter 25 for some tips on how to do this.)

**JUDGE'S TIP**

**Read the case file before your appeals hearing.** The file is a public record, and you have a right to see it (ask the small claims clerk how to get a copy). Sometimes the trial judge will leave notes in the file that the appeal judge will be reading, and you'll want to adjust your case accordingly. In any case, you'll be better prepared if you know what the appeals judge has read.

Once you have decided how to improve your case, practice presenting it to an objective friend. When done, ask your friend which parts of your presentation were convincing and which need more work.

### Some Cures for Prehearing Jitters

What should you do if your appeal will be conducted in a style you find intimidating?

- Read *Represent Yourself in Court: How to Prepare & Try a Winning Case*, by Paul Bergman and Sara Berman (Nolo). This book explains how to conduct a contested civil trial in a formal courtroom setting, including how to present testimony and cross-examine witnesses. It should quickly increase your comfort level.
- Ask the judge, in advance, to conduct your appeal as informally as possible. You can do this on the day of your hearing or, better yet, by writing a brief, polite letter to the court ahead of time. Explain that, as a nonlawyer, you are thoroughly prepared to present the facts of your case, but because you are unfamiliar with formal rules of evidence and procedure, you would appreciate it if your small claims appeal could be conducted so that a citizen who has not spent three years at law school is given a fair opportunity to be heard.
- During your small claims appeal, if there is some procedure you don't understand, politely ask the judge for an explanation. If necessary, remind the judge that you are entitled to understand the rules and procedures that control the presentation of your case, and at the very least, you should be allowed a brief break to compose yourself (then use the time to Google the issue).

In some states, small claims appeals can be presented to the judge just as informally as any small claims court case. At the other extreme, some states' small claims court appeal rules require that an appeal be conducted with all the pomp and circumstance of a regular trial court case. Because procedures can differ even within the same state, this book can't tell you exactly what type of hearing you will face. So, again, it is important to take the time to check out exactly what type of appeal hearing rules you will encounter. For example, you might learn you'll need to be prepared to present your testimony while sitting in the witness box. You might also have to question your witnesses using the formal lawyer style you have seen so often on TV, and introduce evidence according to a strict, step-by-step script.

> CAUTION
> **Jury trials.** A few states permit jury trials on appeal. Most states don't. Check with your court clerk and the appendix.

## Further Appeals

If a defendant loses the appeal, there is usually no right to file a second appeal. However, it is sometimes possible to file an extraordinary writ (a special request for review based on extraordinary circumstances) to a court of appeal claiming that either the small claims court or first appeals court made a serious legal mistake in handling the case (for example, the court had no power to consider the issues involved in your case). In some states, the lower court judge might have the power to recommend that the court of appeal hear your case. But because of the relatively small amounts of money involved, extraordinary writs based on small claims judgments are almost never filed. And when they are, they are seldom granted. For these reasons, this procedure isn't covered here.

# Collecting Your Money

Y ou won. Congratulations! You undoubtedly want to collect every penny from the opposing party as soon as possible. If the other party is cooperative, that won't be much trouble. But some defendants have figured out that the court will not make them pay and that you must take action. That's where this chapter comes in. Here's where you'll learn when you can start your collection efforts and how to enforce your judgment. With patience and careful planning, you should be able to collect by garnishing wages, attaching a bank account, or taking other legal steps.

> CAUTION
> **Don't harass the debtor.** Businesses that regularly attempt to collect debts for another business's consumer customers are subject to the federal Fair Debt Collection Practices Act (15 U.S.C. §§ 1692–1692p), and in most states, are subject to similar state laws. These laws protect consumer debtors from abusive or unfair conduct. The rules prohibit conduct such as calling the debtor so often it's harassing, causing the debtor's phone to ring continuously, using profane language, or badmouthing the debtor in the community. Some state laws apply even when doing your own collections, so consult with a lawyer or review your state law carefully. Even if you are trying to collect debts not covered by these consumer protection laws, avoid inappropriate conduct. Other laws against abusive or unfair tactics might apply.

## The Timing of Collecting Your Money

Because there's always a chance that the judgment debtor will file for bankruptcy and wipe out the money judgment, you'll want to start collecting as soon as possible. But you might have to wait for a time depending on the case.

### Contested Cases

If the defendant appeared in court, fought the case, and lost, you might have to wait to see whether there is an appeal before you start trying to collect the judgment amount. Some states prohibit collection efforts while a defendant can still appeal. Other states do not require you to wait, but you'll likely want to hold any funds you collect until you know the outcome of any appeal. Depending on your state's rules, you must file an appeal immediately after the case—typically, within ten to 30 days. (See Appendix A.)

> **TIP**
> **Exception.** In a few states, no appeals are allowed, and in others, only a losing defendant can appeal. (See Appendix A.) If the other party can't appeal, you can begin collection activities immediately.

After the allowed time to appeal has passed, check with the small claims court clerk to make sure an appeal hasn't been filed. If appealed party files an appeal, you'll get notice in the mail of the appeal date. (Learn more about appeals in Chapter 23.)

After the appeals court makes its decision, it will notify the small claims court. If the appeal was decided in your favor, you can proceed to enforce the judgment immediately in all situations.

## Default Judgments

If you got your judgment because the defendant defaulted (that is, didn't show up), the defendant usually can't appeal without first asking the court to set aside or vacate the default. Most defendants who don't show up in the first place don't bother to do this. Nevertheless, in some states, you might have a waiting period. (See Chapter 15 for more on setting aside default judgments.)

If the defendant loses on the request to set aside the judgment, then appeals that decision, some states might require you to wait until the court decides that appeal before you can begin to enforce your judgment.

# How to Collect

Once the relevant waiting period is up, what should you do? There are a few possibilities.

## Ask for Payment

You can start by asking politely for your money. This might work if you have sued a responsible person or business. But keep in mind that the judgment debtor has already had numerous opportunities to pay you. If the judgment debtor doesn't make arrangements soon after receiving the judgment, you should plan to take action. If, however, you want to start with a payment request and you don't have personal contact with the party who owes you money, try a note like the sample below.

### Sample Request for Payment

> P.O. Box 66
> Bangor, ME 12345
> February 15, 20xx
>
> Mildred Edwards
> 11 Milvia Street
> Bangor, ME 12345
>
> Re: *Toller v. Edwards* (Small Claims Case No. 200600)
>
> Dear Mrs. Edwards:
>
> As you know, a judgment was entered against you in small claims court on January 15 in the amount of $1,457.86. As the judgment creditor, I would appreciate your paying this amount within ten days.
>
> Thank you for your attention to this matter.
>
> Very truly yours,
>
> *John Toller*
> John Toller

## Payment Through the Court

Your judgment debtor might be willing to pay up—but doesn't want to deal directly with you. In some states, the judgment debtor can pay the judgment to the court instead. Contact your small claims court clerk to find out whether this is an option in your state. If so, it might make sense to write a short note explaining that the judgment debtor can make payment to the court. (See the sample letter below.) Once the court receives payment, it will notify you, so keep your current address on file with the court.

## Collecting the Money

If you receive no payment after sending a polite note, you will have a choice: Either get serious about collecting your money or forget it. The court will not enforce your judgment and collect the money for you—you have to do it yourself.

Fortunately, a few ways to legally collect money from a debtor are relatively easy if the debtor has money to collect. Hopefully, you gave some thought to collection before you brought your case. If you only now realize that your opponent doesn't have the funds to buy a toothbrush, let alone pay off your judgment, you are better off not wasting more time and money trying to get your money, at least for the present. Sometimes you'll want to sit on your judgment just in case the judgment debtor's economic life improves in the future.

But if the debtor owns real estate, you'll want to immediately put a lien on the property so that money from a sale will be held back and go to pay your judgment. (See "Property Liens," below.)

TIP
**Collection rules are getting tighter.** A few states are putting teeth into their collection rules. In New York, if a judgment debtor who is solvent doesn't pay three or more small claims court judgments based on a repeated course of conduct or the debtor's business transactions, a judgment creditor can get triple the judgment as damages, plus attorneys' fees. Contact the small claims court clerk to see about any collection rules in your jurisdiction.

## Sample Payment Request With Information
## on Making Payments to the Court

P.O. Box 18-C

Bangor, Maine 12345

July 2, 20xx

Donald Lee

Donald Lee Industries

14 Western Avenue, S.W.

Bangor, Maine 12345

Re: *Andrews v. Lee* (Small Claims Case No. 200600)

Dear Mr. Lee,

As you know, a judgment was entered against you in small claims court on June 25 in the amount of $4,112.87. If you would prefer to pay the small claims court rather than pay me directly, you can do so. However, please be aware that the court might charge a small fee for processing your payment. To arrange payments directly to the court, contact the small claims clerk at  *[name and address of court where small claims case was decided]* .

As an alternative, you can send the payment directly to me. I would appreciate your handling this matter within ten days from the date of this letter.

Thank you for your consideration.

Very truly yours,

*Alicia Andrews*

Alicia Andrews

---

### When the Debtor Pays by Check

Always make copies of any checks the debtor sends you as partial payment on your judgment. If the debtor fails to pay the entire judgment, you'll need to find a collection source for the unpaid portion—and the debtor's bank account is a great place to start. (See "Levying on Wages, Bank Accounts, and Other Property" below.) Your copy of the check will show the debtor's bank, branch, and account number.

If the debtor's check bounces, you might, depending on your state's law, be entitled to:

- Sue in small claims court for the original amount of the bounced check plus damages. First, you must follow your state's detailed procedures, usually including sending a demand letter to the debtor (often by certified mail).
- See whether your county's district attorney's office has a check diversion program. To avoid prosecution, the person who wrote a bad check must make the check good and comply with other rules. You cannot seek damages if you enlist the district attorney's help—but you'll be spared the hassle of another lawsuit.

---

## Installment Payments

When a court orders the judgment debtor to pay a judgment in installments, and the judgment debtor misses one or more payments, the judgment creditor has the right to collect the missed payments immediately. But here is the problem: The judgment creditor can't collect the part that hasn't come due unless the court first sets aside the installment payment provisions and makes the entire judgment due and payable.

EXAMPLE: Phoebe gets a judgment against Ted for $3,000. The judge grants Ted's request to pay the judgment in installments of $300 per month. Ted misses the first payment, and Phoebe hears he plans to move out of state. She can immediately move to collect the $300. But to collect the rest, Phoebe must either wait until each subsequent payment is missed and then try to collect each one or go back to court and ask the judge to set aside the installment payments portion of the judgment so that she can collect it all.

To set aside an installment judgment, call the small claims court clerk's office and find out whether the court has a form for this purpose. Below is a sample form you can copy if your court doesn't have its own form. File the original form with the small claims clerk, have a copy served on the debtor, and follow up with a Proof of Service form. (See Chapter 11.)

## Judgments Against Government Agencies

If you have a small claims judgment against a government agency, typically you can't use any of the enforcement procedures outlined in the rest of this chapter. Instead, you'll need to follow special procedures to collect. Public entities include your state government, counties, cities, school districts, public authorities, and any other political subdivisions in the state.

Procedures differ slightly from state to state. As soon as you are awarded a judgment against a government agency, you can contact the agency to get information about its payment procedures. In many states, you must take the following steps to collect a judgment from a government agency:

1. Prepare a written declaration under penalty of perjury stating the following:
    - the fact that you have a judgment in your favor
    - the name of the government agency that owes the judgment
    - that you desire payment, and
    - the amount of the judgment.
    The sample declaration below contains all this information.

## Sample Request to Set Aside Payment Terms

CITY OF _____ , SMALL CLAIMS COURT

[*Plaintiff's name*] , PLAINTIFF V. [*Defendant's name*] , DEFENDANT

CASE NO. _____

MOTION OF JUDGMENT CREDITOR

TO SET ASIDE TERMS FOR PAYMENT OF JUDGMENT

The undersigned hereby declares the following:

1. The judgment was entered in the above-entitled action on [*date*] against the judgment debtor(s) _____[*name(s)*]_____ in the amount of: $ _____ principal, $_____ interest, and $_____ costs.

2. The judgment bore terms for payment of the above amount as follows: $_____ to be paid on _[*date*]_ and $_____ to be paid on _[*date*]_ . (Complete the applicable item below.)

   • No "grace period" for late payments was stated on the judgment.

   • If payment is (*specify*): _____ days late, the entire balance is due and owing.

3. The judgment debtor(s) has defaulted in payment of the judgment, and the balance owing is $_____ , including interest and costs awarded at the time of judgment. The last payment by the judgment debtor(s) was made on _[*date*]_ in the amount of $_____ .

4. The judgment creditor therefore petitions the court for an order setting aside the terms for payment of the judgment so that execution on the entire balance of the judgment can issue forthwith.

5. I, the undersigned, am [*specify: "the judgment creditor," or "the agent for the judgment creditor"*] .

I declare under penalty of perjury under the laws of the State of _____ that this declaration is true and correct.

Date: _____

Signature of declarant: _____

Print name of declarant: _____

NOTICE TO THE JUDGMENT DEBTOR(S):

If you dispute any allegation made in this motion, you must file a declaration in opposition to the motion with the small claims court within ten days of the mailing of this motion.

2. Get a certified copy of the judgment from the small claims court clerk.

3. Contact the agency that owes you money and find out the fee to collect the judgment.

4. Take or send the declaration, copy of the judgment, and the fee to the office or individual the agency you have the judgment against identifies as the correct place to send the documents.

5. You might be required to deliver a notice to the judgment debtor (the same government agency) where you filed a request for payment, even though doing so is redundant. To play it safe, have a friend mail photocopies of the declaration and the judgment, and a completed proof of service form to the government agency.

6. Keep the original proof of service and your copies of the declaration and judgment in a safe place.

The government agency will notify its treasurer or controller, who will pay you or deposit the money with the court. Make sure that you have your current address on file with the court—otherwise, you might never get paid.

### Sample Declaration

---

I, Steven Nakamura, declare as follows:

1. I have a judgment against the City of Los Angeles (Los Angeles Small Claims Court case #11212).

2. I desire payment according to the terms of the judgment.

3. The exact amount required to satisfy the judgment is $2,312, plus interest at the rate allowable by law from February 16, 20xx, until the judgment is paid in full.

I declare under penalty of perjury under the laws of the State of California that this declaration is true and correct.

Dated: February 16, 20xx          _____
                                        Steven Nakamura

---

# Finding the Debtor's Assets

Collecting your small claims judgment isn't too difficult if the judgment debtor has some money or property and you know where it is. But what do you do if you suspect that money or other assets exist but you have no idea how to find them? For example, you might know a person works, but not where, or that they have money in the bank, but not which one.

## Judgment Debtor's Statement

Wouldn't it be nice to simply ask the judgment debtor a few questions about their assets? Well, in many states the loser (judgment debtor) must fill out a form listing the judgment debtor's assets. (See "Sample Judgment Debtor's Statement of Assets," below.) Typically, the judgment debtor must send a completed copy of this form to the person who won the case (the judgment creditor) within a certain number of days after the judgment is mailed out by the clerk—unless the judgment debtor pays off the judgment, appeals, or asks the judge to reverse a default judgment. If the judgment debtor fails to complete the statement (which, unfortunately, is all too common), the judgment creditor might be able to ask the court to hold the debtor in contempt of court, and even issue a bench warrant for his arrest. Ask a small claims adviser how to ask the court to hold the debtor in contempt.

## Order for Examination

If the judgment debtor doesn't fill out the Statement of Assets form when required or if no such form exists, another tool is available in most states. The judgment creditor can ask the court clerk to issue an order requiring the judgment debtor to appear in court in person for questioning. In some states, this is called an "order for examination" or "judgment debtor's examination." This order, which you must serve on the judgment debtor, requires the debtor to show up in court and provide the information personally. Typically, if the debtor fails to show up, the judge can issue a bench warrant for the person's arrest.

# Sample Judgment Debtor's Statement of Assets

---

| MAIL TO THE JUDGMENT CREDITOR |
| DO NOT FILE WITH THE COURT |

SC-133

**JUDGMENT CREDITOR** (the person or business who won the case) *(name):*

**JUDGMENT DEBTOR** (the person or business who lost the case and owes money) *(name):*

SMALL CLAIMS CASE NO.:

| **NOTICE TO JUDGMENT DEBTOR:** You *must* (1) pay the judgment or (2) appeal or (3) file a motion to vacate. If you fail to pay or take one of the other two actions, you must complete and mail this form to the judgment creditor. If you do not, you may have to go to court to answer questions and may have penalties imposed on you by the court. | **AVISO AL DEUDOR POR FALLO JUDICIAL:** Usted debe (1) pagar el monto del fallo judicial, o (2) presentar un recurso de apelación o (3) presentar un recurso de nulidad. Si usted no paga el fallo o presenta uno de estos dos recursos, deberá llenar y enviar por correo este formulario a su acreedor por fallo judicial. Si no lo hace, es posible que deba presentarse ante la corte para contestar preguntas y pagar las multas que la corte le pueda imponer. |

## INSTRUCTIONS

The small claims court has ruled that you owe money to the judgment creditor.

1. You may appeal a judgment against you only on the other party's claim. You may *not* appeal a judgment against you on *your* claim.

    a. If you appeared at the trial and you want to appeal, you must file a *Notice of Appeal* (form SC-140) within 30 days after the date the *Notice of Entry of Judgment* (form SC-130 or SC-200) was mailed or handed to you by the clerk.

    b. If you did not appear at the trial, before you can appeal, you must first file a *Notice of Motion to Vacate Judgment and Declaration* (form SC-135) and pay the required fee within 30 days after the date the *Notice of Entry of Judgment* was mailed or handed to you. The judgment cannot be collected until the motion is decided. If your motion is denied, you then have 10 days after the date the notice of denial was mailed to file your appeal.

2. Unless you **pay the judgment or appeal or file a motion to vacate, you must fill out this form and mail it to the person who won the case** within **30 days** after the *Notice of Entry of Judgment* was mailed or handed to you by the clerk. Mailing this completed form does not stay enforcement of the judgment.

3. If you lose your appeal or motion to vacate, you must pay the judgment, including postjudgment costs and interest. As soon as the small claims court denies your motion to vacate and the denial is not appealed, or receives the dismissal of your appeal or judgment from the superior court after appeal, the judgment is no longer suspended and may be immediately enforced against you by the judgment creditor.

4. Unless you have paid the judgment, complete and mail this form to the judgment creditor within **30 days** after the date the clerk mails or delivers to you (a) the denial of your motion to vacate, or (b) the dismissal of your appeal, or (c) the judgment against you on your appeal.

---

If you were sued as an individual, skip this box and begin with item 1 below. Otherwise, check the applicable box, attach the documents indicated, and complete item 15 on the reverse.

    a. ☐ *(Corporation or partnership)* Attached to this form is a statement describing the nature, value, and exact location of all assets of the corporation or the partners, and a statement showing that the person signing this form is authorized to submit this form on behalf of the corporation or partnership.

    b. ☐ *(Governmental agency)* Attached to this form is the statement of an authorized representative of the agency stating when the agency will pay the judgment and any reasons for its failure to do so.

## JUDGMENT DEBTOR'S STATEMENT OF ASSETS

**EMPLOYMENT**

1. What are your sources of income and occupation? *(Provide job title and name of division or office in which you work.)*

2. a. Name and address of your business or employer *(include address of your payroll or human resources department, if different):*

    b. If not employed, names and addresses of all sources of income *(specify):*

3. How often are you paid?
    ☐ daily    ☐ every two weeks    ☐ monthly
    ☐ weekly    ☐ twice a month    ☐ other *(explain):*

4. What is your gross pay each pay period? $

5. What is your take-home pay each pay period? $

6. If your spouse earns any income, give the name of your spouse, the name and address of the business or employer, job title, and division or office *(specify):*

Form Adopted for Mandatory Use
Judicial Council of California
SC-133 [Rev. January 1, 2011]

**JUDGMENT DEBTOR'S STATEMENT OF ASSETS**
**(Small Claims)**

Page 1 of 2
Code of Civil Procedure,
§§ 116.620(a), 116.830
www.courts.ca.gov

## Sample Judgment Debtor's Statement of Assets (continued)

**CASH, BANK DEPOSITS**

7. How much money do you have in cash?. . . . . . . . . . . . . . . . . . . . . . . . . . . . . . . . . . . . . . . . . $
8. How much other money do you have in banks, savings and loans, credit unions, and other financial institutions either in your own name or jointly *(list)*:

| Name and address of financial institution | Account number | Individual or joint? | Balance |
|---|---|---|---|
| a. | | | $ |
| b. | | | $ |
| c. | | | $ |

**PROPERTY**

9. List all automobiles, other vehicles, and boats owned in your name or jointly:

| Make and year | License and vehicle identification (VIN) numbers | Value | Legal owner if different from registered owner | Amount owed |
|---|---|---|---|---|
| a. | | $ | | $ |
| b. | | $ | | $ |
| c. | | $ | | $ |
| d. | | $ | | $ |

10. List all real estate owned in your name or jointly:

| Address of real estate | Fair market value | Amount owed |
|---|---|---|
| a. | $ | $ |
| b. | $ | $ |

**OTHER PERSONAL PROPERTY** (*Do not list household furniture and furnishings, appliances, or clothing.*)

11. List anything of value not listed above owned in your name or jointly *(continue on attached sheet if necessary)*:

| Description | Value | Address where property is located |
|---|---|---|
| a. | $ | |
| b. | $ | |
| c. | $ | |

12. Is anyone holding assets for you? ☐ Yes. ☐ No. If yes, describe the assets and give the name and address of the person or entity holding each asset *(specify):*

13. Have you disposed of or transferred any asset within the last 60 days? ☐ Yes. ☐ No. If yes, give the name and address of each person or entity who received any asset and describe each asset *(specify):*

14. If you are not able to pay the judgment in one lump sum, you may be able to make payment arrangements with the person or business who won the case (the judgment creditor). State the amount that you can pay each month: $_____ , beginning on *(date):* _____ . If you are unable to agree, you may also ask the court for permission to make installment payments by filing a *Request to Make Payments* (form SC-220).

15. I declare under penalty of perjury under the laws of the State of California that the foregoing is true and correct.

Date: _____

▶

_____     _____
(TYPE OR PRINT NAME)                                         (SIGNATURE)

*Mail or deliver this completed form to the judgment creditor at the address shown on the* **Notice of Entry of Judgment** *form.*

SC-133 [Rev. January 1, 2011] | **JUDGMENT DEBTOR'S STATEMENT OF ASSETS** (Small Claims) | Page 2 of 2

There are usually some limitations to using this procedure. You can't require the judgment debtor to travel too far to participate, for example.

---

### Collecting Judgments Across State Lines

What if your judgment debtor moves to another state, or you discover that they own property or assets elsewhere? Collecting on the judgment will become less convenient, but it is still possible. The majority of states have enacted what's called the Uniform Enforcement of Foreign Judgments Act, creating standard procedures for going after a debtor's assets or property across state lines.

Here's how it ordinarily works: Say you file your small claims case in Illinois and get a judgment for $2,500. When you try to collect, you discover that the debtor has moved to Florida. To start your collection efforts, you will need to file your judgment in Florida, the new state. The procedure there, as in most states, is that you mail a certified copy of the original judgment to the Florida court clerk (usually in the area of the state where the judgment debtor lives), along with an affidavit showing your and the judgment debtor's names and addresses. (Some states vary this routine, so check with the court clerk first.)

Once the court receives the certified copy and affidavit, your filing becomes a valid part of the court record. The court may notify the judgment debtor of your filing, or you may need to serve notice on the judgment debtor. When this is done, you can proceed with your collection efforts, following the collection laws of the new state.

---

**TIP**

**Ask for relevant documents.** You may want the judgment debtor to bring certain documents to the examination. Bank statements, vehicle records, and documents regarding property ownership can be helpful when trying to collect. To do this, you must ask the clerk to issue a subpoena for documents. (See Chapter 14 for more information.)

TIP

**At the debtor's examination, some states allow the judgment creditor to ask debtors whether they have cash in their possession.** If so, you can ask the judge to issue a "turnover order," authorizing you to take the money right then and there to satisfy at least a portion of the debt.

## Levying on Wages, Bank Accounts, and Other Property

This section discusses ways to collect a court judgment. One or more may work easily and quickly. However, some judgment debtors hide assets or are otherwise difficult to collect from. If you face this situation and believe the judgment debtor might own or buy real property, your best bet might be to file a lien against that property and wait until the judgment debtor tries to sell the property. (See "Property Liens," below, for details on how to do this.)

TIP

**Think twice before using a collection agency.** If you don't want to bother pursuing the debtor, you can turn your debt over to a real collection agency. However, this probably doesn't make much sense, as the agency will often take up to 50% of what it can collect as its fee. And unless you are a regular customer, the agency probably won't treat your debt with much priority unless it believes your judgment will be easy to collect. Of course, if the debt is easy to collect, you should be able to do the job yourself and avoid paying the collection fee.

If you know where the judgment debtor works, you are in good shape. In most states, you are generally entitled to get approximately 25% of a person's net wages to satisfy a debt. (But if a person has a very low income, the amount might be considerably less than 25% and possibly nothing at all.)

Wage garnishments are not allowed in some states. In others, they are limited to, for example, 10% of a debtor's gross wages, 25% of net wages, or a multiple of the minimum wage, whichever is less. Some other states make it difficult to garnish the wages of the head of a family if the family has a low income and needs all of it to survive. The sheriff's or marshal's office in your area can supply you with the rules in your state, or you can check online.

Knowing where a judgment debtor banks can also be extremely valuable. You can provide the information to a sheriff, marshal, or constable and levy on a bank account. You'll get whatever it contains at the time of the levy, subject to several exceptions. (See "Some Money Is Protected," below.) Of course, a bank account levy will only work if there's money in the account. Most debtors who know you're after the funds will withdraw any funds promptly.

Other types of property can be more difficult to get. Why? All states have debtor's exemption laws that prohibit creditors from taking property the judgment debtor will need to work and live. Items protected typically include a portion of or all equity in a family house, furniture, clothes, and much more. You can find the exempt property laws of all 50 states online at www.nolo.com/legal-encyclopedia/bankruptcy-exemptions-state.

Practically speaking, other than wages and account balances, the only types of personal property (assets other than real estate) worth pursuing are business receipts and motor vehicles with equity exceeding the state's exemption amount.

Theoretically, there are many other assets that you could reach—boats and planes, for example—but in most cases, the judgment debtor won't own such luxurious property. And it won't be worth the time and expense involved if your judgment is for a modest amount.

Real estate can be different. Even if the judgment debtor doesn't have much equity in the property, you will still want to record a judgment lien. Most people refinance or sell at some point, and the judgment debtor will have to pay your lien before getting funding or transferring the property title. (See "Property Liens," below.)

## Writ of Execution

Before you can levy on a person's wages or other property, you must get court permission, usually in the form of a writ of execution, writ of garnishment, writ of attachment, or similarly titled document, which, for convenience, we'll refer to as a "writ." (See "Sample Writ of Execution," below.) Some courts also require that you complete a short application for

## Sample Writ of Execution

EJ-130

| ATTORNEY OR PARTY WITHOUT ATTORNEY: | STATE BAR NO.: | FOR COURT USE ONLY |
|---|---|---|

NAME:

FIRM NAME:

STREET ADDRESS:

CITY:     STATE:     ZIP CODE:

TELEPHONE NO.:     FAX NO.:

EMAIL ADDRESS:

ATTORNEY FOR (name):

☐ ATTORNEY FOR    ☐ ORIGINAL JUDGMENT CREDITOR    ☐ ASSIGNEE OF RECORD

**SUPERIOR COURT OF CALIFORNIA, COUNTY OF**

STREET ADDRESS:

MAILING ADDRESS:

CITY AND ZIP CODE:

BRANCH NAME:

PLAINTIFF/PETITIONER:

DEFENDANT/RESPONDENT:

CASE NUMBER:

**WRIT OF**    ☐ **EXECUTION (Money Judgment)**    ☐ Limited Civil Case (including Small Claims)

☐ **POSSESSION OF**    ☐ **Personal Property**

☐ **SALE**    ☐ **Real Property**    ☐ Unlimited Civil Case (including Family and Probate)

1. **To the Sheriff or Marshal of the County of:**
   You are directed to enforce the judgment described below with daily interest and your costs as provided by law.
2. **To any registered process server:** You are authorized to serve this writ only in accordance with CCP 699.080 or CCP 715.040.
3. (Name):
   is the ☐ original judgment creditor ☐ assignee of record whose address is shown on this form above the court's name.
4. **Judgment debtor** (name, type of legal entity if not a natural person, and last known address):

   ☐ Additional judgment debtors on next page

5. **Judgment entered** on (date):
   (See type of judgment in item 22.)

6. ☐ Judgment renewed on (dates):

7. **Notice of sale** under this writ:
   a. ☐ has not been requested.
   b. ☐ has been requested (see next page).

8. ☐ Joint debtor information on next page.

   [SEAL]

9. ☐ Writ of Possession/Writ of Sale information on next page.
10. ☐ This writ is issued on a sister-state judgment.

    For items 11–17, see form MC-012 and form MC-013-INFO.

11. Total judgment (as entered or renewed)   $
12. Costs after judgment (CCP 685.090)   $
13. Subtotal (add 11 and 12)   $
14. Credits to principal (after credit to interest)   $
15. Principal remaining due (subtract 14 from 13) $
16. Accrued interest remaining due per   $
    CCP 685.050(b) (not on GC 6103.5 fees)
17. Fee for issuance of writ (per GC 70626(a)(l)) $
18. **Total amount due** (add 15, 16, and 17)   $
19. **Levying officer:**
    a. Add daily interest from date of writ (at the legal rate on 15) (not on GC 6103.5 fees) . . . . . . . . . . . . . . . $
    b. Pay directly to court costs included in 11 and 17 (GC 6103.5, 68637; CCP 699.520(j)) . . . . . . . . . . . . . . . $
20. ☐ The amounts called for in items 11–19 are different for each debtor. These amounts are stated for each debtor on Attachment 20.

Date: _____    Clerk, by _____ , Deputy

**NOTICE TO PERSON SERVED: SEE PAGE 3 FOR IMPORTANT INFORMATION.**

Page 1 of 3

Form Approved for Optional Use
Judicial Council of California
EJ-130 [Rev. September 1, 2020]    **WRIT OF EXECUTION**    Code of Civil Procedure, §§ 699.520, 712.010, 715.010
Government Code, § 6103.5
www.courts.ca.gov

the writ. If you have a small claims judgment, you are entitled to a writ, and you'll likely get your writ from the small claims court clerk for a small fee, which is a recoverable cost.

Once the court issues your writ, take or send it to the sheriff, marshal, or constable in the county where the assets are located. Give the officer:

- The original writ and one to three or more copies, depending on the requirements of the sheriff, marshal, or constable. Keep a copy of the writ for your files.
- The required fees. The amount will vary depending on the type of asset. Call ahead or check the county's website—many post collection procedures and fees.
- Instructions on the asset type and location. The sheriff, marshal, constable, or small claims clerk might have a form to use when providing these instructions. Typically, however, they will accept a letter containing all the necessary information.

CAUTION

**Don't delay in serving a writ of execution.** A writ of execution expires if it is not served on the debtor by the sheriff, marshal, or constable within a certain number of days of the date it was issued by the court. If this time runs out, you will have to go back to the small claims court clerk and get another writ of execution issued. So don't get a writ until you have identified the property you want to take. That way, you won't use up part of the time holding a debtor's examination or trying other ways to locate property you can take.

## Wages and Bank Accounts

To seize a person's wages, you will probably need to provide an official copy of the writ of execution form to the sheriff, marshal, or constable in the county where the assets are located, and a letter of instruction (see "Sample Letter Containing Wage Levying Instructions," below). The sheriff or marshal will serve a wage withholding order on the debtor's employer, and you should get some money soon. Typically, an earnings withholding order lasts for a set period of time, such as 90 days, or until the judgment is satisfied or expires.

⚠ CAUTION
**Discrimination against "garnishee" prohibited.** Federal law and the laws of some states prohibit an employer from firing an employee because the employee's wages are garnished to satisfy a judgment. (15 U.S.C. § 1674(a).)

To levy on a bank account, first contact the sheriff, marshal, or constable's office to be sure they handle this work (if not, contact a process server). You'll need the original and one or more copies of the writ, a letter of instruction, and the correct fee. If a bank account is in the name of the defendant and someone else, you may have to post a bond, depending on your state's laws.

## Some Money Is Protected

Not all money in a debtor's bank account is up for grabs. Most states have laws that prohibit you from taking exempt funds, and if taken, the judgment debtor can force you to return them. Typically, approximately 75% of wages placed in a bank account are exempt (100% if there has been a previous wage attachment involving the same money) for 30 days after payment. Generally, Social Security, certain retirement accounts, and financial aid for school are also exempt.

💡 TIP
**Timing is key.** The amount of money in most of our bank accounts fluctuates over a month or year. If the debtor is employed, the debtor's bank account balance is probably the largest around the first of the month. If the debtor has seasonal employment, certain times of the year are probably best for the levy. Before you write your instructions to the levying officer, think about when you will most likely find the money.

**Sample Letter Containing Wage Levying Instructions**

P.O. Box 66
Jackson, New York 12355
March 1, 20xx

Sheriff (Civil Division)
Mapleville, New York 12345

Re: *John Toller v. Mildred Edwards*
    Small Claims Court No. 81-52

Dear Sheriff:

Enclosed you will find the original and one copy of a Property-Income Execution issued by the small claims court in the amount of $ _____ .
I also enclose a check for your fee in the amount of $_____ .

I hereby instruct you to execute on the wages of Mildred Edwards, who works at the Graphite Oil Co., 1341 Chester Street, Mapleville, New York. Please serve the Execution on or before March 15, 20xx. [*For a bank account, you would simply substitute* "execute on all monies in the accounts of Mildred Edwards, located at [*address*]." *You generally do not need to know the account number— although some counties may require it—only the bank and branch, but your chance of collecting is probably better if you can supply the account number.*]

Very truly yours,

*John Toller*

John Toller

## Business Assets

In many states, it is possible to have someone from the sheriff's, marshal's, or constable's office sent to the business of a person who owes you money to collect it from the cash on hand. It is done with a till tap or a keeper. You will want to ask your court clerk about your local rules.

A till tap consists of a one-time removal of all cash and checks from the business. The fees are reasonable. For a keeper, a deputy from the sheriff's, marshal's, or constable's office goes to the place of business, takes all the cash and checks in the cash register, and then stays there for a set period (an eight-hour keeper, a 24-hour keeper, or a 48-hour keeper) to take more money as it comes in. Because you must pay the deputy to stay at the collection site, keepers' fees are relatively high. It is also possible for the business's property to be seized and sold. But the costs of doing so are usually prohibitive.

Talk to the sheriff, marshal, or constable in your area to get more details. This person will want an original and several copies of your writ, as well as collection instructions. You can get the judgment debtor to reimburse you for the money you spend on collection processes if enough money comes in to cover it.

## Motor Vehicles

Seizing a person's motor vehicle tends to be difficult for several reasons, including the following:

- A portion of the equity in a car is exempt from your levy in many, though not all, states. The exempt amount ranges widely, from $1,000 to $20,000.

  EXAMPLE: A judgment debtor in Oregon has a car worth $4,000 on which he owes $3,000 to a bank. This means his equity is $1,000—the bank owns the rest. Equity of up to $3,000 is exempt under Oregon law, so you would end up with nothing.

- The car must be parked in an accessible place, such as a street or driveway, unless you obtain a court order allowing entry into a garage or another private place.
- You can't always be sure that the judgment debtor owns the car he drives. It may be in someone else's name, or he may be leasing it.

Finding out whether a judgment debtor owns the car they drive can be tricky. You might get this information from the judgment debtor's statement of assets or by conducting a debtor's examination (see "Finding the Debtor's Assets," above). Also, for a small fee, you might be able to find out from the Department of Motor Vehicles who owns the car, including whether or not a bank or finance company has an interest.

Once you have this information, you can determine whether the car is worth enough to levy against. Would the sales price be enough to pay off any outstanding car loan, give the debtor the exemption amount, cover the costs of the sale, and leave enough to pay a substantial part of your judgment? If you believe the vehicle is worth enough to cover these costs, then have the sheriff pick up the car and sell it. But remember, the sheriff's fees will be relatively high, and you'll have to pay the fees in advance. Also, the sale price at a public auction will fetch far less than at a private sale. If the car sells for enough, you can get back the money spent on sheriff's fees after the sheriff sells the vehicle.

Call the sheriff, marshal, or constable of the county where the car is to find out how much deposit money and writ copies you'll need. Then write a letter similar to the example below.

CAUTION

**Some states have no exemption for motor vehicles, and some exempt a higher amount of equity.** Check your state's laws, call your local sheriff's or marshal's office, or consult the list of all states' exemptions located online at www.nolo.com/legal-encyclopedia/bankruptcy-exemptions-state.

## Sample Letter to Sheriff Requesting Levy

P.O. Box 66
Jackson, New York 12355
March 1, 20xx

Sheriff (Civil Division)
Cheyenne, New York 12345

Re: *John Toller v. Mildred Edwards*
   No. SC 81-52

Dear Sheriff:

You are hereby instructed, under the authority of the enclosed Property-Income Execution, to execute upon and sell all of the right, title, and interest of Mildred Edwards, judgment debtor, in the following motor vehicle:

[*Enter the description of the car as it appears on the DMV report, including the license number.*]

The vehicle is registered in the name(s) of Mildred Edwards, and is regularly found at the following address(es):

[*List home and work address of owner. Remember that the car must be in a public place, such as parked on a street.*]

Enclosed is my check for $_____ to cover your costs of execution and sale.

Very truly yours,

*John Toller*

John Toller

## Stocks, Bonds, Mutual Funds, and Other Securities

If the judgment debtor owns stock or other securities that are not exempt as part of a retirement plan (see below), you might be able to force the debtor to sell these assets to pay your judgment. Your collection method will depend on whether the debtor personally holds the stock certificates or whether they're held by a stockbroker.

If the judgment debtor personally holds the certificates, you can levy against the certificates themselves as tangible personal property. However, you will first need to get a court order allowing you to reach property in a private home.

If the certificates are held for the judgment debtor by a broker, you can initiate a third-party levy against the branch office of the stock brokerage firm. The sheriff, marshal, or constable will require a writ, written instructions, and fee to handle the levy.

Sometimes stock or mutual fund ownership is not manifested in certificates but is recorded in the company's computers issuing the securities. In this case, it is usually possible to make a third-party levy at a company's in-state headquarters. If the company's headquarters are out of state, however, you will need to use different procedures, such as obtaining a court order assigning you the right to the securities. For assistance with this, ask the small claims clerk.

## Small Items

It usually isn't worth the trouble to try to levy on small items of personal property, such as furniture or appliances, because they are commonly covered by one or another debtor's exemption laws. Even if property isn't exempt, selling it would likely produce less cash than the collection costs. If you identify valuable nonexempt property that's worth selling, you will need a court order to allow a levying officer access to property in a private home.

## Individual Retirement Plans

In some states, you can get at money in the judgment debtor's individual (for example, IRA) or self-employment (for example, Keogh) retirement plans held in banks or savings institutions. You'll need to check your state laws to find out whether individual retirement accounts are fair game. And most afford some type of protection to the owner. If you're entitled to go after this money, you can do so just as you would with any other money kept in a bank. Of course, you need to know where the money is.

It's more likely that you would be able to collect against a distribution from an IRA rather than the IRA itself. Also, some states allow you to collect up to 25% of the periodic payment from an individual retirement or Keogh type retirement plan, just the way you would get a wage garnishment. Private company employee retirement plans and federal, state or local government retirement plans work similarly—generally, the balance can't be touched. However, it's likely that you can collect a percentage of a periodic payment made from the account.

## Judgments From Auto Accidents

In certain circumstances, a judgment debtor's driver's license can be suspended by the Department of Motor Vehicles if the debtor doesn't pay a judgment stemming from an auto accident. Check with your Department of Motor Vehicles for information.

> **TIP**
> **First, try negotiation.** If the debtor needs to drive to work, license suspension might cause the person to lose his or her job. To get rid of the debt and therefore avoid the suspension, the debtor might decide to declare bankruptcy. If you are a creditor and intend to ask the Department of Motor Vehicles to suspend the debtor's license, first negotiate with the debtor. You might be able to work out a payment plan, which is a win-win result: You get your money, and the debtor doesn't have to declare bankruptcy.

336 | EVERYBODY'S GUIDE TO SMALL CLAIMS COURT

## Property Liens

Another way to collect money from a person or business against whom you have a small claims judgment is by putting a lien on real estate owned by the debtor. In some states, the entry of a court judgment automatically creates a lien on any real property the debtor owns in the county where the judgment was obtained. In the rest of the states, you must record the judgment with the county to create a lien on the debtor's real property.

Once you have a lien on the judgment debtor's property, especially real property, there is a good chance you'll eventually be paid. It usually works like this: When the judgment debtor wishes to sell the real estate, the title will be clouded by your lien and the debtor will probably pay you off to be able to transfer clear title to a third party. Likewise, if the debtor wishes to refinance, it almost certainly will be contingent on paying off all liens. Sooner or later, you should get your money. Remember, however, that a portion of the debtor's equity in the home is exempt from collection.

Before you record your lien, make sure you wait until the time to appeal has passed. In many states, here's how to record a property lien against all the debtor's real estate that you know about:

1. Get an Abstract of Judgment form from the small claims clerk's office at the court where your case was heard (a small fee is required).
2. Take or mail the Abstract of Judgment form to the County Recorder's office in each county where property is located or you think the debtor might buy property, and pay the required fee. The recorder's office will record your lien and notify the judgment debtor.

## Collection Costs

Using formal collection methods like wage garnishments and property liens to get a judgment debtor to cough up the money owed can be expensive. You will want to make the judgment debtor pay you back for these costs, if possible. You can be compensated for many—but not all—costs of collecting a judgment. Generally speaking, you can get your direct costs of collecting, which include costs like:

- sheriff, marshal, or constable fees
- costs to get copies of required court papers, like a writ of execution or abstract of judgment, and
- fees to file a lien against a debtor's real estate.

However, you won't be able to get compensated for indirect costs such as:

- babysitting costs
- lost wages
- transportation costs, or
- postage or photocopying.

You are entitled to collect interest on your judgment according to your state's law. Interest begins to accrue on the date the judgment was entered. If the judge has entered a judgment to be paid in installments, you can charge interest only on installments that have become due, unless the judgment specifically says interest is to be earned earlier. Apply any payments you receive first toward interest and then to the unpaid balance of the judgment. You cannot claim interest on accrued unpaid interest.

## Renew Your Judgment

Judgments expire after a certain number of years—usually between five and 20, depending on the state. To find out your state's rule, see "Time Limits to Collect Court Judgments," below. Be aware that the expiration periods could differ if you are collecting on a judgment that was originally entered in another state. Also, use the information as a general guideline. You'll need to determine the particulars that apply in your case by reading the law governing your judgment.

Fortunately, most states allow you to renew your judgment—and any liens based on it—if you do so before the expiration date (a few states allow you to revive an expired judgment, too). For information on how to renew a judgment, contact your small claims court clerk's office.

## Time Limits to Collect Court Judgments

This chart is for general guidance only—do not rely on it. You must conduct independent research. These statutes explain how long you have to collect general court judgments. The chart doesn't address reviving judgments and doesn't include rules for particular judgment types. You must read your state statutes before you can determine whether a time limit applies or consult with an attorney.

| State | Statute | Time Limit (years) |
|---|---|---|
| Alabama | Ala. Code § 6-2-32 | 20 |
| Alaska | Alaska Stat. § 09.10.040 | 10 |
| Arizona | Ariz. Rev. Stat. Ann. §§ 12-544, 12-1551 | 10 |
| Arkansas | Ark. Code Ann. §§ 16-56-114, 16-19-1002 | 10; 5 in Justice of Peace Courts |
| California | Cal. Civ. Proc. Code § 683.020 | 10 |
| Colorado | Colo. Rev. Stat. § 13-52-102 | 20; 6 if entered in county courts |
| Connecticut | Conn. Gen. Stat. Ann. § 52-598 | 20 for execution, 25 to bring an action; in small claims court: 10 for execution, and 15 to bring an action |
| Delaware | Del. Code Ann. tit. 10, § 4711 | 10 |
| District of Columbia | D.C. Code Ann. § 15-101 | 12 |
| Florida | Fla. Stat. Ann. § 95.11 | 20 |
| Georgia | Ga. Code Ann. §§ 9-3-20, 9-12-60 | 7 |
| Hawaii | Haw. Rev. Stat. §§ 657-1, 657-5 | 10 |
| Idaho | Idaho Code § 5-215 | 11 |
| Illinois | 735 Ill. Comp. Stat. §§ 5/12-108, 5/13-218 | 7 |
| Indiana | Ind. Code Ann. § 34-11-2-11 | 10 |
| Iowa | Iowa Code § 614.1(6) | 20 |
| Kansas | Kan. Stat. Ann. § 60-2403 | 5 (with 5-year renewals possible) |
| Kentucky | Ky. Rev. Stat. Ann. § 413.090 | 15 |
| Louisiana | La. Civ. Code Ann. Art. 3501 | 10; unlimited renewals |
| Maine | Me. Rev. Stat. Ann. tit. 14, § 864 | 20 |

## Time Limits to Collect Court Judgments (continued)

| State | Statute | Time Limit (years) |
|---|---|---|
| Maryland | Md. Code Ann. [Cts. & Jud. Proc.] § 5-102(a)(3) | 12 |
| Massachusetts | Mass. Gen. Laws ch. 260, § 20 | 20 |
| Michigan | Mich. Comp. Laws § 600.5809 | 10 |
| Minnesota | Minn. Stat. Ann. § 541.04 | 10 |
| Mississippi | Miss. Code Ann. § 15-1-43 | 7 |
| Missouri | Mo. Rev. Stat. §§ 511.370, 516.350 | 10 |
| Montana | Mont. Code Ann. § 27-2-201 | 10 |
| Nebraska | Neb. Rev. Stat. §§ 25-205, 25-1515 | 5 |
| Nevada | Nev. Rev. Stat. Ann. § 11.190 | 6 |
| New Hampshire | N.H. Rev. Stat. Ann. § 508:5 | 20 |
| New Jersey | N.J. Stat. Ann. § 2a:14-5 | 20 |
| New Mexico | N.M. Stat. Ann. §§ 37-1-2, 39-1-6 | 14 |
| New York | N.Y. C.P.L.R. Law § 211 | 20 (10 years against land unless renewed) |
| North Carolina | N.C. Gen. Stat. § 1-47 | 10 |
| North Dakota | N.D. Cent. Code § 28-01-15 | 10 |
| Ohio | Ohio Rev. Code Ann. §§ 2325.18, 2329.07 | Generally 5 years to execute judgment |
| Oklahoma | Okla. Stat. Ann. tit. 12, §§ 95, 735 | 5 |
| Oregon | Or. Rev. Stat. Ann. § 12.070 | 10 |
| Pennsylvania | 42 Pa. Cons. Stat. Ann. § 5525 | 4 |
| Rhode Island | R.I. Gen. Laws § 9-1-17 | 20 |
| South Carolina | S.C. Code Ann. §§ 15-3-600, 15-35-810 | 10 |
| South Dakota | S.D. Codified Laws § 15-2-6 | 20 |
| Tennessee | Tenn. Code Ann. § 28-3-110 | 10 |
| Texas | Tex. Civ. Prac. & Rem. Code Ann. § 34.001 | 10 |
| Utah | Utah Code Ann. § 78B-2-311 | 8 |

| Time Limits to Collect Court Judgments (continued) | | |
|---|---|---|
| **State** | **Statute** | **Time Limit (years)** |
| **Vermont** | Vt. Stat. Ann. tit. 12, § 506 | 8 |
| **Virginia** | Va. Code Ann. § 8.01-251 | 10 (as of January 1, 2022) |
| **Washington** | Wash. Rev. Code Ann. § 4.16.020 | 10 |
| **West Virginia** | W. Va. Code § 38-3-18 | 10 |
| **Wisconsin** | Wis. Stat. § 893.40 | 20 |
| **Wyoming** | Wyo. Stat. Ann. § 1-17-307 | 5 |

# Legal Research

When you're involved in a dispute, there might come a time when you need to know more about the relevant law. Usually, all you'll need to know is how to find the local ordinances, state statutes, or judicial opinions that speak to your particular problem. City and county agencies and offices can often give you good advice and information. For example, a zoning or planning office might answer questions about fence height restrictions or building permits. Also, all state laws are available for free online, as well as many cities' local laws and some judicial decisions. Or, you can make a trip to your local law library.

---

### Where's the Law Library?

Public law libraries are usually located in or near the main county courthouse. You can search online using the term "Law Library." If that fails, call the clerk of the local court for information.

---

This chapter gives basic guidelines for using the Internet and libraries to find answers to legal questions that frequently arise in small claims disputes. If you wish to delve more deeply into the law, Nolo publishes a comprehensive book called *Legal Research: How to Find & Understand the Law,* by the Editors of Nolo. Or another resource with links to small claims court information is Freeadvice.com/legal/small-claims/small-claims-small-claims.

## Local Laws

Most cities' and counties' official websites contain a large body of helpful information, including local ordinances available for searching and downloading. You should be able to find the official website by typing in the following into the Google search bar: <name> <town, city, county, state> website." For instance, searching for "boulder county website" brings up the official Boulder County website in the first position.

If your city's website does not include the text of local ordinances, try finding local laws on one of these sites:

- State and Local Government on the Net (statelocalgov.net), and
- the Municipal Code Corporation (municode.com).

If you don't succeed online, your local laws might be available at your local public library or the city or county law library (usually located near the courthouse). You can also try getting a copy of local ordinances from the relevant city or county office or special district. For example, the zoning board might give you a copy of your town's zoning ordinances; your regional water district might have copies of local water usage ordinances. These departments usually charge a small fee to cover photocopying costs.

Once you've found a copy of your town's local laws, look for your topic in the index or table of contents. Be prepared to look under several different terms. Some indexes are not as helpful as they should be. For instance, if you're quarreling with neighbors about the excessive height of their new fence, you might start by looking under "height" and "fence." If you are unsuccessful, try "zoning laws."

## State Laws

The easiest way to find a copy of a state law (also called a "statute") is using its citation—that is, the number of the specific statute. If you don't know the statute's citation, you can use online and print resources to find statutes on a particular subject.

## If You Know the Citation

Citations to state statutes normally refer to the title (or volume) and section numbers. The three examples shown in Figure 1 are typical.

---

**Sample State Statute Citations**

| 23 | Vt. Stat. Ann. | § 1185 |
|---|---|---|
| title (volume number) | Vermont Statutes Annotated | section number |

| N.J. Stat. Ann. | 2A: | 170-90.1 |
|---|---|---|
| New Jersey Statutes Annotated | volume number | section number |

| Mich. Comp. Laws Ann. | 421.27 | (c)(2)(ii) |
|---|---|---|
| Michigan Compiled Laws Annotated | section number | subsection letter |

---

**Figure 1**

Some states' laws are divided up into several different topical sections. In states such as New York and California, citations look like those shown below.

---

**Sample California and New York Citations**

| P.C. | § 518 |
|---|---|
| Penal Code | section number |

| Penal Law | § 14025 |
|---|---|
| Collection of Penal Statutes | section number |

---

**Figure 2**

When you know the statute's citation, then you can search online or at a local law library to get a copy.

## Using the Internet

Every state maintains its statutes online. You'll often find them on state legislature websites. The websites vary in their format, but almost all of them allow you to search for statutes by topic, keyword, or citation.

If your state's official website does not allow you to search by topic or keyword, then check the Cornell Legal Information Institute website (law.cornell.edu). It lets you search for statutes by topic as well as by name.

---

### Finding Your State's Website

Every state has its statutes online. State websites usually use the following format:

<state postal code abbreviation>.gov

Example: ny.gov, ca.gov, mn.gov

But you'll need to look for a link to legislature or laws on the state site, which might take some searching. If you'd prefer to go straight to the source, insert your state's name in a "statute" search. For instance, try "Florida statutes," Minnesota statutes," or "Kansas statutes." Each request brings up the specific website where you'll find the online version of your state's code sections. (Hint: You'll usually find your state statutes on your state legislature's website.)

---

## Using the Library

You can find state laws in your local public law library. Use the annotated version of the statute book if possible because that version includes additional information that will help with research, such as references to cases that will help you understand how the statute is applied. These books also have subject indexes or tables of contents that you can use to find laws on particular topics. For example, if someone has cut down your tree, you'd look under "trees." Nothing useful there? Try anything else you can think of, such as "timber" or "trespass." Sometimes finding a particular state statute is easy. But don't be discouraged if it takes a bit of time and patience. A few states have pretty bad indexes.

## Make Sure the Law Is Current

Once you've found the law you need, make sure it hasn't been changed or repealed. If you're reading an ordinance online, the source will tell you what year's version of the law you're looking at. At the library, check the front or back of the book of statutes for updates. Just look for the number of the law in the update material. If nothing is there under that number, it means there has been no change. If you find a change, it replaces the law printed in the hardbound volume. If there is nothing but the word "repealed" after the number of the law, the law printed in the hardbound volume is no longer in effect.

## Reading and Interpreting a Statute

When you find a statute on your subject, read it carefully. Remember that lawyers write the laws, and many of them seem unable to write in plain English. Figure 3 shows a page from a volume of state statutes. This state law on spite fences is from the annotated laws of Massachusetts. Let's look at the different pieces of information on the page:

- **(1)** the topic of the statute
- **(2)** the section number of the statute
- **(3)** the name of the statute
- **(4)** the text of the statute
- **(5)** historical information including when the statute was enacted (1887), and when it was modified
- **(6)** a listing of reference materials that discuss the statute
- **(7)** a subject index of cases interpreting the statute
- **(8)** a citation to a case discussing the statute, and
- **(9)** the page number of the book in which the statute appears.

(1)

## SPITE FENCES

**§ 21.** **Definition; remedy of injured occupant**

(2) (3) (4)

A fence or other structure in the nature of a fence which unnecessarily exceeds six feet in height and is maliciously erected or maintained for the purpose of annoying the owners or occupants of adjoining property shall be deemed a private nuisance. Any such owner or occupant injured in the comfort or enjoyment of his estate thereby may have an action of tort for damages under chapter two hundred and forty-three.

**Historical Note** —— (5)

St.1887 c. 348.    R.L.1902 c. 33 § 19.

**Library References** —— (6)

Nuisance ☞3(12).
C.J.S. Nuisance § 39.

Comment. Damnum absque injuria, see M.P.S. vol. 14, Simpson, § 1373.

**Notes of Decisions**

(7)

Constitutionality 1
Distance from boundary line 3
Motive in erecting fence 2
Persons liable 4
Subsequent proceedings 5
Validity 1

(8)

—————

**1. Validity**

St.1887, c. 348, declaring fences unnecessarily exceeding six feet in height for annoyance of adjoining owner to be private nuisances, applies to existing structures subsequently maintained as well as those afterward erected and is consti-

tutional. Rideout v. Knox (1889) 19 N. E. 390, 148 Mass. 368, 2 L.R.A. 81, 12 Am.St.Rep. 560; Smith v. Morse (1889) 19 N.E. 393, 148 Mass. 407.

**2. Motive in erecting fence**

Under St.1887, c. 348, purpose of annoyance must be dominant motive for erecting and maintaining fence. Rideout v. Knox (1889) 19 N.E. 390, 148 Mass. 368, 2 L.R.A. 81, 12 Am.St.Rep. 560.

**3. Distance from boundary line**

Where defendant maliciously erected fence unnecessarily more than 6 feet

5A M.G.L.A.—29    **449**

(9)

Figure 3

Sometimes you'll want to read a judicial decision interpreting a particular statute—for example, if the phrasing of the statute is unclear or if you want to know how the court applied the statute in a particular situation. To find cases interpreting a statute, check the listings after the statute's text in an annotated version of your state's statutes, which you can find in the law library.

In the annotated code, one-sentence summaries of court cases that interpret the statute directly follow the notes on the statute's history. (See Number 8 in Figure 3.) Some statutes have been interpreted by the courts so many times that the publisher includes a little index to the case summaries, which are organized by issues raised by the statute. (See Number 7 in Figure 3.) It is often difficult to tell from a brief summary whether a case is relevant to your problem. Fortunately, the summaries also contain a case citation that allows you to look up the case and read it for yourself. It is essential that you read the case itself and not just rely on what it says in the annotation.

Annotated statutes are not available online except for a fee. At Westlaw (Westlaw.com), you can pay by credit card and then enter the citation for a statute and receive a list of all court cases discussing the law. But it's expensive, so check whether your local law library offers online legal searching at no cost—many do.

## Case Law

A judicial opinion, decision, or case is a written opinion of a court ruling on one or more issues of a particular lawsuit. These opinions are called "case law." Often, they interpret the laws created by the legislature, which is why you might need to read them. Even if your state laws address a particular topic, the language of the law might not give you a clear-cut answer to your question. If you find a particular statute that looks as if it will help you, it's always helpful to know how courts have interpreted the law.

You might need to read a judicial decision for another reason, too. Although most common small claims court issues are addressed either by local law or state statute, some issues are governed entirely by the courts. When there are no state statutes or local ordinances to help you, you can find help in what's called the "common law." The common law is the body of law that is entirely developed by the courts through their written decisions.

## Finding Cases on the Internet

Unfortunately, the full text of many judicial decisions is not available online unless you're able to pay a (usually reasonable) fee.

### Free Research Sites

Google has state court cases going back to 1950. Go to "Google Scholar," select "Case law," and type in a case name.

Also, all states make their more recent cases available free online, though they usually don't go as far back as Google. To find these cases for your state:

**Step 1:** Go to www.law.cornell.edu/co.html.

**Step 2:** Locate the link to the court opinions for your state. There could be one link, or separate links for your state's supreme court and courts of appeal (the lower trial courts seldom publish their opinions, so you probably won't be able to find them).

### Fee-Based Research Sites

If you can't find what you need for free, you'll need to try a site that charges for access to cases. A good place to start is VersusLaw, a fee-based system for finding both current and past (archived) state and federal cases. VersusLaw (Versuslaw.com) offers state and federal court opinions that range from the most recent to those decided 75 years ago.

Other fee-based legal research sites include Westlaw (Westlaw.com) and LexisNexis (Lexisnexis.com). Your local law library might offer use of one of these legal research sites at no cost.

## Finding Cases in the Library

Even if you start your legal research online, you might find yourself needing a law library, especially if you're looking for case law and are unable or unwilling to pay a fee for searching. In the law library, you can read the full text of court cases once you know the citation (see "Understanding Case Citations," below), or use reference materials to find cases on particular subjects.

Ask the librarian to point you to some reference books or to a general legal encyclopedia. These books can give you background information and might also mention cases that will bear on your situation.

**Legal encyclopedias.** Some states have their own; if yours doesn't, use a national one, such as *American Jurisprudence* (called "Am. Jur." for short). Like traditional encyclopedias, these books are arranged alphabetically by topic. The encyclopedia articles discuss how courts have ruled in actual court cases.

Some encyclopedias have more than one series; you want the most recent. For instance, the current series of Am. Jur. is Am. Jur. 2d. Also be sure to check the back of the books (called "pocket parts") for more recent updates.

Figure 4 shows a page from Am. Jur. 2d, discussing uncertain boundary lines—the example involves neighbors setting a boundary by building a fence. You can see the short summaries of court decisions that follow each issue raised. Let's look at the different sections of the page:

① the volume you're currently reading

② the topic

③ the section number within that topic

④ the name of the section

⑤ explanatory text

⑥ citation to a relevant case

⑦ a cross-reference to A.L.R., a set of volumes whose full name is *American Law Reports*, where you'll find another article about this topic, and

⑧ the page number.

*American Law Reports* is another national compilation of court decisions, books, and published articles concerning all areas of the law. A.L.R. also comes in several series—the 7th is the latest—and has updated material in the back. A.L.R. has separate index volumes that list the topics in alphabetical order. A.L.R. is also available online but it's costly—you'll do better using it at your local law library.

① ② ③

mutual acquiescence and recognition by the adjoiners is essential to practical location, provided that there is, at the time of the location, a disputed, indefinite, or uncertain boundary line between the adjoining owners.[11] A practical location of a boundary line has been said to be simply an actual designation on the ground, by the parties, of the monuments and bounds called for by the conveyances,[12] and it has also been said that when a disputed or uncertain boundary line is fixed by practical location it is binding, not by way of transfer of title, but by way of estoppel.[13]

### § 88. Erection of fence. ④

Where there is doubt and uncertainty as to the location of the true boundary line[14] between adjoining landowners, they may agree that a fence may be the division line between their lands.[15] To constitute the fence the boundary line it is not necessary that the agreement be express; it may be inferred from or ⑤ implied by the conduct of the parties, especially where the fence is acquiesced to as the boundary line for the period of the statute of limitations.[16] It has

**11.** Drury v Pekar, supra, quoting Kincaid v Peterson, 135 Or 619, 297 P 833.

The practical location of a boundary line can be established in any one of three ways: (1) the location relied upon must have been acquiesced in for a sufficient length of time to bar a right of entry under the statute of limitations; (2) the line must have been expressly agreed upon between the parties claiming the land on both sides thereof and afterward acquiesced in; or, (3) the parties whose rights are to be barred must have silently looked on, with knowledge of the true line, while the other party encroached upon it or subjected himself to expense in regard to the land which he would not have done had the line been in dispute. Fishman v Nielson, 237 Minn 1, 53 NW2d 553.

**12.** Wells v Jackson Iron Mfg. Co. 47 NH 235.

Boundary lines may be determined by physical indications of the lines on the ground accepted by the parties over a period of time. Fallone v Gochee, 9 App Div 2d 569, 189 NYS2d 363, app den 9 App Div 2d 699, 191 NYS2d 560.

The actual location of a deed may be satisfactorily established, not only by the natural objects found on the ground, but by the fact that all the parties who knew the facts and were interested in the land located the deed in a certain way. Kenmont Coal Co. v Combs, 243 Ky 328, 48 SW2d 9 (holding that location of deed by grantor and his grantee, subsequently acquiesced in for more than 30 years, could not be disputed).

**13.** Adams v Warner, 209 App Div 394, 204 NYS 613, quoted with approval in Drury v Pekar, 224 Or 37, 355 P2d 598.

**14.** Uncertainty of or dispute as to the location of the true boundary line is essential in order that a fence built on a line agreed as the boundary line may operate to preclude the parties from later claiming a different boundary line. Vowinckel v N. Clark & Sons,

217 Cal 258, 18 P2d 58; Pederson v Reynolds, 31 Cal App 2d 18, 87 P2d 51; Blank v Ambs, 260 Mich 589, 245 NW 525; Talbot v Smith, 56 Or 117, 107 P 480, 108 P 125. Annotation: 170 ALR 1146.

But it is not necessary that there should be an actual dispute between the parties regarding the true division line; it is sufficient if it appears that they were uncertain as to the true line and therefore agreed to a designated and certain boundary upon which they constructed a fence and occupied and cultivated or improved their respective portions to that division fence for more than the statutory period. Martin v Lopes (Cal App) ⑥ 164 P2d 321, superseded 28 Cal 2d 618, 170 P2d 881.

When the real boundary line between contiguous landowners is known to them, neither of them may acquire title by acquiescence beyond such line by merely building a fence upon the other's property and cultivating and claiming the land to that point, since title to land by acquiescence is founded on an agreement and an uncertainty exists as to the true line. Martin v Lopes, supra.

**15.** An oral agreement fixing an uncertain and disputed dividing line of lands, and execution thereof by the building of a fence thereon, is not in violation of the statute of frauds, since the parties do not thereby undertake to acquire and pass title to real estate, but merely fix the location of the boundary of the land that they already own, the purpose being to identify their several holdings and make certain that which they regard as uncertain. Holbrooks v Wright, 187 Ky 732, 220 SW2d 524.

Generally as to oral agreements fixing boundary lines, see §§ 78 et seq., supra.

**16.** Hannah v Pogue, 23 Cal 2d 849, 147 P2d 572; Roberts v Brae, 5 Cal 2d 356, 54 P2d 698; Kandlick v Hudek, 365 Ill 292, 6 NE2d 196.

*Annotation:* 170 ALR 1145.

**623**

⑦ ⑧

**Figure 4**

## Reading a Case

A court case contains a lot of information before you even get to the court's actual opinion. Let's look at an example. You find a case that says that a neighbor could not collect money for damage caused by a neighbor's healthy tree. The case is *Turner v. Coppola,* 102 Misc.2d 1043, 424 N.Y.S.2d 864 (N.Y. Sup. Ct. 1980). Figure 5 shows a copy of this page. Let's evaluate what you see there:

(1) the page number

(2) the name and volume of the reporter (collection of cases) you're reading

(3) the official citation for the case

(4) the name of the case

(5) the name of the court

(6) the date the opinion was decided

(7) a summary of the case, including what this court ruled, and

(8) a topic and key number.

The West Publishing Company has given thousands of discrete issues of law their own "key numbers," ordered under topic headings. You can use the topic and key number of a particular rule to find other cases on the same point.

All published cases begin with this kind of introductory information. Once you have gone over the introduction, it is time to read the opinion itself. Never depend on what a reference book, or even the case summary, tells you about an opinion. The people researching the cases for these books are only human, so occasionally, summaries are misleading.

## Make Sure the Case Is Still Valid

Once you've located a case that addresses the issue you're interested in, you'll want to make sure the case is still valid and hasn't been overturned or reversed by another court decision before you use the case in your small claims dispute. You can check that a case is still good law by using an online service called KeyCite, available from Westlaw (Westlaw.com) for a fee. You also get a complete list of all cases that refer to the case, which could lead you

① ②

864           424 NEW YORK SUPPLEMENT, 2d SERIES

"8. The instruction and supervision given * * * were so negligently given as to result in the * * * injuries sustained."

No other factual averment was made by plaintiff which in any way indicates a basis for his conclusion of negligence (*Koppers Co. v. Empire Bituminous Products, Inc.*, 35 A.D.2d 906, 316 N.Y.S.2d 858); and, such is not satisfied by a mere repetition of the complaint without factual evidence upon which to impose liability upon the movant (*Golding v. Weissman*, 35 A.D.2d 941, 316 N.Y.S.2d 522).

Defendant, Senior's motion is granted.

③ ———— 102 Misc.2d 1043

**Barbara G. TURNER, Plaintiff,**

v.

④ **Caroline COPPOLA, Richard Petersen, Minna Petersen and Freda Amster, Defendants.**

⑤ ———— Supreme Court, Special Term, Nassau County, Part I.

⑥ ———— Feb. 13, 1980.

⑦ Plaintiff, who alleged that branches on defendants' trees encroached on plaintiff's property, caused cosmetic damage to her garage and prevented her lawn from receiving adequate sunlight and that twigs, branches and buds from the trees constantly fell on her property, brought action for omnibus relief. On defendants' motion to dismiss complaint for failure to state cause of action, the Supreme Court, Nassau County, Special Term, B. Thomas Pantano, J., held that: (1) the trees were not a "nuisance per se," in such a sense as to sustain an action for relief; (2) complaint did not state cause of action for relief from private nuisance; (3) plaintiff did not have a cause of action in trespass; (4) plaintiff did not

have a cause of action in negligence; but (5) plaintiff could protect herself by self-help consisting of a reasonable cutting of branches to extent that they invaded her property.

Motion to dismiss complaint granted.

**1. Nuisance** ⟸1

Essence of a "private nuisance" is interference with the use and enjoyment of land amounting to an injury in relation to a right of ownership in that land.

    See publication Words and Phrases for other judicial constructions and definitions.

**2. Nuisance** ⟸3(1)

In light of fact that defendants' trees, whose branches allegedly encroached on plaintiff's property and from which twigs, branches and buds were alleged to have constantly fallen onto such property, were not poisonous or noxious in their nature, the trees were not a "nuisance per se," in such a sense as to sustain an action for relief.

    See publication Words and Phrases for other judicial constructions and definitions.

**3. Nuisance** ⟸42

Right to recover damages from overhanging branches depends on presence of actual injury to plaintiff or plaintiff's property.

**4. Nuisance** ⟸48

Complaint, in which it was alleged that branches on defendants' trees encroached on plaintiff's property, caused cosmetic damage to her garage and prevented her lawn from receiving adequate sunlight and that trees, branches and buds from the trees constantly fell on plaintiff's property, did not state cause of action for relief from private nuisance. RPAPL § 871.

**5. Nuisance** ⟸3(1) ———— ⑧
    **Trespass** ⟸10

If an invasion of plaintiff's interest in exclusive possession of his land also deprives him of use and enjoyment of the land, trespass and nuisance would jointly arise, so long as the interference causes

**Figure 5**

to additional cases on the subject you're interested in. Westlaw is expensive to use, but most law libraries offer Westlaw or a similar service for free.

You can check a case's validity using books in the law library—it's an old process called Shepardizing. For instructions, see Nolo's book *Legal Research: How to Find & Understand the Law*, by the Editors of Nolo.

---

### Understanding Case Citations

A case's citation is like its address: It tells you exactly where to locate the published opinion. A citation will tell you the name of the case, the book it is published in, which court decided the case, and the year in which it was published.

Courts publish cases in books called "reporters." There are two kinds of reporters: One, called a "state reporter," publishes just the court cases from a particular state; the second, called a "regional reporter," includes cases from a group of states in the same book. A case's citation will usually tell you where to find the case in either the state or the regional reporter.

Let's take an example: You find a citation for a case stating that a tree owner might have to pay for damage caused to his neighbor's property by his tree. The case citation is *Israel v. Carolina Bar-B-Que, Inc.*, 292 S.C. 282, 356 S.E.2d 123 (Ct. App. 1987). The citation tells you the case name, the two different reporters the case is published in, the court that heard the case, and and the date. Here's how to decode the information.

- The case name: *Israel v. Carolina Bar-B-Que, Inc.*
- The first reporter information is 292 S.C. 282, and it tells us that the case is published in volume 292 of the South Carolina Reporter on page 282. Abbreviations for particular reporters are listed in the front of the volumes of reporters.
- The second reporter information, 356 S.E.2d 123, tells us the case is in volume 356 of the Southeastern Reporter, 2nd Series, at page 123.
- The court that published the opinion: We know the case is from South Carolina because the South Carolina Reporter publishes only cases from that state. We can see that the case comes from a Court of Appeals of South Carolina from the "Ct. App." language in the parentheses.
- The date: 1987.

# Small Claims Court Rules for the 50 States (and the District of Columbia)

⚠️ CAUTION

**Always check your small claims court rules for updates and changes.** Laws may change after this book goes to press and local court rules may vary from one county to the next, so be sure to check your local small claims court rules before making any legal decisions. Whether you are a plaintiff or a defendant, you should either call your local small claims court clerk or see if the information you need is on the Internet. This appendix lists websites for each state's small claims information. (All links are accurate at the time of publication.) You will also find links to small claims courts on Nolo's website (www.nolo.com).

## Alabama

**Court:** District Court, Small Claims Docket.

**Statutes:** Ala. Code §§ 6-3-2; 6-3-7; 12-12-31; 12-12-70; 12-12-71.

**Court rules:** Alabama Small Claims Rules, Rules A to N; Alabama Small Claims Forms, 1 to 8.

**Court information:** http://judicial.alabama.gov/library/SmallClaimsRules
www.alabamalegalhelp.org/resource/small-claims-court?ref=Pnvky
http://guides.ll.georgetown.edu/c.php?g=275769&p=1838373 (state statutes).

**Dollar limit:** $6,000.

**Where to sue:** County or district where any defendant resides or where injury or property damage occurred. Corporation, where injury or property damage occurred, where principal place of business is located, or where plaintiff resides (if defendant does business there).

**Service of process:** Sheriff or other person approved by court; or certified mail, if requested.

**Defendant's response:** Defendant must file written answer within 14 days of service to avoid default.

**Transfer:** No provision.

**Attorneys:** Allowed; required for assignees (collection agencies).

**Appeals:** Allowed by either party within 14 days from the date of the judgment or the denial of a post-trial motion.

**Evictions:** No.

**Jury trials:** Not allowed.

## Alaska

**Court:** District or Magistrate Court, Small Claims Docket.

**Statutes:** Alaska Stat. §§ 22.15.040; 22.15.050.

**Court rules:** Alaska District Court Rules of Civil Procedure Rules 8 to 22; Appellate Court Rules 204, 217.

**Court information:** www.courts.alaska.gov/forms/#sc (select "Self-Help" and "Small Claims")
https://public.courts.alaska.gov/web/forms/docs/sc-100.pdf
www.legis.state.ak.us/basis/folio.asp (state statutes).

**Dollar limit:** $10,000.

**Where to sue:** Court nearest to defendant's residence or place of employment, district in which injury or property damage occurred, district where defendant does business, or a place that will not cause unnecessary expense or inconvenience for defendant.

**Service of process:** Approved process server, Alaska State Trooper, or certified mail sent by court clerk. The clerk notifies plaintiff regarding the service status of defendant.

**Defendant's response:** Defendant must file written answer within 20 days of service (40 days if outside the U.S.) to avoid default. The judge can allow a defendant with a valid excuse to respond later if default hasn't been entered.

**Transfer:** Defendant (or plaintiff against whom a counterclaim has been filed) can request transfer to regular district court by asking for the "formal Rules of Civil Procedure."

**Attorneys:** Allowed; required for assignees (collection agencies).

**Appeals:** Allowed by either party within 30 days from the date shown in the clerk's certificate of distribution of judgment.

**Evictions:** No.

**Jury trials:** Not allowed.

## Arizona

**Court:** Justice Court, Small Claims Division.

**Statutes:** Ariz. Rev. Stat. Ann. §§ 12-401; 22-501 to 22-525.

**Court information:** www.azcourts.gov/selfservicecenter/Small-Claims www.azleg.gov/arstitle (state statutes).

**Dollar limit:** $3,500.

**Where to sue:** Precinct where any defendant resides, where a transient is found, where a spouse resides (unless living separately), where the transaction or injury occurred, where the obligation was to be performed, or any other venue (location) over which the court has jurisdiction if the defendant fails to object.

**Service of process:** Authorized officer or process server approved by court, or registered or certified mail with return receipt requested.

**Defendant's response:** Defendant must answer in writing within 20 days to avoid default.

**Transfer:** Defendant can file motion to transfer venue (court location). Transfer to justice court allowed if defendant objects to small claims court at least ten days before hearing. Case must be transferred to preserve right to appeal.

**Attorneys:** Allowed only if both parties agree in writing.

**Appeals:** Appeals are not allowed, but a party can file a "Motion to Vacate Judgment" asking the court to set aside the judgment based on certain reasons such as error.

**Evictions:** No.

**Jury trials:** Not allowed.

**Notes:** Justice courts have a limit of $10,000. Each justice court has a small claims division for debt, damage, tort, injury, and some contract cases with a value of $3,500 or less. Rules can be found at Ariz. Rev. Stat. Ann. §§ 22-101, et al.

## Arkansas

**Court:** District Court, Small Claims Division.

**Statutes:** Ark. Const. amend. 80 § 7; Ark. Code Ann. § 16-17-706.

**Court rules:** Arkansas District Court Rules 1-11, except where modified by Rule 10; Administrative Order 18.

**Court information:** www.arkansasag.gov/consumer-protection/resources/
column-one/legal-resources/guide-to-small-claims-court
www.lexisnexis.com/hottopics/arcode (state statutes).

**Dollar limit:** $5,000.

**Where to sue:** County where any defendant resides, where the obligation was to be performed, or where the injury occurred.

**Service of process:** Clerk shall serve defendant by certified mail unless the plaintiff requests service by the sheriff or another authorized person.

**Defendant's response:** Defendant must file a written answer setting forth reasons for denial and any affirmative defenses (see court form) within 30 days of service. Defendant must mail a copy of the answer to plaintiff.

**Transfer:** Case will be transferred to regular district court if a party is represented by an attorney or if case value exceeds limits.

**Attorneys:** Not allowed.

**Appeals:** Either party can appeal to circuit court within 30 days of entry of small claims judgment.

**Evictions:** No.

**Jury trials:** Not allowed.

## California

**Court:** Superior Court, Small Claims Division.

**Statutes:** Cal. Civ. Proc. Code §§ 116.110 to 116.950.

**Court information:** www.courts.ca.gov/selfhelp-smallclaims.htm
www.dca.ca.gov/publications/small_claims/index.shtml
https://leginfo.legislature.ca.gov/faces/codes.xhtml (state statutes).

**Dollar limit:** Individuals can generally sue for up to $10,000 (but only two claims can be over $2,500 each year); $6,500 against a guarantor who promised to be responsible for someone else; $2,500 against a guarantor who didn't charge for the guarantee; up to $10,000 against the Registrar of the Contractors as guarantor. Public entities and businesses limited to $5,000, or $4,000 against a guarantor who charged for the guarantee. Until February 1, 2025, court may hear claims for COVID-related rental debt of any amount (limit of two filings per year does not apply to such actions).

**Where to sue:** In the county where any defendant resides; where bodily injury or property damage occurred; where a contract was signed, broken, or to be carried out; where a buyer made a purchase or lived when making a purchase.

**Service of process:** Personal service by sheriff or disinterested adult; substituted service; service by Certified mail sent by court clerk.

**Defendant's response:** No written answer required. Filing a counterclaim isn't required. However, a defendant's claim must be filed at least five days before the hearing (or one day before if plaintiff served the complaint ten days or less before the hearing).

**Transfer:** If defendant counterclaims over the dollar limit, case will be heard in higher court if the small claims court agrees to the transfer.

**Attorneys:** Not allowed.

**Appeals:** Defendant (or plaintiff who loses a counterclaim) must file a Notice of Appeal within 30 days of the date the court mails the small claims judgment. The court will send a superior court trial date. Plaintiff can make a motion to correct a clerical error or a decision that is based on a legal mistake.

**Evictions:** No.

**Jury trials:** Not allowed.

## Colorado

**Court:** County Court, Small Claims Division.

**Statutes:** Colo. Rev. Stat. §§ 13-6-401 to 13-6-417.

**Court rules:** Colorado Rules of County Court Civil Procedure, Rule 411; Colorado Rules of Civil Procedure for Small Claims Courts, Rules 501 to 521.

**Court information:** www.courts.state.co.us/Self_Help/smallclaims
https://leg.colorado.gov/agencies/office-legislative-legal-services/colorado-revised-statutes (state statutes).

**Dollar limit:** $7,500; plaintiff can waive balance over amount but cannot split claims into multiple claims. No more than two claims per month and 18 per calendar year.

**Where to sue:** County in which any defendant resides; is regularly employed; is a student at an institution of higher education; has business office; or for a security deposit dispute or action to enforce restrictive covenants, where the real estate is located.

**Service of process:** Personal service by process server or disinterested adult; or certified mail sent by court clerk.

**Defendant's response:** Defendant must file written and signed response on or before trial date.

**Transfer:** Allowed by defendant who has a counterclaim over $7,500.

**Attorneys:** No attorneys are allowed except for pro se (attorneys can represent themselves) or if the person is an authorized full-time employee of the entity bringing or defending the lawsuit or is an active general partner (partnership), authorized active member (union), a full-time officer (corporation), or active member (association), of the entity that is a party to the lawsuit. Seven day written notice of attorney representation required. If an attorney does appear as permitted above, the other party can have one also.

**Appeals:** Allowed by either party within 14 days after the date of entry of judgment.

**Evictions:** No.

**Jury trials:** Not allowed.

## Connecticut

**Court:** Superior Court, Small Claims Docket.

**Statutes:** Conn. Gen. Stat. Ann. §§ 47a-34 to 47a-42; 51-15; 51-345 to 51-347; 52-57; 52-259.

**Court rules:** Connecticut Superior Court Procedure in Civil Matters, Rules 24-1 to 24-33.

**Court information:** www.jud.ct.gov/faq/smallclaims.html www.jud.ct.gov/lawlib/statutes.htm (state statutes).

**Dollar limit:** $5,000; higher for landlord-tenant security deposit claims and home improvement and new home construction contract breach claims.

**Where to sue:** If plaintiff is corporation or company, county or geographical area where defendant resides or does business or where transaction or injury took place. If plaintiff is individual, where plaintiff resides, where defendant resides, or where transaction or injury took place.

**Service of process:** Priority mail with delivery confirmation, by certified mail return receipt requested or with electronic delivery confirmation, by a nationally recognized courier service providing delivery confirmation, or by a proper officer. Out-of-state business entity service requirements found in C.G.S.A. § 52-57.

**Defendant's response:** Must file answer or a motion to transfer on or before the "answer date" that appears on the answer form sent by the court clerk. A setoff or counterclaim should be filed by the answer date (or the date given after a successful motion to open). The answer date will be between 15 and 45 days after the writ and accompanying documents are filed in the court.

**Transfer:** Transfer allowed to regular superior or housing court upon filing of a counterclaim over $5,000 or if a good defense exists such that the case should be heard by a jury. Jurisdiction is challenged by a motion to dismiss.

**Attorneys:** Allowed; required for corporations.

**Appeals:** Appeals are not allowed in small claims court. However, a party can file a "motion to open judgment" to reopen the case for certain reasons such as a lack of actual notice.

**Evictions:** No.

**Jury trials:** Not allowed; case will be transferred to regular superior court.

## Delaware

**Court:** Justice of the Peace Court.

**Statutes:** Del. Code Ann. tit. 10, §§ 9301 to 9640.

**Court rules:** Justice of the Peace Courts, Rules 1 to 72.1.

**Court information:** www.courts.delaware.gov/JPCourt
www.courts.delaware.gov/help/proceedings
https://delcode.delaware.gov

**Dollar limit:** $25,000.

**Where to sue:** County where defendant resides; in eviction cases, county where property is located.

**Service of process:** Court serves the complaint with the exception of out-of-state parties or if the filer requests a special process server.

**Defendant's response:** In all debt or trespass claims, defendant must file written answer within 15 days after service is made to avoid default. If defendant files counterclaim above $25,000, can still pursue the counterclaim in justice of the peace court. (There is no provision for transfer to higher court.) If defendant wins counterclaim, there are two options: (1) the court will note the outcome on the record and defendant may take the case to a higher court, or (2) defendant may waive the excess over $25,000 and accept $25,000 as the judgment.

**Transfer:** No provision. Complaints and counterclaims exceeding $25,000 should be filed in proper court.

**Attorneys:** Allowed.

**Appeals:** In landlord/tenant summary possession cases, the appeal must be filed within five business days starting from day after judge signs judgment. In all other cases, within 15 actual days (not business days) starting from the day after judge signs judgment.

**Evictions:** Yes.

**Jury trials:** Generally not allowed. Permitted in eviction cases; defendant must make request within ten days of being served.

## District of Columbia

**Court:** Superior Court, Small Claims and Conciliation Branch.

**Statutes:** D.C. Code Ann. §§ 11-721; 11-1301 to 11-1323; 16-3901 to 16-3910; 17-301 to 17-307.

**Court rules:** District of Columbia Superior Court Rules of Procedure for Small Claims and Conciliation Branch, Rules 1 to 19.

**Court information:** www.dccourts.gov/services/civil-matters/requesting-10k-or-less; www.dccourts.gov/sites/default/files/SmallClaimsHandbook.pdf https://code.dccouncil.us/dc/council/code (statutes).

**Dollar limit:** $10,000 for all actions involving money recovery, with the exception of cases involving real property interests.

**Where to sue:** In D.C. if defendant resides in, transacts business in, has the right to use or have property in, or agreed to insure or act as a surety within the District of Columbia; or if the harm occurred in D.C.

**Service of process:** Can be made personally by an uninterested adult or a U.S. Marshal approved by court; or sent by court clerk registered or certified mail, return receipt requested.

**Defendant's response:** No written response required, except where the defendant asserts a set-off or counterclaim.

**Transfer:** Transferable to regular superior court if justice requires, if defendant's counterclaim affects interest in real property (land or housing), or if either party demands jury trial.

**Attorneys:** Allowed; required for corporations. (Certified law students may also appear.)

**Appeals:** Must file an application for an allowance to appeal within three days from the date of judgment and show that an undecided question of law should be before the DC Court of Appeals.

**Evictions:** No.

**Jury trials:** Either party can demand one by filing a jury request before the first court date. The case will transfer to the civil division of superior court.

## Florida

**Court:** County Court.

**Statutes:** Fla. Sm. Cl. Rule 7.010-7.300; Fla. Sm. Cl. Form 7.310-7.350

**Court rules:** Fla. Sm. Cl. Rule 7.010-7.300; Fla. Sm. Cl. Form 7.310-7.350; Florida Rules of Appellate Procedure, Rules 9.110.

**Court information:** https://help.flcourts.org/Other-Resources/Small-Claims www.leg.state.fl.us/statutes (state statutes).

**Dollar limit:** $8,000.

**Where to sue:** County where a defendant resides; where the harm or event occurred; where contract was entered; location agreed to in the contract or if none, where payment was to be made; where an unsecured promissory note was signed or where the borrower lives; where property to be recovered or foreclosed is located.

**Service of process:** Peace officer or adult approved by court; or (for Florida residents only) certified mail, return receipt requested, sent by court clerk or attorney of record.

**Defendant's response:** Must appear personally or by counsel at pretrial conference. No answer required, but must file any counterclaim in writing at least five days before pretrial conference.

**Transfer:** Allowed to regular county court if defendant counterclaims over $8,000. To transfer county court locations, the defendant must orally request a transfer at first court date or file written transfer request seven days before and serve on plaintiff.

**Attorneys:** Allowed; if attorneys are involved, parties are subject to discovery.

**Appeals:** Appeals must be filed within 30 days of the rendition of the order to be reviewed.

**Evictions:** Yes.

**Jury trials:** Allowed. Plaintiff must make demand when filing suit; defendant must make demand within 5 days after service or notice of suit or at pretrial conference.

## Georgia

**Court:** Magistrate Court.

**Statutes:** Ga. Code Ann. §§ 15-10-1; 15-10-2; 15-10-40 to 15-10-54; 15-10-80; 15-10-87.

**Court information:** www.consumer.georgia.gov/consumer-topics/magistrate-court https://sos.ga.gov/index.php/elections/georgia_code_-_lexisnexis (state statutes).

**Dollar limit:** $15,000 (no limit in eviction cases).

**Where to sue:** County where defendant resides; where an unincorporated business is physically located; or where a corporation's registered agent is located.

**Service of process:** The magistrate court serves defendant with a summons to appear and a copy of the claim

**Defendant's response:** Defendant must answer within 30 days (either in writing or in person) to avoid default.

**Transfer:** To appropriate court if defendant's counterclaim is over $15,000; or defendant submits a written request for a jury trial.

**Attorneys:** Allowed.

**Appeals:** Either party can appeal within 30 days from the judge's decision. No appeal rights from a default or dismissal due to plaintiff's nonappearance at trial.

**Evictions:** Yes.

**Jury trials:** Not allowed.

## Hawaii

**Court:** District Court, Small Claims Division.

**Statutes:** Haw. Rev. Stat. §§ 604-5; 633-27 to 633-36.

**Court rules:** Hawaii District Court Rules, Small Claims Division, Rules 1 to 14.

**Court information:** www.courts.state.hi.us/self-help/small_claims/small_claims

**Dollar limit:** $5,000; no limit in landlord-tenant residential security deposit cases. For return of leased or rented personal property, the property must not be worth more than $5,000.

**Where to sue:** Where defendant resides, or if defendant doesn't reside in the judicial circuit, where claim arose. If claim arose outside the judicial circuit, where defendant can be found. If defendants reside in different divisions, where claim arose. If claim arose outside the judicial circuit, where any defendant can be found. In security deposit disputes, where defendant resides, or the property location, if defendant is out of state.

**Service of process:** Authorized process server; registered or certified mail with return receipt requested, to be delivered to addressee only (requires oath, clerk certification, or filing of receipt); uninterested adult.

**Defendant's response:** No formal written answer required. Counterclaims up to $40,000 are allowed.

**Transfer:** The case will be transferred to the circuit court upon a proper demand for a jury trial.

**Attorneys:** Allowed (except in landlord-tenant security deposit cases).

**Appeals:** Not allowed. However, the court can alter or set aside a judgment if an application is made within ten days after entry of judgment (or longer upon a failure to receive notice of entry of judgment).

**Evictions:** No.

**Jury trials:** A party entitled to a jury trial can demand a jury and pay fees before trial. The case will be transferred to the circuit court.

## Idaho

**Court:** Magistrate Division, Small Claims Department.

**Statutes:** Idaho Code §§ 1-2301 to 1-2315.

**Court information:** www.isc.idaho.gov/irsca
https://courtselfhelp.idaho.gov/Forms/claims
www.ilga.gov/legislation/ilcs/ilcs.asp (state statutes).

**Dollar limit:** $5,000 for recovery of money and personal property cases. No pain and suffering or punitive damages.

**Where to sue:** Judicial district in which defendant resides or where the cause of action arose.

**Service of process:** Personal service; or certified or registered mail, return receipt requested, sent by court clerk.

**Defendant's response:** Must file written answer within 21 days of being served.

**Transfer:** No provision.

**Attorneys:** Not allowed.

**Appeals:** Allowed by either party within 30 days.

**Evictions:** No.

**Jury trials:** Not allowed.

## Illinois

**Court:** Small Claims Court.

**Statutes:** 735 Ill. Comp. Stat. §§ 5/2-101 to 5/2-208; 705 Ill. Comp. Stat. § 205/11.

**Court rules:** Illinois Supreme Court Rules, Rules 281 to 289.

**Court information:** www.ag.state.il.us/consumers/smlclaims.html
www.ilga.gov/legislation/ilcs/ilcs.asp (state statutes).

**Dollar limit:** $10,000.

**Where to sue:** County in which any defendant resides, or transaction or injury occurred. Private corporation, where it does business; public corporation, where its principal office is located.

**Service of process:** Sheriff, other law enforcement officer, licensed detective, or court-approved adult; or certified or registered mail, restricted delivery, return receipt requested, by court clerk.

**Defendant's response:** No formal written answer required. Must appear by date on court summons.

**Transfer:** No provision.

**Attorneys:** Allowed; required for corporations.

**Appeals:** Allowed by either party if filed within 30 days of entry of judgment.

**Evictions:** Yes.

**Jury trials:** The plaintiff must demand a jury when filing claim. The defendant can demand a jury up until the first appearance.

**Notes:** An alternative procedure exists for claims of $3,000 or less in Cook County's Pro Se Court. Plaintiffs represent themselves, and lawyers are allowed for defendants.

## Indiana

**Court:** Circuit, Superior, and County Court, Small Claims Docket; Marion County Small Claims Court.

**Statutes:** Ind. Code Ann. §§ 33-28-3-2 to 33-28-3-10 (circuit court); 33-29-2-1 to 33-29-2-10 (superior court); 33-34-3-1 to 33-34-3-15.1 (Marion County Small Claims Court).

**Court rules:** Indiana Rules for Appellate Procedure, Rule 9; Indiana Rules for Small Claims, Rules 1 to 16.

**Court information:** www.in.gov/judiciary/2710.htm
www.in.gov/judiciary/rules/small_claims
http://iga.in.gov/legislative/laws/2019/ic/titles/001 (state statutes).

**Dollar limit:** $10,000 (Marion County might have different limit.)

**Where to sue:** County in which any defendant resides or is employed; where transaction or occurrence took place; or where obligation arose or was to be performed by defendant. For landlord-tenant disputes, in county or town where property is located.

**Service of process:** Certified mail with return receipt requested; by delivering a copy to the defendant personally; or by leaving a copy at the defendant's dwelling house or usual place of abode and sending copy of claim to last known address by first-class mail. Marion County: Personal service or registered or certified mail.

**Defendant's response:** No formal written answer required.

**Transfer:** No.

**Attorneys:** Allowed.

**Appeals:** Within 30 days after entry of final judgment.

**Evictions:** Yes, if total rent due does not exceed $10,000 (Marion County might be different).

**Jury trials:** Defendant must request jury trial within ten days following service of complaint and deposit fees or else the right to jury trial is waived. Once requested, transferred from small claims to formal court.

## Iowa

**Court:** District Court, Small Claims Docket.

**Statutes:** Iowa Code §§ 631.1 to 631.17.

**Court information:** www.iowacourts.gov/for-the-public/representing-yourself/small-claims

www.legis.iowa.gov/law/iowaCode (state statutes).

**Dollar limit:** $6,500.

**Where to sue:** County in which any defendant resides or if resident is out of state, where resident can be found, where transaction or injury occurred, or obligation was to be performed.

**Service of process:** Peace officer or disinterested adult; or certified mail, restricted delivery, return receipt requested, sent by court clerk. For eviction cases, must be served personally.

**Defendant's response:** The defendant must appear within 20 days after service is made to avoid default. A nonresident has 60 days to appear.

**Transfer:** At judge's discretion if defendant counterclaims over the dollar limit.

**Attorneys:** Allowed.

**Appeals:** Allowed by either party upon oral notice at end of hearing or by written notice within 20 days after judgment is rendered. Heard in district court; no new evidence on appeal.

**Evictions:** Yes.

**Jury Trials:** Not allowed.

## Kansas

**Court:** District Court, Small Claims Docket.

**Statutes:** Kan. Stat. Ann. §§ 61-2701 to 61-2714; 61-3003; 61-3402 to 3409.

**Court information:** www.kscourts.org/Public/Small-Claims
www.kslegislature.org/li/b2019_20/statute (state statutes).

**Dollar limit:** $4,000; limit of twenty claims per calendar year.

**Where to sue:** Individual: Where defendant lives; where plaintiff resides if defendant is served there; defendant's place of business or employment; or where the cause of action arose. Corporation: Where registered office is located; where the cause of action arose; or where the defendant was transacting business at the time of the filing of the petition.

**Service of process:** Sheriff by return receipt delivery (including certified mail, priority mail, commercial courier service, etc). A party can ask the clerk to direct the sheriff to use personal or residential service. Service by publication is also available. A party can serve with permission from clerk. Acknowledgment of receipt or voluntary appearance constitutes service.

**Defendant's response:** No formal written answer required.

**Transfer:** If more than jurisdictional amount is claimed, the judge can dismiss the action, let the filer waive the excess, or allow the filer to bring claim in court of competent jurisdiction. A judge can hear a defendant's cross-claim if the amount is within the court's general jurisdiction.

**Attorneys:** Not allowed. However, if the claimant is an attorney, the other side is entitled to an attorney.

**Appeals:** Allowed by either party if filed within 14 days of entry of judgment.

**Evictions:** No.

**Jury trials:** Not allowed.

## Kentucky

**Court:** District Court, Small Claims Division.

**Statutes:** Ky. Rev. Stat. Ann. §§ 24A.200 to 24A.360.

**Court information:** https://kycourts.gov/Courts/District-Court/Documents/
   P6SmallClaimsHandbookweb.pdf
https://kycourts.gov/Legal-Help/Pages/default.aspx
https://apps.legislature.ky.gov/law/statutes (state statutes).

**Dollar limit:** $2,500

**Where to sue:** Judicial district in which defendant or defendant's agent resides
or does business.

**Service of process:** Certified or registered mail by court clerk.

**Defendant's response:** Must appear for hearing (20 to 40 days from service of
process). Must file counterclaim within five days of hearing.

**Transfer:** Allowed to regular district court or circuit court if defendant's
counterclaim is over $2,500, if defendant demands jury trial, or if judge decides
the case is too complex for small claims division.

**Attorneys:** Allowed.

**Appeals:** Either party can file an appeal within ten days of the judgment.

**Evictions:** Yes.

**Jury trials:** Not allowed. Plaintiff waives right to jury trial by filing case. Jury
trial request by defendant transfers case to regular district court.

**Notes:** Professional moneylenders and collection agents cannot sue in small
claims court.

## Louisiana

**Court:** City Court, Small Claims Division. (Parish Courts and the Justice of the
Peace might handle small claims. Contact your local court.)

**Statutes:** La. Rev. Stat. Ann. §§ 13:2586; 13:5200 to 13:5211.

**Court information:** https://lasc.libguides.com/JOP
www.lsba.org/Public/CourtStructure.aspx
www.brla.gov/FAQ.aspx?TID=27 (Baton Rouge)
www.shreveportla.gov/1044/Small-Claims Shreveport)
www.legis.la.gov/legis/Laws_Toc.aspx?folder=75&level=Parent (state statutes).

**Dollar limit:** $5,000.

**Where to sue:** Parish in which defendant resides. Corporation or partnership, in
parish or district in which business establishment located.

**Service of process:** Certified mail with return receipt requested; or sheriff, marshal, or constable, if certified mail is unclaimed or refused. Specific small claims notice must be served.

**Defendant's response:** Must file written answer within ten days of service to avoid default. A request to transfer case to regular docket (to preserve appeal) must be filed within ten days of service. Counterclaims must be filed with answer.

**Transfer:** Before trial, a defendant with a counterclaim over the dollar limit can file in the proper court and have the case transferred.

**Attorneys:** Allowed.

**Appeals:** Not allowed.

**Evictions:** Not allowed.

**Jury trials:** Not allowed.

## Maine

**Court:** District Court, Small Claims Docket.

**Statutes:** Me. Rev. Stat. Ann. tit. 14, §§ 7481 to 7487.

**Court rules:** Maine Rules of Civil Procedure, Rule 4. Maine Rules of Small Claims Procedure, Rule 1 to 18.

**Court information:** www.courts.maine.gov/help/small-claims/index.html http://legislature.maine.gov/statutes (state statutes).

**Dollar limit:** $6,000.

**Where to sue:** District court division in which defendant resides or has place of business, where the transaction occurred, or where registered agent resides if corporation.

**Service of process:** Certified mail, private process (personal service), constable, or sheriff.

**Defendant's response:** No formal written answer required.

**Transfer:** No provision.

**Attorneys:** Allowed.

**Appeals:** Allowed by either party within 30 days. Heard in superior court. Plaintiff's appeal on questions of law only; defendant's appeal on law and fact.

**Evictions:** No.

**Jury trials:** No provision.

## Maryland

**Court:** District Court. Small Claims Docket.

**Statutes:** Md. Code Ann. [Cts. & Jud. Proc.] §§ 4-405; 6-403.

**Court rules:** Maryland Court Rules, Rules 3-701, 7-104, 7-112.

**Court information:** www.mdcourts.gov/legalhelp/smallclaims
http://mgaleg.maryland.gov/mgawebsite/Laws/Statutes (state statutes).

**Dollar limit:** $5,000.

**Where to sue:** County in which any defendant resides, is employed, or does business; if multiple defendants from different counties, where injury to person or property occurred. Corporation may also be sued where it maintains principal office.

**Service of process:** Sheriff, constable, or disinterested adult, personally or by certified mail.

**Defendant's response:** Defendant has 15 days from receipt of summons to file "Notice of Intention to Defend" in order to avoid default (out-of-state defendant has 60 days).

**Transfer:** To regular civil docket if counterclaim exceeds $5,000 or if defendant demands jury trial.

**Attorneys:** Allowed.

**Appeals:** Allowed by either party within 30 days from entry of judgment or order. The other party can file a notice of appeal within ten days after the filing date of the first notice.

**Evictions:** Yes, as long as the rent claimed does not exceed $5,000. Review district court procedures for housing cases.

**Jury trials:** Not allowed. If demand is filed, the matter is transferred to regular civil docket.

## Massachusetts

**Court:** District Court, Small Claims Division; Boston Municipal Court.

**Statutes:** Mass. Gen. Laws ch. 218, §§ 21 to 25; ch. 223, § 6; ch. 93A, § 9 (consumer complaints).

**Court rules:** Massachusetts Rules of Court, Uniform Small Claims Rules, Rules 1 to 10; Small Claims Standards, 1:00 to 9:05.

**Court information:** www.mass.gov/small-claims
https://malegislature.gov/laws/generallaws (state statutes).

**Dollar limit:** $7,000. No limit for the following: property damage caused by motor vehicle, statutory award if actual damages are $7,000 or less; or double or treble damages awarded pursuant to a consumer protection law.

**Where to sue:** Judicial district in which plaintiff or defendant resides, is employed, or does business. Actions against landlords can also be brought in district in which property is located.

**Service of process:** First-class mail sent by court clerk for in-state defendants. For out-of-state defendants, sheriff or registered or certified mail.

**Defendant's response:** Written answer is optional, not required.

**Transfer:** Allowed to regular civil docket only at court's discretion .

**Attorneys:** Allowed.

**Appeals:** Not allowed for plaintiff or a defaulting defendant. A defendant who appeared at trial must file a Claim of Appeal form requesting review by a judge or jury, a small fee, and a $100 bond (more for a landlord) within 10 days after receiving written notice of the magistrates decision.

**Evictions:** No.

**Jury trials:** Not allowed.

**Notes:** Consumer complaint small claims: (1) plaintiff must make written demand for relief at least 30 days before filing suit; (2) attorneys' fees available; (3) triple damages available.

## Michigan

**Court:** District Court, Small Claims Division.

**Statutes:** Mich. Comp. Laws §§ 600.8401 to 600.8427.

**Court information:** www.courts.mi.gov/administration/scao/forms/pages/small-claims.aspx
www.michiganlegalhelp.org/self-help-tools/money-and-debt/i-have-small-claims-case
www.legislature.mi.gov/(S(rnl4xaxomfznr5545torg1r2))/mileg.aspx?page=home (state statutes).

**Dollar limit:** $6,500.

**Where to sue:** County where defendant resides or is employed, or where transaction or injury occurred.

**Service of process:** Plaintiff pays to have court clerk serve defendant by certified mail, return receipt requested, or personal service.

**Defendant's response:** No formal written answer required.

**Transfer:** Either party can transfer to regular district court before trial. If defendant's counterclaim is over $6,000 or if defendant wants attorney, case will be transferred.

**Attorneys:** Not allowed.

**Appeals:** Not allowed. Exception: If action is heard by district court magistrate, parties can appeal to small claims division for new trial within seven days of judgment.

**Evictions:** No.

**Jury trials:** Not allowed.

## Minnesota

**Court:** Conciliation Court.

**Statutes:** Minn. Stat. Ann. §§ 491A.01 to 491A.03.

**Court rules:** Minnesota General Practice Rules, Rules 501 to 525.

**Court information:** www.mncourts.gov/Help-Topics/Conciliation-Court.aspx www.revisor.mn.gov/statutes (state statutes).

**Dollar limit:** $15,000 ($4,000 for consumer credit cases).

**Where to sue:** County in which any defendant resides. Corporation, any county in which it has registered agent, place of business, or office; in certain circumstances, county in which plaintiff resides. Landlord-tenant disputes (other than evictions), county where rental property is located.

**Service of process:** First-class mail by court administrator; or by electronic means if party has agreed to or is required to accept electronic service. If claim is over $2,500, certified mail by plaintiff. If defendant is out-of-state, plaintiff must arrange service.

**Defendant's response:** No formal written answer required. Defendant must file counterclaim at least five days of the trial date. A counterclaim over $15,000 must proceed in district court. A plaintiff who doesn't receive a district court summons and counterclaim after 30 days can reinstate small claims action.

**Transfer:** To district court on demand for a jury trial or defendant's counterclaim above jurisdictional limit.

**Attorneys:** Not allowed.

**Appeals:** Either side can appeal by filing a Demand for Removal, an Affidavit of Good Faith, and an Affidavit of Service with the Court Administrator within 20 days of the date the judgment was mailed.

**Evictions:** No.

**Jury trials:** Not allowed.

## Mississippi

**Court:** Justice Court.

**Statutes:** Miss. Code Ann. §§ 9-11-9 to 9-11-33; 11-9-101 to 11-9-147; 11-25-1; 11-51-85.

**Court information:** www.courts.ms.gov/trialcourts/justicecourt/justicecourt.php

**Dollar limit:** $3,500.

**Where to sue:** County in which defendant resides or where the cause of action arose. A defendant who does not reside in the State of Mississippi or has no fixed place of residence shall be sued in the county where the cause of action arose.

**Service of process:** Clerk executes process. If returned within ten working days, the clerk directs the sheriff to execute process, or in case of emergency, another reputable process server.

**Defendant's response:** No formal written answer required.

**Transfer:** No provision.

**Attorneys:** Allowed.

**Appeals:** Either party can appeal. The appeal must be demanded and bond given within 10 days after the rendition of the judgment.

**Evictions:** Yes.

**Jury trials:** Either party can demand jury trial.

## Missouri

**Court:** Circuit Court, Small Claims Docket.

**Statutes:** Mo. Rev. Stat. §§ 482.300 to 482.365.

**Court rules:** Missouri Supreme Court Rules of the Small Claims Division of Circuit Court, Rules 140.01 to 152.

**Court information:** www.mo.gov/government/judicial-branch
https://missourilawyershelp.org/wp-content/uploads/2021/06/Small-claims-
 handbook-2021.pdf
https://revisor.mo.gov/main/Home.aspx (state statutes).

**Dollar limit:** $5,000.

**Where to sue:** County in which at least one defendant resides, or in which one plaintiff resides and at least one defendant may be found, or where transaction or injury occurred. If defendant is a business, where the business or registered agent is located, or where the transaction or injury occurred.

**Service of process:** Certified mail, return receipt requested or by personal service.

**Defendant's response:** No formal written answer required. Must file counterclaim within ten days after service of process.

**Transfer:** Allowed to regular circuit court if defendant counterclaims over $5,000, unless all parties agree to stay in small claims court.

**Attorneys:** Allowed.

**Appeals:** Allowed by either party if file demand within ten days of the issuance of the decision (the date appearing on the decision, not the date received).

**Evictions:** No.

**Jury trials:** Not allowed.

## Montana

**Court:** Small Claims Court.

**Statutes:** Mont. Code Ann. §§ 25-2-118; 3-12-101 to 3-12-107 (district court); 25-33-101 to 25-33-306 (appeals); 25-35-501 to 25-35-807; 3-10-1001 to 3-10-1004 (justice court).

**Court information:** www.dojmt.gov/consumer/guide-to-small-claims-court
https://leg.mt.gov/statute (state statutes).

**Dollar limit:** $7,000.

**Where to sue:** County or judicial district in which any defendant resides; if defendant does not live in state, where transaction or injury occurred.

**Service of process:** Sheriff or constable; other process server (justice court only).

**Defendant's response:** No formal written answer required. Defendant must serve counterclaim involving same dispute on plaintiff at least 72 hours before hearing. Counterclaims can't exceed $6,500 or if the court finds against plaintiff, defendant can pursue excess in justice or district court.

**Transfer:** Allowed by defendant to regular justice court if request filed within ten days of receipt of complaint.

**Attorneys:** Not allowed, unless all parties have attorneys.

**Appeals:** Allowed by either party if made within ten days of the original entry of judgment.

**Evictions:** No.

**Jury trials:** Not allowed. Defendant may request transfer to regular justice court for jury trial.

## Nebraska

**Court:** Small Claims Court.

**Statutes:** Neb. Rev. Stat. §§ 25-505.1; 25-2801 to 25-2807

**Court information:** www.supremecourt.nebraska.gov/self-help/small-claims
https://nebraskalegislature.gov/laws/browse-statutes.php (state statutes).

**Dollar limit:** $3,900 from July 1, 2020, through June 30, 2025 (adjusted every five years based on the Consumer Price Index).

**Where to sue:** County where the defendant or defendants agent resides or is doing business, or in the county in which the cause of action arose.

**Service of process:** Personal service by disinterested adult, certified mail, or designated delivery service; return receipt requested.

**Defendant's response:** Written answer not required, unless the case is transferred to the regular docket. Counterclaim: must file and deliver to plaintiff at least two days prior to trial.

**Transfer:** Transferable to regular civil court on defendant's request at least two days prior to the hearing or counterclaim over $3,500. Defendant must file an answer when the case is transferred.

**Attorneys:** Not allowed.

**Appeals:** Either party can demand appeal within 30 days after the entry of judgment by filing a Notice of Appeal, Appeal Bond, Transcript, and Bill of Exceptions.

**Evictions:** No.

**Jury trials:** Not allowed in small claims court. Defendant may request transfer to regular docket of county court by giving notice at least two days before hearing. Defendant must file an answer when the case is transferred, and demand for a jury trial must be made on or before the date the answer is filed with the court.

## Nevada

**Court:** Small Claims Court.

**Statutes:** Nev. Rev. Stat. Ann. §§ 73.010 to 73.060.

**Court rules:** Nevada Justice Court Rules of Civil Procedure, Rules 4; 88 to 100.

**Court information:** www.lasvegasjusticecourt.us/divisions/small_claims (Las Vegas) www.washoecounty.us/rjc/divisions/civil/services (Reno) www.civillawselfhelpcenter.org/self-help/small-claims www.leg.state.nv.us/nrs (state statutes).

**Dollar limit:** $10,000.

**Where to sue:** Where the defendant resides, does business, or is employed currently (or at time of incident); where the injury or property damage occurred; or where a contractual obligation is (or was) supposed to be performed.

**Service of process:** Personal or substitute service by sheriff, constable, or disinterested adult. Service by certified or registered mail if allowed by the court.

**Defendant's response:** No formal written answer required.

**Transfer:** No provision.

**Attorneys:** Allowed.

**Appeals:** Either party can appeal the decision within five business days from the date the decision was filed (plus three calendar days if the decision was mailed).

**Evictions:** No.

**Jury trials:** No provision.

## New Hampshire

**Court:** District or Municipal Court, Small Claims Docket.

**Statutes:** N.H. Rev. Stat. Ann. §§ 503:1 to 503:11.

**Court rules:** New Hampshire Rules of the Circuit Court - District Division, Rules 4.1 to 4.28.

**Court information:** www.courts.state.nh.us/district/eclaims
www.doj.nh.gov/consumer/complaints/small-claims.htm
www.gencourt.state.nh.us/rsa/html/nhtoc.htm (state statutes).

**Dollar limit:** $10,000.

**Where to sue:** Municipal court in the town in which the defendant or the plaintiff resides. If none, with the clerk of the district court in which district the defendant or the plaintiff resides.

**Service of process:** First class mail sent by court; if returned as undelivered, plaintiff must provide a new or alternate address. The court will forward the new notice to the defendant.

**Defendant's response:** Must respond to claim in writing within 30 days from the date the court mails the notice (the response date appears on the summons) to avoid default. Any counterclaim related to plaintiff's claim must be included in response; otherwise, defendant will have to show good cause to include a counterclaim at a later date.

**Transfer:** To superior court if defendant requests a jury trial (claim must be more than $1,500).

**Attorneys:** Allowed.

**Appeals:** The party against whom the judgment has been issued can appeal within 30 days of the rendition of judgment or of the clerk's notice of the judgment, whichever is later.

**Evictions:** No.

**Jury trials:** Not allowed; must transfer to superior court. Defendant must file request for jury trial within five days of plaintiff's claim, but only permitted for claims over $1,500.

## New Jersey

**Court:** Superior Court, Law Division, Special Civil Part, Small Claims Section.

**Statutes:** N.J. Stat Ann. §§ 2A 18-66, 67, 69, 71.

**Court rules:** New Jersey Rules of Court, Rules 1:40-6; 2:4-1; 6:1 to 6:12-2.

**Court information:** https://njcourts.gov/selfhelp/index.html
www.njcourts.gov/selfhelp/small_claims.html
https://nj.gov/state/dos-statutes.shtml (state statutes).

**Dollar limit:** $3,000 generally; $5,000 for claims relating to security deposits. Landlord/tenant claims for rent or money damages only.

**Where to sue:** County in which at least one defendant in the action resides. A business entity resides in the county in which its registered office is located or a county in which it is doing business. For a security deposit claim, the county where the landlord lives or where the rental property is located.

**Service of process:** Certified and regular mail by the court; if service not made, by mail or, at the request of the plaintiff, personal service by court officer.

**Defendant's response:** Written answers not allowed.

**Transfer:** Not allowed. Defendant must file jury demand at least five days before appearance date to transfer claim to the Special Civil (to $15,000) or the Law Division (unlimited) depending on the amount of damages.

**Attorneys:** Allowed.

**Appeals:** Either side can appeal the case to the Appellate Division of the Superior Court within 45 days from the date of judgment.

**Evictions:** No.

**Jury trials:** Defendant must submit demand at least five days before return of summons (case is then transferred to special civil part).

## New Mexico

**Court:** Metropolitan Court (Bernalillo County); Magistrate Court.

**Statutes:** N.M. Stat. Ann. §§ 34-8A-1 to 34-8A-10 (metropolitan court); 35-3-3, 35-3-5, 35-8-1 and 35-8-2 (magistrate court); 35-11-2, 35-13-1 to 35-13-3 (appeals).

**Court rules:** New Mexico Rules of Civil Procedure for the Magistrate Courts, Rules 2-101 to 2-804; New Mexico Rules of Civil Procedure for the Metropolitan Court, Rules 3-101 to 3-804.

**Court information:** https://metro.nmcourts.gov/self-help-center.aspx
www.nmcourts.gov/about-the-courts.aspx
www2.nmcourts.gov/othercourts/magistrate_brochure.pdf
https://lawlibrary.nmcourts.gov/general.aspx (state statutes).

**Dollar limit:** $10,000.

**Where to sue:** District in which plaintiff or defendant resides or may be found, or where the cause of action (transaction or injury) occurred.

**Service of process:** Service by sheriff or individual over 18 years who isn't party to the action. Personal service or service by first-class mail with signed acknowledgment.

**Defendant's response:** Must file answer on or before appearance date in summons. Counterclaims within jurisdictional limit can be filed. Counterclaims exceeding jurisdictional limit will be dismissed.

**Transfer:** No provision.

**Attorneys:** Allowed.

**Appeals:** Either party can file an appeal in the district court within 15 days after the judgment or final order appealed from is filed in the magistrate or metropolitan court. Once filed, the other side can file an appeal within ten days after the first notice of appeal was served or within the time otherwise prescribed by the rule, whichever is last.

**Evictions:** Yes.

**Jury trials:** Allowed.

## New York

**Court:** City, Town, and Village Courts; New York City Small Claims Court; Nassau County District, Small Claims Court; Suffolk District, Small Claims Court.

**Statutes:** N.Y. Uniform City Ct. Act § 1801; N.Y. Uniform Justice Ct. Act § 1801; N.Y. Dist. Ct. Act § 1801; and NYC Civ. Ct. Act § 1801

**Court rules:** N.Y. Uniform Trial Court Rules, Rules 208.41, 208.41-A, 210.41, 210.41-A, 212.41, 212.41-A, 214.10.

**Court information:** www.nycourts.gov/courthelp/SmallClaims/index.shtml
http://ww2.nycourts.gov/lawlibraries/nycodesstatutes.shtml (state statutes)
www.courts.state.ny.us/courthelp/pdfs/SmallClaimsHandbook.pdf
www.nycourts.gov/COURTS/nyc/smallclaims/pdfs/smallclaims.pdf

**Dollar limit:** $10,000 in New York City; $5,000 in Nassau County, Western Suffolk County, and City Courts (excluding NYC); $3,000 in Eastern Suffolk County, Town Courts, and Village Courts.

**Where to sue:** In a City Court if the defendant lives, works, or has a place of business in a city. If the defendant lives, works, or has a place of business in a town or village, in the Town or Village Court, or the City Court in the County.

**Service of process:** Certified mail, return receipt requested or ordinary first-class mail by court clerk. If after 21 days the notice isn't returned as undeliverable, then notice presumed.

**Defendant's response:** No written answer required. Defendant to file counter-claim within five days of receiving plaintiff's claim but it cannot exceed the $5,000 limit.

**Transfer:** Allowed by court's discretion.

**Attorneys:** Allowed.

**Appeals:** Allowed only on the ground that "substantial justice" was not done. Must file appeal within 30 days if received judgment in court or by personal delivery, or within 35 days of the mailing date if mailed by the court clerk. Heard in county court or appellate division of supreme court (for New York City) on law, not facts. There is no appeal from arbitrator's decision.

**Evictions:** No.

**Jury trials:** Defendant may request jury trial at least one day prior to hearing. Must file affidavit stating issues that require jury trial.

**Notes:** Corporations and partnerships cannot sue in small claims court, but may appear as defendants. (Does not apply to municipal and public benefit corporations and school districts. Partnerships can bring a small claims action in Western Suffolk County or Nassau District Court.) Instead, they can bring commercial claims, which have similar rules to small claims courts but are subject to these additional restrictions: (1) Same limits and procedures as regular small claims except claim is brought by corporation, partnership, or association. (2) Business must have principal office in NY state. (3) Defendant must reside, be employed, or have a business office in the county where suit is brought.

## North Carolina

**Court:** Small Claims Court.

**Statutes:** N.C. Gen. Stat. §§ 7A-210 to 7A-232; 42-29.

**Court information:** www.nccourts.gov/courts/small-claims-court
www.ncleg.gov/Laws/GeneralStatutes (state statutes).

**Dollar limit:** Varies by county from $5,000 to $10,000.

**Where to sue:** County in which defendant resides. Corporation, where it maintains place of business.

**Service of process:** Personal service, registered or certified mail, signature confirmation, or designated delivery service. (Alternate method is permitted in eviction cases; see N.C. Gen. Stat. § 42-29.)

**Defendant's response:** Not required. If answer is not filed, general denial of all claims is assumed. Counterclaims over $10,000 not allowed. Failure to assert counterclaim will not bar claim in separate action.

**Transfer:** No provision; but defendant can bring separate action in proper court.

**Attorneys:** Allowed.

**Appeals:** Either party can give notice of appeal orally in open court or by filing notice of appeal in the office of the clerk of superior court within 10 days after entry of judgment.

**Evictions:** Yes.

**Jury trials:** Not allowed. If case is not assigned to magistrate, it is treated as regular civil case. Plaintiff may request jury trial within five days of receiving notice of nonassignment, and defendant may make request either before or at same time as filing answer.

## North Dakota

**Court:** Small Claims Court.

**Statutes:** N.D. Cent Code §§ 27-08.1-01 to 27-08.1-08.

**Court rules:** North Dakota Rules of Court, Rule 10.2.

**Court information:** www.ndcourts.gov/legal-self-help/small-claims www.legis.nd.gov/general-information/north-dakota-century-code (state statutes).

**Dollar limit:** $15,000.

**Where to sue:** Generally, where the defendant resides. Collection of a bad check claim: where check was passed, or where defendant resides or does business. Collection of an open credit account claim: where defendant resides or does business, or, if less than $1,000 and not from a telephone or mail order transaction, where transaction occurred, or where defendant resides or does business. Real property lease, dispute over earnest money, or real estate purchase deposit claim: where real property is located unless written agreement to proceed elsewhere exists. When suing a corporation, limited liability company, or a partnership: location of place of business or where claim occurred.

**Service of process:** Personal service by disinterested adult or by certified mail.

**Defendant's response:** Defendant must return form requesting hearing within 20 days of service. An answer isn't required. Defendant must file and serve counterclaim at least 48 hours before hearing.

**Transfer:** Defendant can transfer case to District Court (regular civil court procedure) if request made within 20 days of service.

**Attorneys:** Allowed.

**Appeals:** Not allowed.

**Evictions:** No.

**Jury trials:** Not allowed.

**Notes:** Plaintiff can't dismiss a small claims action. If plaintiff fails to prosecute, claim will be dismissed with prejudice (plaintiff cannot refile claim).

## Ohio

**Court:** County and Municipal Courts, Small Claims Division.

**Statutes:** Ohio Rev. Code Ann. §§ 1925.01 to 1925.18.

**Court rules:** Ohio Rules of Civil Procedure, Rules 3 and 4.1; Ohio Rules of Appellate Procedure, Rule 4.

**Court information:** www.ohiojudges.org/citizen-guide-brochures www.supremecourt.ohio.gov/JudSystem/trialCourts http://codes.ohio.gov/orc (state statutes).

**Dollar limit:** $6,000.

**Where to sue:** County where the defendant resides or does business; where the activity or injury occurred; where the claim for relief arose; where the property subject to the claim is located.

**Service of process:** Sheriff; or certified mail by clerk, return receipt requested.

**Defendant's response:** No written answer required. Must file and serve counterclaim at least seven days before trial date.

**Transfer:** To regular civil court upon defendant's counterclaim over $6,000 or court's motion. Defendant (or plaintiff if counterclaim is made) can request transfer, but must file affidavit stating grounds of defense.

**Attorneys:** Allowed.

**Appeals:** Two-levels of appeal: A party may file written objections to the Magistrates decision within 14 days of that decision. A municipal judge will then review the Magistrates decision and enter a Final Judgement. That Final Judgment may then be appealed to the Court of Appeals within 30 days.

**Evictions:** No.

**Jury trials:** Not allowed.

## Oklahoma

**Court:** District Court, Small Claims Procedure.

**Statutes:** Okla. Stat. Ann. tit. 12, §§ 131 to 141; 1751 to 1773.

**Court information:** https://oklacountyjudges.org/small-claims
www.oklegislature.gov/osstatuestitle.html (state statutes).

**Dollar limit:** $10,000.

**Where to sue:** County where the defendant resides or does business; where the activity or injury occurred; where the claim for relief arose; where the property subject to the claim is located. Collection of open account, note, or other instrument of indebtedness in any county allowed by law, where the debt was contracted, or where other instrument of indebtedness was given.

**Service of process:** Certified mail by clerk, return receipt requested. Plaintiff may request personal service by sheriff or other disinterested adult.

**Defendant's response:** No formal written answer required. Defendant must file counterclaim at least 72 hours before appearance date.

**Transfer:** Defendant can request transfer up to 48 hours before date to appear. A counterclaim exceeding $10,000 will be transferred to another docket unless both parties agree to submit to small claims procedures.

**Attorneys:** Allowed.

**Appeals:** Allowed by either party if filed within 30 days of entry of judgment.

**Evictions:** Yes.

**Jury trials:** Not allowed unless claim or counterclaim is more than $1,500. Then either party may demand jury trial at least two working days before time set for defendant's appearance.

**Notes:** Collection agencies may not sue in small claims court.

## Oregon

**Court:** Circuit and Justice Courts, Small Claims Department.

**Statutes:** Or. Rev. Stat. §§ 46.405 to 46.570; 55.011 to 55.140.

**Court information:** www.osbar.org/public/legalinfo/1061_SmallClaims.htm
www.courts.oregon.gov/forms/Pages/small-claims.aspx
www.oregonlegislature.gov/bills_laws/pages/ors.aspx (state statutues).

**Dollar limit:** $10,000.

**Where to sue:** County where defendant resides or can be found, where injury or damage occurred, or where contract or obligation was to be performed.

**Service of process:** Certified mail, or sheriff or court-approved adult. (In justice court, if claim is over $50, must use personal service.)

**Defendant's response:** Defendant must answer within 14 days of service to avoid default, and must request hearing. If counterclaim is over $10,000, must file motion to transfer to regular circuit court or counterclaim will be ignored. Plaintiff must reply to defendant's counterclaim within 20 days of service.

**Transfer:** To regular docket or other appropriate court if counterclaim is more than $10,000 and defendant requests transfer; or if defendant demands jury trial and counterclaim is for more than $750.

**Attorneys:** Not allowed without judge's consent.

**Appeals:** From circuit court, no appeal. From justice court, allowed by defendant on claim, or by plaintiff on counterclaim, within ten days after entry of the judgment.

**Evictions:** No.

**Jury trials:** Not allowed. If claim is over $750, defendant can request jury trial. Request must be made at same time as answer, within 14 days of service. Case is then transferred to appropriate court.

## Pennsylvania

**Court:** Magisterial District Court; Philadelphia Municipal Court.

**Statutes:** 42 Pa. Cons. Stat. Ann. §§ 1123, 1515.

**Court rules:** Pennsylvania Rules of Civil Procedure, Rules 400 to 405, 1002, 1006, 2179; Rules of Civil Procedure Governing Actions and Proceedings Before Magisterial District Judges, Rules 301 to 342; Philadelphia Municipal Court Rules of Civil Practice, Rules 101 to 144.

**Court information:** www.pacourts.us/courts/minor-courts
www.pabar.org/clips/bringingsuitBeforeDJ.pdf
www.legis.state.pa.us (state statutes).

**Dollar limit:** $12,000.

**Where to sue:** Wherever defendant can be served; where cause of action arose; or where transaction or occurrence took place. Wherever a corporation or partnership regularly conducts business; has its registered office; has principal place of business; or where transaction or occurrence took place.

**Service of process:** Magisterial court will arrange service by personal service, substitute service, or certified mail with return receipt.

**Defendant's response:** In magisterial court, defendant must file counterclaim at least five days before hearing; at least 10 days before trial in Philadelphia Municipal Court unless the counterclaim is less than $2,000.

**Transfer:** In Philadelphia Municipal Court, a defendant with a counterclaim over $12,000, must bring suit in court of common pleas within 30 days or any overage is considered waived. There is no provision for transfer from magisterial court.

**Attorneys:** Allowed.

**Appeals:** Allowed by either party within 30 days of entry of judgment.

**Evictions:** No.

**Jury trials:** Either party can request jury trial and case will be transferred in magisterial court. Not allowed except on appeal in Philadelphia Municipal Court.

**Notes:** If claiming more than $2,000 personal injury or property damage, must submit statement of claim signed under oath (Philadelphia Municipal Court).

## Rhode Island

**Court:** District Court, Small Claims Docket.

**Statutes:** R.I. Gen. Laws §§ 10-16-1 to 10-16-16; 9-4-3; 9-4-4; 9-12-10 (appeals).

**Court rules:** Rhode Island District Court Rules of Small Claims Procedure, Rules 1.00 to 7.01; Rhode Island District Court Rules of Civil Procedure, Rule 73.

**Court information:** www.courts.ri.gov/Courts/districtcourt/Pages/smallclaims.aspx http://webserver.rilin.state.ri.us/Statutes (state statutes).

**Dollar limit:** $2,500.

**Where to sue:** District where either party resides or where defendant can be found; if plaintiff is corporation, where defendant resides or can be found.

**Service of process:** To an individual by personal or substitute service. To a corporation by delivering to an officer, managing, or general agent, or by leaving with authorized person at corporate office or agent appointed to receive service of process.

**Defendant's response:** Defendant must file written answer, defense, or counterclaim either before or on date set for answering.

**Transfer:** If defendant's counterclaim is for over $2,500 and judge finds for defendant, defendant can still file claim in district court.

**Attorneys:** Allowed; required for all corporations other than close corporations with assets under $1 million.

**Appeals:** Defendant must file appeal on plaintiff's claim (plaintiff has right to appeal on defendant's counterclaim) within two days of entry of judgment, exclusive of Saturdays, Sundays, and legal holidays. Exception: In consumer plaintiff claim, if manufacturer or seller defendant loses by default, no appeal allowed.

**Evictions:** No.

**Jury trials:** No provision.

## South Carolina

**Court:** Magistrates Court.

**Statutes:** S.C. Code Ann. §§ 22-3-10 to 22-3-320; 15-7-30; 18-7-10 to 18-7-30.

**Court rules:** South Carolina Rules of Magistrates Court, Rules 1 to 24.

**Court information:** www.sccourts.org/selfHelp/FAQMagistrate.pdf www.scstatehouse.gov/code/statmast.php (state statutes).

**Dollar limit:** $7,500.

**Where to sue:** County where at least one defendant resides or where the most substantial part of the cause of action arose. Against a domestic company, county where it has principal place of business.

**Service of process:** Sheriff, the sheriff's deputy, a magistrate's constable, or other disinterested adult; commercial delivery service; personal service or certified mail, return receipt requested and delivery restricted to the addressee.

**Defendant's response:** May answer in writing or orally and file counterclaims within 30 days or time period stated in summons.

**Transfer:** Counterclaim amounts over $7,500 that aren't waived will be transferred to the circuit court of the county.

**Attorneys:** Allowed.

**Appeals:** Either party can file for appeal within 30 days after delivery of written notice of judgment to the party or attorney.

**Evictions:** Yes.

**Jury trials:** Either party may request jury trial in writing at least five days before trial date.

## South Dakota

**Court:** Circuit or Magistrates Court, Small Claims Procedure.

**Statutes:** S.D. Codified Laws Ann. §§ 15-39-45 to 15-39-78; 16-12B-6; 16-12B-12; 16-12B-16; 16-12C-8; 16-12C-13 to 16-12C-15.

**Court information:** http://ujs.sd.gov/Small_Claims/ http://sdlegislature.gov/Statutes/Codified_Laws/default.aspx (state statutes).

**Dollar limit:** $12,000.

**Where to sue:** County in which any defendant resides, or where transaction or injury occurred. Corporation, partnership, or LLC, any county where defendant has place of business.

**Service of process:** Certified or registered mail first, return receipt requested (service is binding on defendant who refuses to accept and sign for the letter). If undeliverable, then service must be made by another method, determined by court. If plaintiff elects not to pursue further notification of the defendant or if the further notification is unsuccessful after 90 days, the clerk may dismiss the action without prejudice.

**Defendant's response:** Defendant must comply with the instructions provided in the notice; otherwise, a default will be taken. The clerk is instructed to put the substance of defendant's defense in the docket and to deem it an answer.

**Transfer:** Defendant must petition at least five days before appearance or answer date and provide affidavit giving reasons that justify transfer.

**Attorneys:** Allowed.

**Appeals:** Not allowed. However, a party can file a "Motion to Vacate Judgment" asking the court to set aside the judgment for reasons such as error or a failure to be served the claim.

**Evictions:** No.

**Jury trials:** Not allowed. Defendant must apply for transfer to circuit court five days before trial date.

## Tennessee

**Court:** General Sessions Court, Small Claims Docket.

**Statutes:** Tenn. Code Ann. §§ 16-15-501 to 16-15-505; 16-15-710 to 16-15-735; 16-15-901 to 16-15-905; 20-4-101; 20-4-103.

**Court rules:** Tennessee Rules of Civil Procedure, Rule 38.03.

**Court information:** http://tncourts.gov/programs/self-help-center www.tsc.state.tn.us/Tennessee%20Code (state statutes).

**Dollar limit:** $25,000. No limit in eviction suits or suits to recover personal property.

**Where to sue:** County where defendant resides or where the cause of action arose. In certain cases involving property, county where either all or a portion of the property is located.

**Service of process:** Personal or substituted service by a disinterested adult; certified mail, with return receipt.

**Defendant's response:** No formal written answer required.

**Transfer:** Defendant may request transfer to circuit court at least three days before hearing (must provide affidavit that defense is either substantial, complex, or expensive enough to require transfer).

**Attorneys:** Allowed.

**Appeals:** Allowed by either party. Heard in circuit court as new trial. May demand jury trial within ten days after appeal filed.

**Evictions:** Yes.

**Jury trials:** Not allowed except on appeal or transfer.

**Notes:** Tennessee has no actual small claims system, but trials in general sessions court are normally conducted with informal rules.

## Texas

**Court:** Justice Court.

**Statutes:** Tex. Gov't. Code Ann. §§ 27.031; 27.060.

**Court rules:** Texas Rules of Civil Procedure, Rules 500 to 507.

**Court information:** https://guides.sll.texas.gov/small-claims www.tyla.org/tyla/assets/File/HowToSueInJusticeCourt-SB0119E-1013_Web.pdf https://statutes.capitol.texas.gov (state statutes).

**Dollar limit:** $20,000.

**Where to sue:** County and precinct in which defendant resides; or county where obligation was to be performed, incidents giving rise to the claim occurred, or property at issue is located. If the defendant is a nonresident of Texas, or if defendant's residence is unknown, file the suit in the county and precinct where the plaintiff resides.

**Service of process:** Sheriff, constable, process server, or (with court approval) disinterested adult. Certified mail by court clerk, upon request by plaintiff. Service by publication in a newspaper if the defendant can't be found.

**Defendant's response:** Defendant must file a written answer with the court and serve a copy on the plaintiff. If the defendant was not served by publication, the answer is due by the end of the 14th day after the day the defendant was served with the citation. If the defendant was served by publication, the answer is due by the end of the 42nd day after the citation was issued. In either case, there are exceptions for weekends, holidays, and days the court is closed before 5:00 p.m.

**Transfer:** Transfer allowed to another precinct in same county upon written motion of defendant based on improper venue, by either party with affidavits of two credible people that the party can't get a fair and impartial trial in the precinct or in front of a specific judge, or by consent of both parties.

**Attorneys:** Allowed.

**Appeals:** Either party can file an appeal within 21 days after the judgment was signed or a motion for new trial was denied.

**Evictions:** Separate small claims courts have been abolished as of August 2013; both small claims cases and evictions are heard in Justice Court. Evictions cases are governed by Rules 500–507 and 510 of Part V of the Rules of Civil Procedure.

**Jury trials:** Either party may demand jury trial by filing a request no later than 14 days before the trial date.

**Notes:** No professional moneylenders or collection agents may sue in small claims court.

## Utah

**Court:** District Court, Small Claims Department.

**Statutes:** Utah Code Ann. §§ 78A-8-101 to 78A-8-109.

**Court rules:** Utah Rules of Small Claims Procedure, Rules 1 to 12, A to K.

**Court information:** www.utcourts.gov/howto/smallclaims
https://le.utah.gov/xcode/code.html (state statutes).

**Dollar limit:** $11,000.

**Where to sue:** County in which defendant resides or debt was incurred.

**Service of process:** Sheriff, constable, marshal, or their deputy; a person over 18 years old who is not a party or a party's attorney; courier service or mail, return receipt requested.

**Defendant's response:** No answer required. Must file counter affidavit (counter-claim) at least 15 days before trial; counter affidavit cannot exceed $11,000 and it must arise out of same transaction or occurrence as plaintiff's claim.

**Transfer:** No provision.

**Attorneys:** Allowed.

**Appeals:** Either party can appeal within 28 business days of entry of judgment. Heard in district court as new trial.

**Evictions:** No.

**Jury trials:** No provision.

## Vermont

**Court:** Superior Court, Small Claims Procedure.

**Statutes:** Vt. Stat. Ann. tit. 12, §§ 5531 to 5541; 402.

**Court rules:** Vermont Rules of Small Claims Procedure, Rules 1 to 14.

**Court information:** www.vermontjudiciary.org/self-help/debt-collection-small-claims https://legislature.vermont.gov/statutes (state statutes).

**Dollar limit:** $5,000.

**Where to sue:** County in which either party resides.

**Service of process:** Court will serve by first-class mail; if defendant does not return form acknowledging receipt, plaintiff must arrange service by sheriff or another person authorized to serve process.

**Defendant's response:** Answer required within 30 days of mailing date by plaintiff or receipt of service. Answer may include any related counterclaim but judgement can't exceed small claims limits.

**Transfer:** A claim or counterclaim cannot be transferred.

**Attorneys:** Allowed.

**Appeals:** Allowed by either party within 30 days of entry of judgment.

**Evictions:** No.

**Jury trials:** Defendant may request jury trial at least one day prior to appearance.

## Virginia

**Court:** District Court, Small Claims Division.

**Statutes:** Va. Code Ann. §§ 8.01-262; 16.1-76; 16.1-77; 16.1-106; 16.1-113; 16.1-122.1 to 16.1-122.7.

**Court information:** www.courts.state.va.us/resources/small_claims_court_ procedures.pdf
www.courts.state.va.us/courts/gd/home.html
www.courts.state.va.us/courtadmin/library/va.html (state statutes).

**Dollar limit:** $5,000.

**Where to sue:** District in which defendant resides, is employed, or regularly conducts business; where transaction or injury occurred; or where property is located. For a nonindividual defendant, where its principal office or principal place of business is located, or where the defendant has a registered office or agent for service.

**Service of process:** Court shall serve defendant or plaintiff can use a private process server.

**Defendant's response:** No formal written answer required. May file counterclaim any time before trial, counterclaim cannot exceed $5,000.

**Transfer:** To circuit court if defendant wants attorney representation.

**Attorneys:** Not allowed in small claims division; if defendant wants attorney representation, can request transfer.

**Appeals:** Allowed by either party within ten days after entry of judgment on cases over $50.

**Evictions:** No.

**Jury trials:** Not allowed unless case is appealed.

**Notes:** General district courts, similar to small claims court but with more procedures, can hear claims up to $25,000. See Va. Code Ann. §§ 16.1-77 to 16.1-80.

## Washington

**Court:** District Court, Small Claims Department.

**Statutes:** Wash. Rev. Code Ann. §§ 12.36.010 to 12.40.120; 3.66.040.

**Court information:** www.courts.wa.gov/newsinfo/resources/?fa=newsinfo_jury.
  scc&altMenu=smal
www.atg.wa.gov/small-claims-court-0
https://apps.leg.wa.gov/rcw (state statutes).

**Dollar limit:** $10,000 if brought by natural person; $5,000 all other cases.

**Where to sue:** County where any defendant resides or, if residence cannot be determined by reasonable efforts, place of employment. Corporation, where it transacts business or has office.

**Service of process:** Sheriff, deputy, or disinterested adult; personal service or certified or registered mail, return receipt requested.

**Defendant's response:** No formal written answer required. Defendant with counterclaim over $5,000 may file separate suit in superior court while plaintiff's case proceeds in small claims court.

**Transfer:** Allowed only upon judge's decision, following a hearing.

**Attorneys:** Not allowed without judge's consent, unless case transferred from regular civil court.

**Appeals:** Within 30 days of entry of judgment. The party who files a claim or counterclaim can't appeal unless the claimed amount exceeds $1,000; no party can appeal unless amount claimed was $250 or more.

**Evictions:** No.

**Jury trials:** No provision.

## West Virginia

**Court:** Magistrate Court.

**Statutes:** W. Va. Code §§ 50-2-1 to 50-6-3; 56-1-1.

**Court rules:** Rules of Civil Procedure for Magistrate Courts, Rules 1 to 21.

**Court information:** www.courtswv.gov/lower-courts/magistrate-courts.html
www.wvlegislature.gov/wvcode/code.cfm (state statutes).

**Dollar limit:** $10,000.

**Where to sue:** County in which any defendant resides or can be served, or where transaction or injury occurred. West Virginia corporations, where principal office is located; other corporations, where they do business. For eviction suits, county where property is located.

**Service of process:** Sheriff or disinterested adult; certified or registered mail by court at plaintiff's request, return receipt requested.

**Defendant's response:** Defendant must file written answer within 20 days of service to avoid default (30 days if service is made on defendant's attorney or agent). Defendant can also file a counterclaim for $10,000 or less.

**Transfer:** Before trial, an action involving less than $5,000 can be removed to circuit court if all parties agree. Defendant can request transfer to another venue in answer or within reasonable time.

**Attorneys:** Allowed.

**Appeals:** Allowed by either party within 20 days after a judgment is entered or within 20 days after the magistrate has denied a motion for new trial.

**Evictions:** Yes.

**Jury trials:** Either party may demand jury trial if claim is over $20 or involves possession of real estate. Must be made in writing within 20 days of service of defendant's answer, or in eviction cases, five days after service of complaint.

## Wisconsin

**Court:** Circuit Court, Small Claims Action.

**Statutes:** Wis. Stat. §§ 799.01 to 799.445; 421.401; 801.50; 808.03.

**Court information:** www.wicourts.gov/services/public/selfhelp/smallclaims.htm https://docs.legis.wisconsin.gov/statutes/statutes (state statutes).

**Dollar limit:** $10,000. No limit in eviction suits.

**Where to sue:** County in which any defendant resides or does substantial business, where transaction or injury occurred, or where property is located. County where contract claim arose or, if claim arose from consumer transaction, county where contract was signed or where purchase or loan took place. For landlord-tenant claims, county where property is located.

**Service of process:** Sheriff, process server, or disinterested adult; or by certified mail by court clerk, return receipt requested.

**Defendant's response:** No formal written answer required.

**Transfer:** Upon defendant's counterclaim over $10,000, case will be tried according to regular circuit court civil procedure.

**Attorneys:** Allowed.

**Appeals:** Allowed by either party within 15 days after the entry of judgment. No appeal from default judgment.

**Evictions:** Yes.

**Jury trials:** Either party may request a jury trial.

## Wyoming

**Court:** Circuit Court, Small Claims Docket.

**Statutes:** Wyo. Stat. Ann. §§ 1-21-201 to 1-21-205; 5-9-128; 5-9-136.

**Court rules:** Wyoming Rules and Forms Governing Small Claims Cases, Rules 1 to 7, Forms 1 and 2.

**Court information:** www.courts.state.wy.us/court_rule/rules-and-forms-governing-small-claims-cases

www.courts.state.wy.us/legal-assistances-and-forms/court-self-help-forms

www.wyoleg.gov/StateStatutes/StatutesConstitution (state statutes).

**Dollar limit:** $6,000.

**Where to sue:** County in which defendant has an address.

**Service of process:** Sheriff, deputy, or disinterested adult; or by certified mail, return receipt requested (by court clerk if defendant lives in the same county as court).

**Defendant's response:** No answer is required.

**Transfer:** No provision.

**Attorneys:** Allowed. If one party appears with an attorney, the other party is entitled to a continuance to obtain one.

**Appeals:** Allowed by either party within 30 days of entry of judgment.

**Evictions:** No.

**Jury trials:** Either party can demand jury trial.

# Legal Jargon for Small Claims Court

Mercifully, there is not a great deal of technical language used in small claims courts. But there are a few terms that might be new to you and that you will have to become familiar with. Don't try to learn all of these terms now. Refer back to these definitions when you need them.

**Abstract of Judgment.** An official document issued by the small claims court clerk's office indicating that you have a money judgment in your favor against another person. Filing it with the County Recorder places a lien on real property owned by the judgment debtor. (For more information about property liens, see Chapter 24.)

**Appeal.** In the small claims context, a request that the superior court rehear the case and reverse the decision of the small claims court. Some states allow only a defendant to appeal; others allow the parties to appeal based only on a mistaken application of law and not a retrial of the facts. (See Chapter 23 and Appendix A.)

**Calendar.** A list of cases heard by a small claims court on a particular day. A case taken "off calendar" will not be heard on the original court date.

**Claim of Exemption.** A procedure by which a judgment debtor can claim that, under federal or state law, money or property is exempt from being seized to satisfy a debt.

**Conditional Judgment.** A conditional judgment consists of certain actions or requirements that are contingent on other actions (for instance, return the property in ten days or pay $2,000).

**Continuance.** A court order postponing a court appearance to a later date.

**Counterclaim.** When a defendant sues the plaintiff for damages arising from the same lawsuit.

**Default Judgment.** A court decision in favor of the person filing suit—a plaintiff or cross-complainant—when the person sued fails to show up to the small claims trial.

**Defendant.** The person or party the plaintiff sues.

**Defendant's Claim.** A claim by a defendant alleging that the plaintiff owes the defendant money. The claim is filed as part of the same small claims action that the plaintiff started. See "Counterclaim."

**Dismissed Case.** A dismissal ends the case. A judge or the filer can dismiss an action "with prejudice" or "without prejudice." An action dismissed without prejudice can be refiled; however, a case dismissed with prejudice cannot. A plaintiff can refile a case dismissed without prejudice, but not a case dismissed with prejudice.

**Equitable Relief.** A small claims court judge can order a nonmonetary remedy in some situations—that is, order a party to do, or not do something, such as return unique property, end a fraudulent contract, fix a mistaken contract, or one of the other acts discussed in Chapter 4.

**Equity.** The value of a particular piece of property that you own. For example, if a car has a fair market value of $10,000 and you owe a bank $8,000 on it, your equity is $2,000.

**Eviction.** See Unlawful Detainer Proceeding, below.

**Exempt Property.** Under federal and state law, certain personal and real property is exempt from being taken to pay (satisfy) court judgments if the debtor follows certain procedures. (See Chapter 24.)

**Formal Court.** This book refers to the formal court as the state court above the small claims court. Depending on the state, a formal state court might be called a "municipal," "superior," "district," "circuit," "supreme," "civil," or another court. For instance, in California, claims too large to qualify for small claims court are heard in superior court.

**Garnish.** To attach (legally take) money—usually wages, or commissions, or a bank account—for payment of a debt.

**Hearing.** The court trial.

**Homestead.** Homestead laws allow homeowners to protect a certain amount of the equity in their homes from attachment and sale to satisfy most debts. Homestead laws can work in one of two ways. In some states, the homeowner must file a paper called a "Declaration of Homestead."

In other states, simply owning a home (and having the deed recorded) is enough to entitle the homeowner to homestead protection. (See Chapter 24.)

**Judge Pro Tem.** A lawyer who hears cases for a regular judge temporarily. Because this person isn't an elected or officially appointed judge, a pro tem can only hear your case with your written consent, which will typically be requested on the day you go to court.

**Judgment.** The court decision signed by a judge.

**Judgment Creditor.** A person owed money under a court judgment.

**Judgment Debtor.** A person who owes money under a court judgment.

**Jurisdiction.** A court's authority to hear and decide a particular type of case. A small claims court has jurisdiction to hear certain types of cases involving money damages up to an amount often called the "jurisdictional amount" or "jurisdictional limit." Some small claims courts also have jurisdiction over certain type of nonmonetary cases, such as unlawful detainer (eviction) actions, and some may award nonmonetary remedies (equitable relief), as discussed in Chapter 4. (For more information about the courts' jurisdiction over people, see Chapter 8.)

**Jury Trial.** A group of citizens assembled to hear evidence at trial and render a verdict. Judges or commissioners hear almost all small claims cases and appeals—most small claims courts do not allow trial by jury. (See Appendix A for your state's rules.)

**Levy.** A legal method to seize property or money for unpaid debts under court order. For example, a sheriff can levy on (take and sell) your automobile if you refuse to pay a judgment.

**Lien.** A legal right to an interest in the real estate (real property) of another for payment of a debt. To get a lien, you first must get a court judgment and then take proper steps to have the court enter an Abstract of Judgment. To establish the lien, you then take the abstract to the County Recorder's office in a county where the judgment debtor has real estate.

**Magistrate.** Another word for judge.

**Mediation.** A process encouraged in many small claims courts by which the parties to a dispute meet with a neutral mediator who attempts to help them arrive at their own solution to the problem. If mediation succeeds, the parties won't need to proceed to trial; if it fails, the dispute can still go to court to be decided on by a judge.

**Motion to Vacate Judgment.** The motion the defendant must file to reopen a proceeding and set aside a default judgment issued because the sued party didn't show up. (See Chapter 15.)

**Order of Examination.** A court procedure allowing a judgment creditor to question a judgment debtor about the extent and location of assets.

**Party.** A participant in a lawsuit. The plaintiff or defendant are often referred to as a "party"—and both together as the "parties"—to a small claims suit.

**Plaintiff.** The person or party who starts a lawsuit.

**Prejudice.** A term used when a case is dismissed. A case dismissed without prejudice can be refiled at any time as long as the statute of limitations period has not run out (see Chapter 5). However, a case dismissed with prejudice is dead (can't be refiled) unless the dismissal is first successfully appealed.

**Process Server.** The person who delivers court papers to a party or witness. (See Chapter 11.)

**Recorder (Office of the County Recorder).** The county office that records and files important legal documents, such as deeds to real property. The County Recorder's office is usually located in the main county courthouse.

**Release.** A written agreement in which a person agrees to waive a right or responsibility; for example, a release of liability.

**Replevin.** A type of legal action in which the owner of movable goods is given the right to recover them from someone who shouldn't have them. It is commonly used in relation to buyers and sellers; for example, a seller might bring a replevin action if the seller delivered goods to a buyer who then failed to pay for them. Some states' small claims courts allow replevin actions.

**Satisfaction of Judgment.** A written statement filed by the judgment creditor when the judgment is paid. (See Chapter 23.)

**Service.** The formal delivery of court papers to a party or witness, which must be done in a manner specified by statute. Also called "service of process."

**Statute of Limitations.** The time during which you must file your lawsuit. It usually starts on the date the act or failure to act giving rise to the lawsuit occurred, and ends one or more years later, with the number of years depending on the type of suit. (See Chapter 5.)

**Stay of Enforcement.** When a defendant appeals a small claims court judgment to the superior court, enforcement (collection) of the judgment is stayed (stopped) until the time for appeal has expired.

**Stipulation.** An agreement on any topic relevant to a case entered into by the parties. A stipulation signed by the judge becomes a court order.

**Submission.** A judge who wants to delay deciding a case until a later time will take it under submission. Some judges announce their decision as to who won and who lost right in the courtroom. More often, they take the case under submission and mail out a decision later.

**Subpoena.** A court order requiring a witness to appear in court. It must be delivered to the person subpoenaed to be valid. (See Chapter 14.)

**Subpoena Duces Tecum.** A court order requiring that certain documents be produced in court.

**Substituted Service.** A method by which court papers can be delivered to a defendant who is difficult to reach by other means. (See Chapter 11.)

**Transfer.** The procedure by which the defendant can have a small claims case transferred to a formal court. In most states, this can be done when the defendant has a claim against the plaintiff for an amount greater than the small claims maximum. In a few states, the defendant can transfer any case to traditional court. In many states, a defendant who wants a jury trial can also transfer to formal court. See Appendix A for details.

**Trial de Novo.** The rehearing of the facts of a small claims case after a defendant appeals. The previous small claims decision has no effect, and the appeal takes the form of a new trial (trial de novo). This is allowed only in some states. Check Appendix A.

**Unlawful Detainer Proceeding.** Legalese for eviction. Also known by other names, such as "summary dispossession" and "forcible entry and detainer." Check Appendix A.

**Venue.** The proper location to bring a suit (discussed in detail in Chapter 9). A suit brought in the wrong court can be transferred to the correct court or dismissed. A case can proceed in the wrong court if both parties appear and agree to it.

**Wage Garnishment.** A collection procedure that withdraws funds directly from a judgment debtor's wages.

**Writ of Execution.** An order issued by a judge that allows a judgment creditor to forcibly collect money through garnishment, levy, or other means.

# Index

# ⚖ NOLO

## *More from Nolo*

Nolo.com offers a large library of legal solutions and forms, created by Nolo's in-house legal editors. These reliable documents can be prepared in minutes.

## Create a Document Online

**Incorporation.** Incorporate your business in any state.

**LLC Formation.** Gain asset protection and pass-through tax status in any state.

**Will.** Nolo has helped people make over 2 million wills. Is it time to make or revise yours?

**Living Trust (avoid probate).** Plan now to save your family the cost, delays, and hassle of probate.

**Provisional Patent.** Preserve your right to obtain a patent by claiming "patent pending" status.

## Download Useful Legal Forms

Nolo.com has hundreds of top quality legal forms available for download:

- bill of sale
- promissory note
- nondisclosure agreement
- LLC operating agreement
- corporate minutes
- commercial lease and sublease
- motor vehicle bill of sale
- consignment agreement
- and many more.

## www.nolo.com

## On Nolo.com you'll also find:

### Books & Software

Nolo publishes hundreds of great books and software programs for consumers and
business owners. Order a copy, or download an ebook version instantly, at Nolo.com.

### Online Forms

You can quickly and easily make a will or living trust, form an LLC or corporation,
apply for a provisional patent, or make hundreds of other forms—online.

### Free Legal Information

Thousands of articles answer common questions about everyday legal issues,
including wills, bankruptcy, small business formation, divorce, patents,
employment, and much more.

### Plain-English Legal Dictionary

Stumped by jargon? Look it up in America's most up-to-date source for
definitions of legal terms, free at Nolo.com.

### Lawyer Directory

Nolo's consumer-friendly lawyer directory provides in-depth profiles of lawyers all
over America. You'll find information you need to choose the right lawyer.